WITHDRAWN

QUEEN'S REBELS

David W. Miller

QUEEN'S REBELS
Ulster Loyalism in Historical Perspective

GILL AND MACMILLAN, DUBLIN
BARNES & NOBLE BOOKS, NEW YORK
(a division of Harper & Row Publishers, Inc.)

First published 1978 by
Gill and Macmillan Ltd
15/17 Eden Quay
Dublin 1
with associated companies in
London, New York, Delhi, Hong Kong,
Johannesburg, Lagos, Melbourne,
Singapore, Tokyo

© David W. Miller

7171 0904 6

Published in the U.S.A. 1978 by
Harper & Row Publishers, Inc.
Barnes & Noble Import Division

Library of Congress Cataloging in Publication Data

Miller, David W.   1940–
Queen's rebels: Ulster loyalism in historical perspective.

Includes bibliographical references and index.
1. Northern Ireland—History.   I.   Title.
DA990.U46M49   1978   941.6   78–16943
ISBN 0–06–494829–3

Printed in Great Britain by
Bristol Typesetting Co Ltd,
Barton Manor, St Philips, Bristol

*To my mother
and the memory of my father*

Contents

Contents continued

'The time might come when Ulstermen would have to become Queen's rebels in order to remain citizens of any kind.'

Rev. Robert Bradford, MP
August, 1975

Preface

THIS is an essay on the Northern Ireland problem. In modern Western society, to call such a situation as that in Northern Ireland a 'problem' is to invite the question, 'What is the solution?' More and more well-informed observers in the past two years or so have been referring to the Northern Ireland problem, however, as 'insoluble'. In that light, it may seem presumptuous for an historian even to address this problem, since one reason commonly given for such a gloomy assessment is that the problem is 'rooted in history'. This assertion rests on a truism : you cannot change history. If only the problem were 'rooted in' something else—economic structures, say, or political institutions or social relations—then we might consult the specialists in those aspects of human society to learn what to change in order to 'solve' the problem. If we are reduced to consulting the historian, then, truly, we may despair.

Is such despair justified? Has the historian nothing to contribute to the solution of great problems of public policy? To answer this question, it is perhaps worthwhile to ask what we mean by a 'problem'. A problem, in the sense ordinarily intended by an expression like 'the Northern Ireland problem', is some practical difficulty to be overcome in the external world. The word 'problem', however, is also used in an older sense to mean a puzzling question. Such a problem is solved not when a practical difficulty is overcome, but when the question has ceased to be puzzling.

The distinction between the two senses of the word 'problem' can help us to understand how history's contribution to problem-solving differs from those of the other social sciences. All social sciences, indeed, all sciences, are concerned with solving puzzles, but the puzzles which interest the historian tend to be particular rather than general. He seeks to understand the unique situation in itself rather than simply as an instance to confirm or refute a proposed universal law. This is not to say, of course, that historians reject all principles of regularity in human affairs: indeed, no explanation of any event carries force without reference to some such principle. The historian tends, however, to use the theories developed by other social scientists eclectically and heuristically. His purpose is not so much to test the validity of such theories as to render comprehensible a particular situation. If a by-product of this activity is to set new problems for those who formulate general theories, that is both desirable and appropriate.

Furthermore, other social scientists work on the assumption that a problem of the 'practical difficulty' sort can be reduced to a puzzle whose solution can easily be translated into policies which will solve the practical difficulty. Indeed, a prime test of the validity of their theories is whether this translation works. Historians, on the other hand, usually confine themselves to solving puzzles: they seek to understand why things happened the way they did in the past, not to make them happen some other way in the future. Indeed, historians, more than other social scientists, are disposed to take a tragic view of human affairs, not only because they have perhaps a wider (vicarious) experience of human folly, but also because they are trained to treat with scepticism the claims made for public men by their admirers that they have decisively altered the course of events.

The public man who consults an historian, therefore, must not expect such ready prescriptions as he may obtain from the economist or the political scientist or the sociologist. He must expect, indeed, to be treated as part of the problem. If he gains only an understanding of the role he is playing in a drama whose outcome he is powerless to affect, that is not valueless: it is what distinguishes a tragic hero from a mere victim. He may, however, gain more: with a better understanding of the forces with which he contends, he may learn to transcend the role in which he has been cast. Not all reality is tragic, even in the North of Ireland, and if the historian is disposed to the tragic view, he is not necessarily the fatalist implied in the observation that a problem 'rooted in history' must be insoluble. He expects to find not only continuity but change in the past, so that if the problem is truly 'rooted in history', so too may be the solution. Clio remains one of the Muses, not one of the Fates.

* * *

I began the line of research which led to this essay in the summer of 1972. I have received support in the form of summer stipends from the National Endowment for the Humanities and from the Falk Foundation. I was able to spend a sabbatical year, 1975–76, as a research fellow of the Institute for Irish Studies in Belfast through the generosity of the Academic Council of Queen's University and the co-operation of the leaves committee of Carnegie-Mellon University. To all these agencies I am most grateful. I want also to express particular gratitude to the staffs of Public Record Office of Northern Ireland, the State Paper Office of Ireland, the Linenhall Library, the National Library of Ireland, and the libraries of Queen's University, Belfast, Carnegie-Mellon University, the University of Pittsburgh and the Pittsburgh Theological Seminary.

Among the many scholars who gave generously of their time in conversations with me, I must single out for special thanks Mr W. H. Crawford, Prof. E. R. R. Green, Mr Aiken McClelland, Prof. T. W. Moody, Prof. Richard Rose, Dr A. T. Q. Stewart, Dr Brian Walker, and Dr John Whyte. Prof. Irving Bartlett, Prof. J. C. Beckett, Prof. Hugh Kearney, Miss Sarah Nelson and Prof. Ludwig Schaefer each read all or part of the manuscript and provided helpful criticisms. The essay was greatly improved by their suggestions, but responsibility for its faults remains mine alone.

Finally I record my debt to my wife Margaret, who reluctantly agreed to go to Belfast for a year, and to my daughter Roberta, who reluctantly agreed to come back.

D.W.M.
Pittsburgh, Christmas, 1977

Introduction

FEW aspects of the contemporary Ulster problem are more perplexing to British and other outside observers than the 'conditional' character of the loyalty professed by those known as 'Loyalists'. A substantial section of the Protestant population often seems to be loudly proclaiming its loyalty to the Queen while simultaneously declining to submit to her government. Indeed, in certain circumstances they maintain that only by disobedience to the Queen's laws can they be loyal to her. The phenomenon has been usefully conceptualised by Richard Rose, who found that 38 per cent of a sample of Protestants interviewed in 1968 took an 'ultra' position, expressing *support* for the regime while refusing unreserved *compliance* with its basic political laws.[1]

In July, 1975, one year after the loyalist general strike which seemed to epitomise these attitudes, a speech by Enoch Powell, M.P. for South Down, threw the differences between English and Ulster concepts of 'loyalty' into sharp relief. It was self-contradictory, Mr Powell told his constituents at Kilkeel, for a person 'who calls himself a Unionist . . . to place limits or conditions upon his obedience to the Crown in Parliament'.[2] It was a characteristically English formulation of the issue which touched a very sensitive nerve in the Ulster body politic and was greeted by a chorus of dissent from Powell's colleagues in the United Ulster Unionist Council (UUUC), in whose interest he had contested the South Down seat in October, 1974. Harry West, leader of the Official Unionist Party, the Rev. Ian Paisley, leader of the Democratic Unionist Party, and the headquarters of William Craig's Vanguard Unionist Party all promptly denounced Powell's definition of loyalty. All three proclaimed loyalty to the

'the will of the British Parliament' (Vanguard), 'the dictates of any British political party in power at Westminster' (West) or 'the so-called will of the British government' (Vanguard), or owed allegiance to 'Westminster' (West), 'the government and parliament at Westminster' (Paisley), 'the British parliament' (West) or 'the Wilsons and Heaths of this world' (Paisley).[3]

Both West and Paisley justified their positions by reference to Westminster's supposed treachery toward Ulster in the past, West alluding to the 1973 Sunningdale agreement, Paisley to the less imaginary threat posed by the 1912 Home Rule Bill. 'If the Crown in Parliament decreed to put Ulster into a United Ireland', Paisley argued, 'according to Mr Powell's theory we would have to obey if we were loyal. This is utter nonsense.' Indeed it was nonsense, as Powell himself agreed in an interview three days later : 'of course, there could be no loyalty to a parliament and a sovereign authority which has kicked you out'; but he dismissed such an action by the U.K. parliament as 'inconceivable'.[4] More fundamentally, his critics had distorted his argument : when he had warned 'that loyalty to the Crown in Parliament must be unconditional, he had not said, or meant, loyalty to the British government.' He had meant that 'so long as Northern Ireland remains part of the United Kingdom, then the loyalty of citizens in Ulster, like that of citizens in Kent or Cornwall, is, of course, to the sovereign, and the sovereign is the Crown in Parliament; nobody can dispute that.'

Powell was, in effect, saying that as the United Kingdom is now a constitutional monarchy, the crown can only be an object of loyalty within the framework of that constitution. In terms of the best current constitutional thinking, his point was indeed indisputable. The only leading UUUC figure who supported him publicly, Jim Kilfedder, M.P. for North Down, pointed out that in the United Kingdom, people 'declared allegiance to Queen Elizabeth, but this was on the basis that the sovereign acted in a constitutional manner, accepting the wishes of the people expressed through parliament and government. The monarchy could not act constitutionally without parliament, . . . and there was no Queen's party.'[5] Neither West nor Paisley chose to address the issue in these terms, though the Vanguard statement did allude to an earlier constitutional principle : 'Ulster's first loyalty is to the British crown and a Protestant established monarchy, and', the statement added, 'not to the will of the Britiish parliament'. Though the stipulation that the monarch must be a Protestant, which Orangemen make an explicit condition of their loyalty, is still a part of the British constitution, it is hardly, for most Englishmen, its essence. Indeed, the fact that neither West nor Paisley mentioned this stipulation, and that even the Rev. Martin Smyth, Grand Master of the Orange Order and a leading Official Unionist politician, glossed over it with the assertion 'that while the loyalty of Orangemen to the Queen was conditional it was nonetheless wholehearted',[6] suggests that it is no longer paramount even in Ulster Protestant political thinking. Moreover, it was certainly not the issue over which Loyalists had been defying Westminster's authority in 1974-75.

Actually the whole matter of loyalty to the crown can easily divert our attention from the heart of the problem, which is illuminated, ironically, by one attack on Powell's speech which was probably unrepresentative of Ulster Protestant opinion as a whole. John Taylor, a prominent Official Unionist, drew an important distinction : 'There is absolutely no doubt that *if they were talking of personages* that their loyalty was to the Queen subject only to her being Protestant'.[7] Implicitly recognizing that loyalty to 'personages' is not the currency of modern political discussion, he went on to maintain 'that the average Loyalist today would state without hesitation that his first loyalty was to Ulster rather than to the United Kingdom parliament'. Now, in fact, in our day loyalty is normally evoked by neither a 'personage', nor a constitution, but a community—in particular that peculiarly modern community known as the 'nation'. The Queen evokes loyalty in Britain because she is a symbol of the British (or 'English') nation. The British constitution, precisely because its exponents no longer make any pretence of its having originated in an original compact, but allow that virtually any aspect of it can be altered by 'the Crown in Parliament', depends more than most constitutions upon an active sense of national community to legitimise the actions of government. Indeed, even societies such as the United States, which formally adhere to an original contract, really depend for their cohesiveness upon the willingness of their component communities to submit to the consensus of the national community.[8] If Loyalist spokesmen generally took Mr Taylor's position—that the community of 'Ulster' was the prime object of their loyalty—their attitude would probably be much more easily understood, perhaps even welcomed, in Britain. The British are familiar with nationalism, not only because they have had so often to deal with it in other peoples, but also because it is a vital, if unacknowledged, element in their own political culture.

In fact, however, efforts by Mr Taylor and others at about this time to promote enthusiasm for an 'Ulster identity' and an 'Ulster allegiance' have met with a disappointing response. It is true that the Protestant community in Ulster does evoke loyalty, but not as a 'nation'. Let me hasten to add that I do not mean to deny that community's right to a self-determination separate from the predominantly Catholic 'Irish nation'. As will become clear in this essay, I do not accept the myth of nationalism which permeates modern political attitudes, and one of whose assumptions is that a group's right to self-determination is contingent upon its possession of a 'nationality'. In suggesting that the Ulster Protestant community is not a nation, I mean in part that its own members do not readily conceive it to be a potential claimant to sovereignty. Sovereignty reposes in the crown, and they have been extraordinarily reluctant to contemplate any alternative arrangement. On the other hand, their loyalty to the Queen does not represent, as does that of her British subjects, a nationalist attachment to Britain. That is, it does not legitimise in Ulster the determination of a national consensus operating through the national institutions which she symbolically heads. I am suggesting that the central peculiarity in Ulster's political culture is that no community—not Britain, not the United Kingdom, not 'Ulster' and certainly not Ireland—has attained for Ulster Protestants all the characteristics which a nation commonly possesses in the modern world. In particular, the 'British' nation never succeeded in evoking in Ulster the kind of semi-automatic trust on which modern democratic nation-states rely to establish consent, or what some political scientists call 'diffuse support', even on the part of citizens who bitterly oppose actions of the government of the day. By exploring the origins of this anomaly I believe we can better understand the character of the Ulster Protestant community and thereby delineate more clearly than has hitherto been done the nature of the Northern Ireland problem.

An editorial published in the *News Letter*, the principal organ of Ulster Unionism, three days after Powell's speech provides a useful clue as to those origins. The leader writer argues that Powell's definition of loyalty could be unreservedly accepted anywhere in the U.K. except Northern Ireland, which is unique because of the danger 'of losing unwillingly its United Kingdom connection'. However, Parliament's authority might be resisted only if it were 'traitorous to a section of its population'—as in the case of Sunningdale. The leader writer was at pains—as none of Powell's critics among the politicians were—to agree with his reasoning in specific instances he had cited, such as illegal possession of firearms by Loyalists. Regretting that Powell's speech had caused 'unease' among Unionists, the editorial concluded:

> Had he remembered that loyalty in politics, in business, in social and in domestic relationships, is a two-way link-up that is interrupted when, just as with an electric current, the flow is stopped on one line, he would not have allowed himself to stray into error.[9]

This technological metaphor expresses a venerable theory of political obligation—that of the social contract thinkers who flourished at the time when Ulster was being colonised from England and Scotland. Indeed, 'conditional loyalty', though it seems anomalous in our own day, was very common in the early modern world, at least among that tiny portion of the population which had anything to do with politics. It resembles, in fact, the classic 'Whig' position: one's relationship to the regime is defined by a social contract (more precisely, a 'contract of government')[10] by which both the ruler and the ruled undertake certain obligations to each other. It reduces political obligation to a simple matter of private ethics: one ought to be loyal to the king for the same reason that one should keep ordinary bargains. If the ruler defaults on his side of the bargain the subjects are absolved of their duty to obey his laws. It resembles even more closely the peculiar Scottish variant of contractarian thought and practice, covenanting, in which the proper course for subjects whose king violates his bargain (or refuses to undertake it in the first place) is not to repudiate his regime, but to refuse compliance with his laws and try to coerce him into keeping (or making) the bargain.

Ulster Protestants do not, of course, regulate their political conduct by copies of Locke's *Second Treatise*, or even of the Solemn League and Covenant, somehow lovingly preserved in their families since the seventeenth century. They often do, however, think in terms reminiscent of those documents, as, for example, when Dr Paisley recently warned the Secretary of State that 'government is not a one-way street. It is a civil contract in which each party has a duty.'[11] We can gain insight into Ulster Protestant attitudes toward the sovereign authority, i.e. toward the parliamentary democracy at Westminster, by being alert in the examination of their history to the concepts and issues which preoccupied social contract thinkers in early modern Europe: the 'state of nature' in which there is no government, the purposes of civil society, and the relationship between order and authority. It is by appreciating how Ulster Protestants have handled such issues in the context of fundamental social change since the seventeenth century that we can understand why they avoided the more 'normal' course of investing the 'nation'—any nation—with the attributes of a divine-right monarch.

'The Commendable Practice of these Kingdoms'
1607-1784

State of Nature

If Thomas Hobbes' picture of the life of man in the absence of settled government—'solitary, poor, nasty, brutish, and short'—was suggested to him by the condition of England at the time he wrote, then the province of Ulster at that time was an even closer approximation of such a 'state of nature'. At the end of 1643, each man stood upon his own keeping, and no civil government enjoyed effective authority in the province. In the hinterland of the fortified town of Derry, known as the Laggan,[1] and in the countryside of south Antrim and north Down, British settlers guarded their homesteads against any renewal of the depredations of the native Irish, who two years earlier had driven their compatriots from much of the soil between these two enclaves on which they had settled during the previous generation.

The Irish, for their part, could call upon no effective authority to protect them from the occasional punitive raids of three distinct 'British' military units in the province : the 'Laggan Force' composed 'almost entirely from among the British farmers, labourers and artisans of Tyrone and east Donegal and officered by the landed gentry of those parts',[2] a similar force consisting of the retainers of the Down and Antrim magnates, Lords Conway, Montgomery and Clandeboye, and a Scottish army commanded by Major-General Robert Monro and normally stationed in the walled town of Carrickfergus. Like other native and 'Old English' Catholics, the Ulster Irish were, to be sure, affiliated with the Confederation of Kilkenny, but that body was probably unable to provide the rudiments of settled government in the North. At this moment, according to a contemporary historian of the Confederation, Ulster was in such a state that 'the Confederates of that province began to desert it, and to be a burden to the neighbours' country with their creaghts [nomadic herds]'.[3]

Both settlers and natives recognised in some sense the right of their nominal sovereign, Charles I, to *be* king—as did also his Puritan subjects in England who were openly at war with him under the banner of parliament—but this fact created no disposition to give practical effect to his royal authority. An uneasy calm which for the moment existed in the province owed something to the cessation of hostilities which had just been arranged between the king's representative in Dublin, the Marquis of Ormond, and the Confederation of Kilkenny. It owed more to the convenience of all parties in Ulster, whose resources to carry on continued hostilities were limited, and none of whom trusted either of the parties who had contracted the cessation. The leader of the native Irish in Ulster, Owen Roe O'Neill, acknowledged the Confederation's authority only when it suited him. The Scottish army at Carrickfergus owed a divided allegiance to two of the king's current antagonists—the Scottish Estates and the English parliament. But most important for our purposes are the reasons the British settlers had for profoundly distrusting the king.

Although the absence of civil authority in Ulster in 1643, as I have described it, might seem to derive from the fact that a Civil War was in progress in England, one precipitating cause of that war was a colossal failure of royal policy in Ulster itself, culminating in the native rebellion of 1641. Ironically, the 'plantation' of Ulster with British settlers, which the rebels had almost succeeded in undoing, had been originally conceived as a solution to what British observers regarded as the problem of public order in the province. Following the earlier pacification of the North, which had cost so much blood and treasure in the last decade of Elizabeth's reign, James I's officials had diagnosed the problem of public order in the province as resulting from the survival there of the old Irish social structure in which land was not held in heritable English fashion by individuals, but rather was considered the property of the entire clan in common and was portioned out by the authority of a clan chief who owed his position not to rights of primogeniture but to selection by the clan from candidates meeting certain elaborate kinship requirements. In British eyes, the system led to frequent strife and uncertainty, and to oppression of the humbler clansmen by their leaders. It was believed to encourage rebellion by perpetuating the 'royal' pretensions of the chieftains. More to the point, perhaps, it was adapted to a restless, semi-nomadic lifestyle throughout a clan's 'country' which still survived but which was giving way to more settled agriculture.

An attempt had been made, in keeping with long-standing Tudor policy, to convert the principal Ulster chieftains, 'the O'Neill' and 'the O'Donnell', into feudal magnates on the English model, with the titles Earl of Tyrone and Earl of Tyrconnell. When, however, Tyrone and Tyrconnell, growing restive in the more restrictive role now assigned them, took ship for the continent in 1607 with their principal retainers, the government decided on a more radical step to eradicate the old social order. Their lands,[4] comprising most of the six modern counties of Armagh, Cavan, Donegal, Fermanagh, Londonderry and Tyrone, were deemed escheated to the crown. Into these counties was to be introduced a class of small and middling gentry from England and Scotland who would 'undertake' to build minor fortifications on the portions of land they received at nominal rent from the crown and to populate the land with English and lowland Scottish tenants. Adjacent, but distinct, portions of land were set aside for the native population.

Had this policy been carried out with consistent regard to its framers' intentions, it is possible that today we might regard the Ulster Plantation as an enlightened and progressive act of state-building. If one posits a settled agricultural lifestyle on the English model, there was indeed more land in Ulster than was 'needed' to support comfortably the greatly reduced native population which had survived the terrible devastations of Elizabeth's Irish wars,[5] even if the plan may be faulted for allotting too little land to natives. However, until the native population had undergone the great transformation in outlook which the plan envisaged— the transition which Sir Henry Maine was to describe as the movement 'from Status to Contract'[6]—they would inevitably look upon this characteristically absolutist act of state as larceny on a grand scale, no matter how skilfully the crown's lawyers decked it out. If the Ulster Irish were to accept their new position as tenants of particular holdings in a new 'English' social order, it was essential that the projected scheme be carried out almost to the letter—in particular that a British population substantial enough to defend itself and the new order be introduced quickly. The problem here was simply that the scheme flew in the face of economic reality. Although the typical 'undertaker' did bring a few retainers from England or Scotland, he soon found it much easier and more profitable to let most of his land, in violation of his undertaking, to existing native occupiers, who, because of a lower standard of living, were prepared to pay higher rents than potential British tenants.[7] Only in the coastal counties of Down and Antrim, which were outside the main plantation scheme, did economic conditions favour the substantial immigration which could, and did, create within a generation a British (in particular, Scottish) settlement sufficiently numerous to be truly secure.[8] Defying, as it did the natural workings of economic forces, the plantation throughout most of the escheated counties could be successful only if the government was determined—as was not inconceivable in an age which was innocent of the doctrine of *laissez-faire*—to use its authority to see that its will was carried out.

This is precisely what did not happen. Successive inquiries demonstrated that the temptation to let to natives land reserved for British tenants was standing in the way of the importation of enough British settlers to secure the new order. By the 1630s, when James's son Charles I finally took action against the massive defaults of the City of London and its companies, which had undertaken to plant the entire county of Londonderry, however, he had already embarked on his ill-fated attempt to govern without parliament in England. In keeping with its policy of 'fiscal feudalism' in England in these years, Charles' government showed itself more anxious to use their proven defaults to mulct the undertakers for money he needed to carry on without parliament, than actually to remedy their principal default, the failure to supplant natives with British tenants.[9] The mere fact that many natives did take leases under the new order suggests that the fundamental social transformation posited by the plantation scheme was underway. Nevertheless, menacing elements of the old society lingered on; the hills swarmed with 'woodkerne', native warriors who, from time to time attacked isolated settlers, and who, in turn, were hunted by the settlers much like the wolves who still inhabited the Ulster woods. The exposed position of those who had settled in the province on faith in the crown's determination to make the plantation work, and the exposed position of the crown in British politics in 1641 were of a piece. Together they virtually guaranteed that the native rising in October of that year would succeed in driving the settlers from all but their strongest positions.

Thus those settlers who still stood upon their guard in the province in 1643 had every reason to distrust a king who, having failed to carry out policies which might have secured their position in Ulster, was now openly trying to obtain an army of the very Irish 'Papists' who had almost been their undoing to extricate him from his difficulties in England. What follows, then, is an account of Ulster Protestants' evolving understanding of their relationship to sovereign authority. We begin at a point when that group had, through no fault of the bulk of its members, but in large measure through the delinquency of the sovereign authority, been denied legitimation of its position in society according to the ordinary ethical canons of the age. It is well to draw here a distinction between *support* for the Stuart regime and *trust* of the Stuart king. All parties in Ireland, with the possible exception of a few Ulster Irish, who may have had lingering hopes for realisation of the royal pretensions of the clan chiefs in the province, recognised Charles I as *the* king, by right. There was as yet no republican party in Ireland and certainly no support for an alternative dynasty. For the British planters in Ulster there was really no effective choice other than support for the present regime, and situated as they were, in a remote corner of the king's dominions, nothing they might do in arms could seriously affect his tenure of the throne. Furthermore, at least the Scots among them possessed, in fuller measure perhaps than the English Puritans, that reverence for the person of the king which is characteristic of traditional societies. As we have seen, however, they had good reasons to distrust Charles' actual exercise of his kingly authority and, by virtue of his isolation from the province, ample scope for effective disobedience to his regime's basic political laws.

'True-Bleu Presbyterian Loyalty'

In April, 1644, an opportunity presented itself for the planters to clarify their relationship to the regime. The chaplains who had accompanied the Scottish Army to Ulster two years earlier and had constituted the first presbytery in Ireland were commissioned by the Scottish General Assembly to administer to the Army the Solemn League and Covenant.[10] The Solemn League, from the perspective of English history, was the document setting forth the terms on which the Scottish Estates agreed to assist the English parliament in its quarrel with the king, namely the establishment of Presbyterianism throughout the three kingdoms. In the context of Scottish history, however, it was the culmination of a peculiar social contract tradition. The proximate origins of that tradition lay in the tug-of-war since 1560 between the crown on the one hand and the Kirk, the magnates and the populace on the other. The claims of the Kirk were set out in thoroughly contractarian form by Scottish thinkers, notably George Buchanan in the late sixteenth century and Samuel Rutherford during the crisis of the 1640s. The growing claims of the monarchy were countered with the theory that power properly belonged to the people, who exercised it in their choice of a king and might call him to account for his stewardship of the kingly office.[11]

More important than this recent intellectual tradition was a contractarian social practice of much longer standing which did not arise out of such theoretical considerations. Through the centuries of weak central government in the kingdom, the nobility and gentry had developed a tradition of entering into 'bands' for mutual protection.[12] In the late sixteenth century this tradition had been appropriated by the Kirk—initially with the young King James's approval—fearing that the Reformation in Scotland would be undone by intrigues of Catholic nobles and agents of France and Spain. By the King's Confession of 1580/81, signed first by James and his court, and then circulated for signatures in the countryside,[13] the king was bound to maintain true religion (defined negatively by an elaborate recital of teachings attributed to the 'Roman Antichrist') and his subjects bound to 'defend his [the King's] person and authority with our geare, bodies, and lives, in the defence of Christ, His evangel, liberty of our country, ministration of justice, and punishment of iniquity'.[14] A mass renewal of this band was undertaken at the order of the General Assembly in 1590, and during the next few years the ancient custom of public banding was transmuted into a weapon of the Kirk in its resistance to the anti-Presbyterian tendencies of the monarchy.[15]

This development was assisted by the transformation, which was going on in Scotland as in the rest of Calvinist Christendom, of Calvin's teachings into a 'federal' or 'covenant' theology stressing, as Calvin had not, the 'covenant of works' and 'covenant of grace' to define God's relationship with man. As James made further and further inroads into what many of his Scottish subjects regarded as 'true religion' in the years after his accession to the English throne, a number of preachers were disseminating the idea that Scotland enjoyed a special covenant relation with the Almighty within the larger covenant scheme which was becoming reformed orthodoxy.[16] Scottish Presbyterians were gripped by a mood of apocalyptic expectancy that their country would assume a special role in a universal fulfilment of prophecy.

It was against this background that Charles I attempted to impose a new liturgy upon the Church of Scotland by royal *fiat* rather than through a general assembly. Popular revulsion at the supposedly 'popish' innovations of the prayer book was skillfully used by opponents of the prerogative who drafted and promoted a new band, the National Covenant of 1638. Though the intentions of its projectors may have been conservative—the office of bishop was not condemned[17]—the 'true religion' which its signatories undertook to defend was soon defined by events as thoroughgoing Presbyterianism. The signatories also confessed their allegiance, in the most profuse terms, to the king, though in the context of a reiteration of the obligations undertaken by his father in 1580/81. The Covenant came to be understood as a contract between God and His people: 'Noblemen, Barons, Gentlemen, Burgesses, Ministers, and Commons',[18] to which the king ought properly also to be a party. It was a contract of government (not, strictly speaking, a social contract executed in the state of nature) *in posse*. The ensuing conflict, known in England as the Civil War, was for Scotland the struggle to compel the king to execute the contract. Full of zeal to reform the world on the Scottish model, the Scots thought they had committed the English Puritans to their peculiar vision in 1643 with the latter's adherence to the Solemn League.

The position of the Scottish Covenanters was in many respects similar to that adopted by the Confederate Catholics in Ireland.[19]

Both groups bound themselves by a solemn oath to support the king's tenure of the throne while withholding compliance with his rule—even taking up arms against his forces—in the interest of compelling him to honour what they conceived to be obligations of the crown. In Rose's terms, both groups were taking an 'ultra' position, and the parallel between them is a pointed reminder that the seemingly peculiar conjunction of attitudes among Ulster Protestants in recent times, whose origins we are seeing, would not have appeared so extraordinary in the seventeenth century.

The army chaplains who set out to administer the Solemn League to Monro's troops in 1644, soon found that 'in those places where the covenant was administered to the army, the whole country about came and willingly joined themselves in the covenant'.[20] They thereupon undertook a tour of Protestant settlements and garrisons, expounding the covenant to populace, as well as soldiers. Up to this point religion, *per se*, had played only a peripheral role in the politics of the Ulster colony. The colonists were Protestants and the natives Catholics, but that was only one difference between the two populations, who, like the Lowlanders and Highlanders of Scotland, exhibited more striking contrasts in language, dress and customs. Moreover, to be a Protestant meant simply to adhere to the Church by law established. Although some of the Scots in Ulster had Presbyterian leanings, and although under the mild and moderately Calvinist rule of Archbishop Ussher some bishops had been willing to make concessions to satisfy the Presbyterian scruples of clergy in the Scottish settlements, the religious enthusiasms of Scotland seem not to have infected the colony very severely. Prior to the 1640s, the Ulster colony, like frontier society in nineteenth-century America, was subject to outbursts of revivalism (notably in 1625 along the Sixmilewater) but was probably not preoccupied with spiritual affairs. During Laud's ascendancy in England, clergy of Presbyterian leanings were deposed in Ulster without creating widespread popular disaffection. The crisis of 1638 in Edinburgh passed off without triggering any systematic effort to administer the covenant in Ulster, though resentment was aroused by the government's ham-handed and probably unnecessary efforts to administer to the Ulster Scots an oath (which came to be known as 'the Black Oath') renouncing the covenant.[21] The relative disinterest over the proceedings in Scotland in 1638, a time, when, if we are to believe the Presbyterian historians of the next generation, the Ulster plantation was full of 'profane and wicked men', the 'scum' of both England and Scotland,[22] contrasts sharply with the outpouring of enthusiasm with which the ministers were received when they went about administering the Solemn League in 1644. We do not have to adopt the pious view that the rebellion was God's plan for disposing of sinners to make way for godly people,[23] to recognise that it had created a wholly new situation.

When the ministers were in Derry they received a request from the local Protestants who constituted the garrison at Enniskillen that they come and administer the covenant to them. When the ministers hesitated to make the journey of nearly fifty miles, partly through hostile country, the garrison proposed to march to Derry themselves, take the covenant and return to their post. The ministers then agreed to go, because had the garrison come to Derry they could not have stayed away from their post long enough for the ministers to inquire carefully into their sincerity before administering the oath. The garrison thought the ministers to be 'over scrupulous',[24] and here we hit upon the real significance of the exercise. Whereas for the ministers the covenant was an engagement to undertake a great spiritual crusade in which the Scots had been singled out by God to reform first the other two kingdoms and ultimately the world, for the Ulster Protestant populace it had much more immediacy. It was, quite simply, a public band against the danger, now all too apparent, from the natives. As the ministers and their retinue travelled from Derry to Enniskillen, the Irish, 'hearing the covenant was coming that way, fled, because they heard that the covenant was to extirpate all Papists'.[25] They had heard not what the Covenant actually said, but probably what some of the local Protestants believed or wanted it to say.

The 1644 situation provides an archetype for Ulster Protestant history. The sovereign authority had tried to create a system of public order—in this instance a pyramid of quasi-feudal relationships between individuals at whose apex was the king himself, and it had failed catastrophically in 1641. Though their removal from Britain had largely isolated the settlers from the ecclesiastical and political controversies which had triggered the 1638 covenanting episode in Scotland, the 1641 rebellion had brought home to them in the starkest possible way realities almost identical with those which had originally prompted the covenanting tradition in Scotland. They learned that public order derived in reality not from the sovereign authority (nor from its representatives in Dublin Castle), but from their own exertions on the ground. The appearance of the Scottish clergy prepared to administer the covenant provided them with a social ritual closely corresponding to their perceived relationship to authority. Those who took the covenant were contracting 'to preserve and defend the King's Majesty's person and authority, in the preservation and defence of the true religion and liberties of the kingdoms'.[26] The support for the king expressed here was of a very conditional sort, for other parts of the document made plain that 'true religion' did not embrace precisely the religion Charles I sincerely held, namely 'Prelacy'. Covenanting was a way of expressing profuse support for the king while withholding compliance until he should himself become a Covenanter. It defined the relationship of a royalist subject to a monarch who could not be trusted. The enthusiasm for the covenant which the ministers met throughout Ulster in 1644 probably derived less from deeply-felt Presbyterian conviction than from the fact that its purpose was 'the preservation *of ourselves* and our religion from utter ruin and destruction, according to the commendable practice of these kingdoms in former times'.[27]

During the Civil War and Interregnum, Presbyterian ministers obtained most of the livings in the areas of intensive Scottish settlement. Although they were ejected from these livings in 1661, the persecuted church they led survived and retained the adherence of the vast majority of the Scottish settlers, though not of the Scottish landlords. (Conformity was a virtual necessity for those who wanted to play the game whose stakes were the millions of acres of land which had changed hands in twenty years of upheaval.) In at least some formal sense the Solemn League and Covenant remained the contract of government by which they regulated their attitude to authority. Moreover, they interpreted that document in accordance with Scottish Presbyterian, not English Puritan, logic. When the English Puritans so missed the point of the covenanting exercise as to chop off the head of the Lord's anointed in 1649, the Ulster presbytery, like its Scottish mother church, roundly condemned them.[28] The

point was not to repudiate the king—still less to execute him—
but to coerce him into signing the covenant. Indeed, in 1650 the
young King Charles II did reluctantly sign a declaration of his
father's errors at Dunfermline, and at his Scottish coronation on
1 January 1651 he subscribed both the National Covenant of
1638 and the Solemn League. Though Cromwell quickly established the Commonwealth's authority in Scotland, as he had
already done in Ireland, the Ulster Presbyterians, like their
counterparts in Scotland, continued to recognise Charles II as
their rightful king and refused to acknowledge the Cromwellian
government.

The Presbyterian clergy did manage to reconcile their non-
recognition of the Cromwellian regime with acceptance of
salaries, in lieu of tithes (the true Kirk's just due) from that
regime. Despite Charles' betrayal of the covenant upon his
restoration, Presbyterians, whose continued practice of their
religion constituted a violation of his basic political laws, considered themselves the staunchest of his supporters and the most
honest and consistent of his subjects. Though they had few
opportunities to state their case publicly before 1690, we do get a
clear statement of it in the early eighteenth century from the
Rev. John McBride, Presbyterian minister of Belfast, in reply to
an episcopalian attack under the ironic title *A Sample of True-
Bleu Presbyterian Loyalty*. He defined the word 'Loyal' as simply
the French word for 'lawful', the description of 'the King's
Liege-man, as he is his *Liege-Lord*; for so he was called of old
by virtue of his allegiance or *liegancy*, signifying a mutual bond,
. . . i.e., *a strict bond, between the King and his Subjects*;
*mutually obliging each to other; the King to protection and just
government; the Subject to pay tribute and due obedience*'.[29]
Indeed, he argued, Charles II himself had taught such principles
to his subjects in his 1650 declaration at Dunfermline :

That the King shall always esteem Them *best Servants* and
most Loyal Subjects, who serve and seek his Greatness, in a
Right line of Subordination to God; Giving unto God the
Things that are God's, and to *Caesar* the Things that are
Caesar's : and resolveth not to Love and Countenance any who
have so little Conscience and Piety, as to follow his Interest,
to the Prejudice of the Gospel and Kingdom of Jesus Christ :

Which he looks not on, as Duty, but Flattery, and driving on
Self-Designs, under pretence of maintaining Royal Authority
and Greatness.[30]

'This', McBride triumphantly concluded in large type, 'is True-
bleu *Presbyteria[n]* Loyalty.'

Around 1670, to the dismay of the episcopal authorities, but
sometimes with the secret connivance of the easy-going king,[31]
the Ulster Presbyterians set about erecting as much as possible of
the mechanism of presbyterian jurisdiction in areas of Scottish
dominance. In their own eyes, their institution was not a mere
sect seeking toleration, but 'ye church off Ireland'.[32] In general,
they avoided the courses by which a minority of Presbyterians in
Scotland eventually came to repudiate the king altogether.[33]
Writing to a friend in Dublin at the time of the Bothwell rising
of 1679 in Scotland, a Ballymoney Episcopalian divided the
Presbyterians into two categories, the 'very impatient' and the
'more moderate':

> The former Sort have their expectations on the good fortunes
> of the present Rebels in Scotland. The latter would seem to
> expect all from the next sessions of Parliament in England;
> saying, their Brethren in Scotland are too hasty with the
> Covena[nt] since it was coming about of it self.[34]

Actually, the 'more moderate' attitude was far more characteristic
among Ulster Presbyterians and is reflected in a contemporary
letter from the Rev. Robert Rule, minister of Derry, to one of the
local gentry concerning the Scottish insurrection:

> . . . though I could not but commiserate and pity them under
> these sad oppressions which provoked them unto it, yet I am
> far from approving such an attempt against lawful authority
> and could heartily have wished they had sitten still under
> them until the lord had given them another issue, and as I
> know none of our persuasion in this country who are for such
> courses (neither have they any temptation thereunto from the
> lenity and indulgence of the magistrate allowing us the free
> exercise of our religion and worship) so, for my own part,
> though we were deprived of that I should hold myself obliged
> quietly and patiently to suffer, for I profess that dangerous
> principle to propagate religion by arms is none of mine. This

is the ingenuous account of my most inward thoughts, who is desirous of nothing earthly more passionately than to approve myself a loyal and faithful subject of his majesty, . . .[35]

What Rule described as 'our religion and worship' was, from the standpoint of the episcopal authorities, the exercise of a competing jurisdiction, not only over doctrine and liturgy but over areas of public morality which the law formally reserved to them. The ministers had authorized the compilation of an official history of their institution, whose author would entitle it 'A true Narrative of the Rise and Progress of the Presbyterian Government in the North of Ireland'—not, as its nineteenth-century redactor preferred, 'of the Presbyterian Church in Ireland'.[36] Though they hoped for a legal Presbyterian establishment through the instrumentality of a change in parliamentary opinion or of God intervening to give 'another issue', which in those days was believed to be a literal possibility, the well-understood reality was that they did exercise the rudiments of Presbyterian government within the territory populated by Presbyterians, and they did so with the King's connivance. It is noteworthy that while Rule denies that any Presbyterians of his acquaintance in Ireland favour the Scottish rebellion, he does not claim to speak for anyone but himself on the question of what would happen if 'the lenity and indulgence of the magistrate' were withdrawn.

The characteristic Presbyterian attitude toward the sovereign authority emerges from the testimony of Rev. William Trail of Lifford, who was called before the Privy Council in 1681 for having appointed a public fast—a power not legally delegated by the king even to archbishops.[37] Trail found himself closely questioned by Primate Boyle as to allegations that he had been trying to dissuade soldiers quartered near Derry from taking the oath of supremacy:

BOYLE But do you acknowledge the king's supremacy?

TRAIL Yes.

BOYLE But do you acknowledge the king's supremacy in ecclesiastical matters?

TRAIL Yes. We allow unto the king a supremacy in ecclesiastical matters.

BOYLE But do you acknowledge that the king has power to establish the ecclesiastical government?

B

TRAIL Yes, and that we do too. But I will deal ingenuously with your grace [addressing Lord Lieutenant Ormond to avoid acknowledging Boyle's ecclesiastical authority]. I do not believe that the king has power to set up what government he pleases in the Church; but that he has power to set up the due and true government of the Church.[38]

This, indeed, was the crux of the matter, and Trail was able to score a point against the Primate by pointing out that many episcopalians took exactly the same position : that the king had no power to establish any church government but the one they regarded as *jure divino*. 'All the difference then is', Ormond interposed with evident amusement at the Primate's expense, 'that when the king sets up the one government you say he is in the right; and when he sets up the other, they say he is in the right.'

Unable to shake Trail's confident assertion of 'support' for the King, Boyle probed his attitude toward compliance. To the Primate's query, 'But you make resistance', Trail replied with incontrovertible fact : 'We make no resistance.' 'But you can or may make resistance', Boyle continued, to which Trail rejoined, 'A man may go mad', evoking laughter from the council. When the Primate pressed on to ask 'But is it not lawful to make resistance?' however, Trail responded with an interesting bit of evasion :

May it please your grace [addressing Ormond, as always] this is hard to put such a mean subject as I am and a man of my coat so to it to answer such questions, which must be determined by judges and lawyers how far it is permittable by law and according to the covenant betwixt the king and the people.[39]

The position of Presbyterianism between the 1640s and the 1680s is relevant to our understanding of public order and the problem of allegiance even though the fundamental problem of public order was 'solved' for a generation by Cromwell's vigorous suppression of Catholic resistance to the Commonwealth, by Charles II's possession of much greater political sagacity than his father, and, probably, by the migration of greater numbers of British settlers to Ulster in the generation after 1641 than in the generation before. Presbyterians came to rest their case for their

exercise of ecclesiastical jurisdiction upon the voluntary acquiescence of their members,[40] which, they maintained, was compatible
with continued allegiance to the crown despite its contravention
of the jurisdiction sanctioned formally by the crown. They were
making a *de facto* assertion of popular sovereignty under the
guise of *jure divino* propositions.

Through this assertion they sustained a lively sense that one's
allegiance to a remote king was quite compatible with a robust
local initiative even in defiance of the king's authority in matters
over which the king might claim formal jurisdiction. In fact, this
particular initiative was confined to a politically tangential aspect
of the problem of public order; deviations of Presbyterians themselves from the norms enjoined by seventeenth-century Calvin-
ism; its objects were the sabbath-breaker, the fornicator and
perhaps the occasional sheep-stealer. Nevertheless, it is a significant episode in the evolution of the idea that the legitimacy of
the sovereign authority is not to be challenged, but its proper role
vis-à-vis Ulster Protestants is to sanction the means they adopt for
preserving public order in their own territory according to their
lights. When the larger threat to public order—the native Catholics' assertion of what they regarded as their patrimonial rights—
should again be posed, the specifically Presbyterian forms of the
public band would be seen to be irrelevant and be discarded.

Indeed, already Presbyterianism was becoming detached from
literal adherence to the covenant. Although the formal ordination rules of 1672 still required candidates for the ministry to
take the covenant,[41] the practice seems already to have been in
decline by that date.[42] Though our information on attitudes
among the laity is much more limited than for the clergy, it is
probable that many laymen continued longer than their clergy
to consider the covenant literally binding not only upon them but
upon their posterity. In 1683 an Anglican gentleman observed
that at Larne, even though a Scottish father would have to do
penance before the congregation if he had 'made bold with his
Bride before hand' still 'generally the people will not omit Christ-
ening with their own Minister, Supposing the Children to be
Christened into the Solemn League and Covenant'.[43]

Though Charles II was clearly untrustworthy, so long as he
was king there was always a chance, however unrealistic it may
appear in retrospect, that he would have a change of heart and

honour his 1651 undertaking. Occasional measures of indulgence
to Presbyterians, such as his secret provision of small stipends for
their ministers in 1672, encouraged such hopes.[44] The accession
of his brother James II in 1685 created a wholly new situation,
for James was not only an uncovenanted king, but an avowed
Roman Catholic. Even if he could have been reduced to such
extremities as had driven his brother to sign the covenant in
1651, his signature would have been worthless, for it was firmly
believed that the pope would release any Catholic from an oath
which conflicted with the Church's interests. Two courses of
action were open. The first was advocated by Rev. David
Houston, the Ulster counterpart of the extreme Cameronians in
Scotland, who became particularly active during James's reign.
There is evidence that Houston was attracting a sufficient following to alarm the majority of Presbyterian clergy, who took steps
to silence him.[45] Presumably he was arguing that the accession of
an avowed Papist absolved Presbyterians of any allegiance to the
regime in London and justified rebellion to obtain some new
covenanted king. His colleagues were steering clear of overt expressions of support for James—fortunately none seem to have been
demanded of them—and taking the alternative course of praying
for deliverance from a dilemma to which their tradition gave no
clear guidelines.[46]

Deliverance was foreshadowed in 1688 when a combination
of magnates in England acted to hasten the 'abdication' of James
in favour of his Protestant daughter Mary and her husband
William, Prince of Orange. In the North of Ireland the crisis
was accompanied by rumours that the Catholics were planning
a general massacre of Protestants such as they were believed to
have attempted in 1641. In settlements throughout the province
Protestants spontaneously entered into new public bands for
mutual defence, but this time without specifically Presbyterian
aims. There are shreds of evidence that the Presbyterian ministers
hoped to extract from William, who could almost be deemed a
Presbyterian himself, an establishment of Presbyterianism for the
northern province alone, within an otherwise episcopal Church of
Ireland.[47] They made no effort, however, to have such aspirations included in the public bands. The Houstonites, who wanted
to admit only covenanters to fight for King William, turned out
to be a derisory minority, and in the end Houston himself agreed

to use his influence for the uncovenanted Protestant cause.[48] In the East of the province, the band took the form of an 'Antrim Association' of prominent landowners 'in behalf of our selves, and Protestant Tenants'.[49] In the fortified towns of Derry and Enniskillen in the West, it took the form of resolutions on the part of townsfolk not to admit Roman Catholic troops which James's government, still in control of Dublin Castle and most of the Irish countryside, was seeking to quarter within their walls.

Though the news of William's landing in England was 'very acceptable to the generality of the Protestants of Ireland',[50] the public bands in their inception were not attempts to meddle in the dynastic struggle. Protestants were acting upon 'the Law of Self-preservation (one of the Ancientest of the World)'[51] to devise 'some method, besides those ordinarily appointed by the Laws, for their own defence; and preserving as much as in them lies, the publick Peace of the Nation, which is so much endeavoured to be disturbed by Popish and Illegal Counsellors, and their Abettors'.[52] Despite the fact that their action blatantly defied his authority, the Derry citizenry still regarded James as their legitimate sovereign when they declared, early in December,

> that as we have resolved to stand upon our guard, and defend our walls, and not to admit of any Papist whatsoever to quarter among us, so we have firmly and sincerely determined to persevere in our duty and loyalty to our sovereign Lord the King, without the least umbrage of mutiny or seditious opposition to his royal commands. . . .
> GOD SAVE THE KING.[53]

There is, of course, a certain irony in a body of citizens professing loyalty in terms which would have excluded the very object of that loyalty from setting foot in their town. Nevertheless, a coherent theory of political obligation, rendered more serviceable by the jettison of Presbyterian baggage by the renewed public bands, is implicit in Ulster Protestant behaviour: the king, whoever he is, is sovereign, but he is also a long way away. The actual maintenance of public order in those wild parts depended, they believed, upon their own efforts, and if those efforts should bring them into opposition to royal authority, that opposition was not 'seditious', as it did not attack his right to *be* king (preferably a long way away). Only when William had clearly won the game in England did the banded Protestants openly declare for him—he was proclaimed king in the besieged town of Derry on 21 March 1689—and finally in 1690 he landed at Carrickfergus, defeated the forces of James at the Boyne on 1 July, and in succeeding months established his authority throughout Ireland. The relationship between the sovereign authority and the public band had been clear enough when the operative band was the Solemn League and Covenant: it was the sovereign's duty to join the band and, so long as he refused, his subjects, while not repudiating him, should not comply with his laws. The demise of the covenant meant that in the 1688–90 crisis this relationship was somewhat hazy. Developments in Ulster and Ireland during the eighteenth century would clarify the relationship on a new basis.

True Whigs and Lurking Enemies

The Williamite Revolution determined the shape of Irish politics and society for the succeeding ninety years, and we must therefore consider some of the consequences of that revolution. In the first place, William solved what we might call the 'Presbyterian question'. To understand this we must first remember that the northern Presbyterians were already disposed to accept the reality of an episcopal establishment in Ireland, though they hoped for as advantageous a position as possible within that framework. This reality was dictated by the simple fact that, since the Restoration, power throughout the British Isles had found its way back into the hands of the propertied, and the Presbyterian church in Ulster, despite its social strength, was essentially an institution of men of little or no property. William had happened upon the scene at a moment when it was possible to disarm religion of its political sting by satisfying the claims of the religious professionals. One of his first acts upon landing in Ulster was to order small salaries (the *regium donum*) to be paid to the Presbyterian clergy out of royal funds. As this was a public transaction (unlike Charles II's secret promise of such salaries in 1672) ministers could plausibly maintain that they had a sort of quasi-establishment status alongside the Church of Ireland clergy in Presbyterian districts. Despite infringements of full civil liberties (which in any event caused serious inconvenience only for that tiny minority of Presbyterians with enough property to participate in politics) the *regium donum* was regularly paid until 1870, except for a brief interval near the end of Queen Anne's reign.

The covenanting phenomenon virtually disappeared in Ulster, as it did also in Scotland with the attainment in 1690 of 'Presbyterianism in one country'. The antecedent tradition of public banding also lost its relevance in Scotland with the growing imposition of public order upon the country. In Ireland, however, there *was* a continuing threat to public order, however exaggerated that threat might have been in Protestant minds— unlike Scotland,[54] the country really *was* full of Catholics. In effect, public banding was not abandoned, but from 1688 was transmuted into an exercise embracing not only Presbyterians, but those English (and indeed Scottish) settlers who were attached to the episcopal establishment as well. Whether under the name of the Antrim Association in 1689, the militia in 1715, 1719, 1745, 1756 and 1760, or the Volunteers in 1778, the Protestant tenantry were accustomed to being arrayed in arms under their landlords' leadership to maintain order whenever the French/ Spanish/Catholic/Jacobite threat with the presumed native threat accompanying it, reared its ugly head. The habit sustained in the Protestant community the sense that public order really derived more from their exertions than from the activities of the sovereign authority. Indeed, the central government might find itself bestowing its sanction on the militia only after the latter had in fact been constituted in the countryside.[55] Given Presbyterian abandonment of their insistence that the king be a Presbyterian, and the fact, established in 1689 and confirmed in the 1701 Act of Settlement, that the monarchy would be perpetually Protestant, the relationship between the public band and the crown itself ceased to be a problem.

However, another consequence of the Williamite Revolution was a major change in the position of the crown. Although English parliaments had occasionally attempted to legislate for Ireland, in constitutional theory Ireland was a distinct kingdom, and such legislation was applied to Ireland only at the king's pleasure. Moreover, although the Irish parliament's initiative was severely constrained by Poynings' Law of 1494, that Act gave powers of revision and veto over Irish legislation not to the English parliament, but to the King's privy council in England.

These points of constitutional theory were formally unaffected by the Revolution, but William and Mary's renunciation of various prerogatives in the Bill of Rights, and their recognition of parliament's dominance in England, crucially altered the constitutional reality. The crown could no longer effectively stand in the way of the English parliament's desire to control Irish affairs, and in 1719 that parliament even formally asserted in the Declaratory Act, the famous 'Sixth of George I', its power to pass legislation binding on Ireland. Moreover, during the next several decades executive power came to be exercised by ministers accountable in practice, if not yet in theory, to parliamentary majorities in England.[56] Thus, just as the problem of the Ulster Protestant community's relationship to the sovereign authority of the crown was 'solved', the crown was ceasing to be in practice the ultimate repository of public authority in Ireland. To understand how the relationship between public order, reposing in the bands, and the public authority of the English (after 1707, British) political system, we must consider the landed elite whose leadership in Ulster was still an essential feature of the bands.

This elite consisted not only of the heirs of the undertakers in the North, but also of Protestant gentry throughout Ireland whose propertied position (except for a few Gaelic and Anglo-Norman families who had converted to Protestantism) derived from subsequent forfeitures. Though the Ulster Irish had little left to forfeit when they initiated the rebellion of 1641, Catholics still owned 59 per cent of the land in the whole of Ireland at that time.[57] The English parliament had raised money to suppress the rebellion by selling shares of 'adventure' redeemable in land to be forfeited by the rebels. The settlement of this transaction by the Cromwellian regime, the payment of soldiers' arrears in Irish land, and the adjustment of a variety of other claims after the Restoration had reduced the proportion of Irish land owned by Catholics to 22 per cent. During James II's brief reign in Dublin, a virtually all-Catholic parliament passed Acts which, had the Jacobite cause succeeded, would have reconfiscated the land of virtually all Protestants and restored the Catholic gentry to their patrimony. Not surprisingly, therefore, the Williamites implemented further forfeitures so that by 1703 Catholics owned a mere 14 per cent of the land of Ireland.

Though the Irish ascendancy, like the English governing class, was divided into Whigs and Tories in day-to-day politics, even the Tories were Whiggish on the fundamentals of the Revolution settlement. Indeed, the ascendancy developed elaborate rituals[58] for acting out their Whiggish principles in commemoration of their deliverance by the great King William from 'popery, slavery and arbitrary power'. Now in England, Whiggery was associated with the contractarian theory of political obligation embodied in the famous resolution by which the Commons of the English Convention in 1689 rationalised the Revolution:

> That King James II, having endeavoured to subvert the constitution of his kingdom by breaking the original contract between the king and people, and by the advice of Jesuits and other wicked persons, having withdrawn himself out of the kingdom, has abdicated the Government; . . .[59]

This notion that the English constitution embodied an original contract between prince and people became the accepted orthodoxy of political life in the eighteenth century, despite manifold difficulties in specifying just when and how the bargain had been entered into.[60] Even Tories found it easy to adopt the Whig orthodoxy, at least after 1714, as the reality that power now rested firmly in the hands of the propertied class gave its members few reasons to anticipate any further 'violation' of the contract.

For Englishmen of property, the theories of John Locke could provide a neat, self-contained myth accounting for both the origin of their property and the political power they now exercised by virtue of it.[61] Property had arisen out of the innocuous activity of gathering acorns in the primeval woods. In this 'state of nature', individuals contracted to form a civil society and entrusted power to a government in order to protect those pre-existing property rights; in England James II had violated his trust by invading those rights; Englishmen of property thereupon entrusted a new prince with power, taking care this time to make him answerable to themselves. Although civil society is formed by a social contract according to Locke, the relationship between the society and its government is not strictly speaking a contract, but a trusteeship. The community retains all the rights, the government all the duties, like a trustee in ordinary law. The concept of trusteeship became part of the Whig vocabulary, though popular contractarian thought did not always distinguish clearly between a contract and a trust. The Whig notion of political obligation—that the people were bound to support the regime only so long as the regime fulfilled its undertaking to protect their rights (primarily rights of property)—was in any event practically the same whether the undertaking was regarded as a contract or a trust.

To be sure, Locke's state of nature was simply a fiction invented to meet the needs of the theory, but it did have a certain element of reality for the only people whose attitude toward political obligation mattered very much in early eighteenth-century England, the aristocracy and gentry. In Locke's state of nature, each man, by natural right, supposedly performed the function of maintaining order. In early modern England, each *gentleman*, by a right which seemed just as natural, really did perform the function of maintaining order in his own neighbourhood. No government of that day could contemplate carrying out this vital role of the state with paid civil servants; all governments relied upon the gentry in the role of magistrates to maintain order in the countryside. (Indeed, it can be argued that James II's downfall came when he appeared to be tampering with accepted practice in this matter.) If conceived as embracing the whole population, Locke's state of nature was not only fictitious, it was unthinkable. If conceived as a description of the rights and relationships of the landed elite on the hypothesis that the central authority should disappear, it seemed natural, inevitable and right. Locke's theory, as understood by eighteenth-century Whiggery, was a rationale for the political obligation not of the citizen, but of the proconsul.

For Irishmen of property, matters were not so simple. Manifestly, Irish property had not originated in acorn-gathering. Nearly every Irish Protestant landowner knew he had a Catholic counterpart who considered the land rightfully his, who believed it had been taken from his ancestors by violence or chicane, and who might very well leave his heirs a testamentary deed to keep alive the memory of their patrimony.[62] The Irish alternative to Locke's acorn-gathering story was the myth of the 1641 massacre. In calling the massacre a myth I do not mean to deny that very many killings did occur. What was mythical was the widespread belief that literally hundreds of thousands of Protestants had been murdered. The most popular figure, 150,000, probably owed its currency to the fact that it corresponded closely to the number of Ulster Protestants believed available for massacring.[63] The myth amounts to an assertion that the Catholic Irish attempted what would today be called genocide against the British Protestants and that therefore not just the particular culprits but the entire race was justly deprived of its land, which arrangement the Williamite settlement confirmed.

It was impossible to integrate this myth into a satisfactory larger myth of the origins of political authority. The landed class in Ireland, unlike their English counterparts, tended to be dissatisfied with the political power they derived from their propertied position, for the Irish parliament was becoming more obviously subordinate to the British Government after the Revolution. When an Irish Whig, such as William Molyneux, tried to construct a theory that the Irish parliament was entitled to powers established by a contract of government between king and people, he was up against the unavoidable reality that if any such transaction had occurred, it must have been a contract with the ancestors of the very people who had been deprived of their property. His English critics were not taken in by the preposterous fiction to which he resorted : that 'the great Body of the present People of *Ireland* are the Progeny of the *English* and *Britains*, that from time to time have come over into this kingdom; and there remains but a meer handful of the antient *Irish* at this day; I may say, not one in a thousand'.[64] Actually, there would not be any Irish Protestants, William Atwood unkindly but realistically pointed out, without 'the Protection of England'. 'If the *Irish Natives* are not conquered', he continued, and if just conquest gives no more title to the conqueror than Molyneux was willing to allow, then

> let the *English* in *Ireland* look to it how to justifie those Possessions which they enjoy by the help of the Crown and Kingdom of England; and if their Consciences are squeamish, let them renounce their Right to the Lands of the Natives but let them not bring in to question the Right of *Engl.* to all Foreign Plantations : and let them never fear that equal Power here to which a great part of the *English Nation*, [i.e., the unenfranchised] are resigned, without any other kind of

consent than the people of *Ireland* have given, to the Laws made in *England,* with intention to bind them, and be published there.[65]

The popularity of Molyneux's argument that only the King, Lords and Commons of Ireland had power to legislate for her was probably undiminished among the Irish ascendancy by attacks such as Atwood's. Nevertheless, the hard truths stated by Atwood accurately reflected the position they had to adopt toward an English nation which regarded itself as having bailed them out twice in fifty years. However great their Whiggish disdain for arbitrary power in the person of the monarch, their own understanding of the origins of their own propertied position led inexorably to a need, for the time being at least, to acquiesce in what could be depicted as arbitrary power on the part of the British political system over them.

Actually the exercise of British authority in the Irish political system was not wholly arbitrary—most British ministries were anxious to obtain their objectives in Ireland by persuasion. Moreover, although the Irish parliament failed to attain the dominance over the executive which its English counterpart achieved, parliaments could no longer be ignored after the Revolution, even in Ireland. It was quite possible before 1689 for monarchs to govern Ireland without calling a parliament for many years at a stretch—the last previous Irish parliament had met in 1665—but within a few years after the Revolution a parliament was meeting regularly in Dublin every second year. There was thus, for the first time, an institutional focus for the political life of the landed elite, whose members controlled representation in the Commons even more completely than did their English counterparts. From the very first Williamite parliament, the Irish ascendancy chafed against the restrictions upon their parliamentary independence. Though the beginnings of a 'Patriot Party' can be discerned in the 1720s, it was only in the 1750s that such a party, regularly opposing the government on 'constitutional' issues, became a force to be reckoned with.[66] Commenting on one of the early victories of the Patriot Party in 1753, the rejection of a bill for applying a revenue surplus to the reduction of the national debt after the privy council had amended it to imply that the king had given his 'previous consent'. i.e., that the crown, and therefore the British ministry, controlled the surplus anyway, Lord Charlemont wrote :

> Men were . . . accustomed to turn their thoughts to constitutional subjects, and to reflect on the difference between political freedom and servitude, a reflection which for many years had been overlooked, or wholly absorbed in the mobbish misconception of Whig principle. They were taught to know that Ireland had, or ought to have, a constitution, and to perceive that there was something more in the character of a Whig than implicit loyalty to king George, a detestation of the Pretender, and a fervent zeal for the Hanover succession—excellent qualities when they flow from principle, but trivial at best when every principle is made to flow from them.[67]

Although Charlemont composed these remarks many years later, they do reflect the understanding the Patriot Party came to have, if not their actual thinking in the 1750s. In particular, his ambiguity over whether Ireland 'had' or 'ought to have' a constitution reflects an emerging rationalisation of political obligation compatible with some sort of action to remedy the Irish ascendancy's growing political frustration.

Did Ireland have a constitution or not? The constitution Charlemont referred to was the one described by Molyneux as having originated in a compact between the Irish people and the king shortly after the Anglo-Norman invasion of the twelfth century, and which provided that Ireland be governed by the King, Lords and Commons of Ireland. By rights Ireland still 'had' this constitution, and Charlemont's phrase 'or ought to have ' was intended to assert that its practical effect had been nullified by British constitutional developments since 1688, and by specific actions of the British government and parliament, such as the Sixth of George I. Now actually, the Irish parliament had never in practice possessed substantially greater powers than it was exercising in the mid-eighteenth century. The Patriot Party was suffering from a sense of relative deprivation because the Irish parliament's powers had not been increased, like those of its English counterpart, by virtue of the Williamite Revolution. Put slightly differently, Ireland indeed had a 'constitution'—one which included Poynings' Law and, by now, the Sixth of George I—but she had never had an opportunity to establish its

contractual character in the minds of Englishmen. It was not this
actual constitution, but the contractual constitution of Molyneux
which Ireland 'ought to have' and to which Patriots were referring when they profusely expressed loyalty to King *and Constitution*.

The efforts of the Patriot Party were directed toward getting
the British political system to endorse Molyneux's 'constitution'
much as in the preceding century the Covenanters had sought to
get the King to sign the covenant. Might this constitution provide
the needed link between the public order maintained by the
bands and public authority at Westminster and Dublin Castle?
To establish such a link would require a more innovative outlook
than was exhibited at the outbreak of war with France in 1756
by Samuel Blacker of Tanderagee, who called it a time

> to show true patriotism in arming ourselves with the spirit of
> liberty in favour of our king and country against the gasconad-
> ing insolence of the French. If Ireland is to be attacked, it will
> be by our lurking enemies at home, who are bred up with
> notions of eternal salvation by the utter annihilation of
> Protestants.[68]

Significantly, however, some of the Patriot Clubs formed in
the aftermath of the 1753 victory over the revenue surplus, were
willing, at least cautiously, to associate the danger of oppression
at the hands of French and native Catholics with that posed by
the ministerial opponents of their constitutional programme. The
County Down Patriot Club, 'animated by that Spirit of Liberty,
which alone is productive of true Loyalty' resolved to

> plight our Faith on the present critical Juncture to his Majesty
> King George and his Royal House, the Publick, and to each
> other, that we will arm Ourselves and Tenants, subject to, and
> under the auspicious Direction of our most gracious Sovereign,
> in Defence of his Majesty and the essential Rights of Com-
> munity, against all Usurpations of his Neighbours and
> Treachery of his Servants, that Source of Hope to his
> Enemies.[69]

This linkage of the public band to the emerging ideology of the
Patriot Party was made more explicit by the County Antrim
Club. In resolving to defend the King's person, dominions and

royal house, 'and that most excellent Constitution which has placed him at the Head of these Nations', they took the occasion to declare their inflexible opposition to 'all measures tending to infringe the sacred Rights of the People, by subjecting them in an undue Degree to the Power and Influence of ministerial Cabals, and to sap the Basis of our Security and Happiness, by violating that matchless Constitution which our Ancestors established by their Blood'.[70]

Latent in this posturing was a conception of political obligation which might justify turning the public band against the Westminster regime in the name of loyalty to a constitution which that regime was deemed to have infringed. In 1778 a situation arose in which such a possibility might be realized. The revolt in the American colonies had drained the island of troops, the coasts of naval protection, and the treasury of money. With the entry of France into the conflict on the American side, French ships began to appear menacingly off the Irish coast. The government appeared powerless to act, and, as Lecky has written, 'the greatest disasters were to be feared unless the gentry took the matter into their own hands and acted very much as if Government had been dissolved'.[71] In keeping with the habit of public banding, the Protestant gentry began organising their Protestant tenants as independent companies of 'volunteers'. At first there was little indication that this public band would do anything but stand on its guard against French invasion and potential Catholic insurrection, except that the earliest and most enthusiastic volunteering took place in Down and Antrim whose Presbyterian population were known to be sympathetic to the cause of the American colonists, whose numbers included many of their emigrant kinsmen and whose grievances were uncomfortably analogous to those of the Patriot Party in Ireland. The government lacked funds to pay the volunteers as a militia, but William Brownlow of Lurgan probably spoke for many Protestant gentry when he wrote to Charlemont that he had 'always preferred' independent companies to a regular militia.[72] Though the government did, after considerable hesitation, supply some arms to certain volunteer units,[73] the volunteers remained an essentially paramilitary force, not bound by an oath of allegiance, though they were fulsome in their expressions of 'loyalty'.

The military pageantry associated with the movement was

promptly incorporated into the established ritual of Remembering 1690. As early as 1 July 1778, the annual celebration of the
Battle of the Boyne at Newtownards included a parade of Volunteers wearing orange cockades.[74] By the time of William's birthday, 4 November, volunteering had spread throughout the island,
and we find the 'armed Societies' of Cork parading and firing
volleys in honour of the day, the Dublin Volunteers parading to
St Werburgh's Church to hear a sermon to mark the occasion,
and the Belfast Volunteers calling for a special performance of
The Tragedy of Tamerlane the Great, commonly interpreted as
an allegory of the Jacobite-Williamite contest, in commemoration
of the anniversary.[75] The anniversary of the shutting of Derry's
gates (7 December) was celebrated by the first Volunteer company of Coleraine with a parade, volleys, 'several evolutions and
firings' and 'a sumptuous entertainment' at the Royal George
tavern.[76] Indeed, for several years the Williamite festivals would
be regularly enlived by organized Volunteer display.

It soon became apparent that the Williamite settlement was
being remembered not only as confirmation of Protestant ascendancy in Ireland, but also as a decisive victory for representative
principles over absolutism—principles which ought properly to
apply to Ireland as well as England. A volunteer company in Co.
Monaghan declared its aims to be

> to defend ourselves from our natural enemies; to evidence our
> loyalty to his Majesty King George, and our attachment to our
> *civil* constitution, founded upon Revolution principles; for the
> establishing of which our fore-fathers fought and bled; and
> which, at this time, require the exertion of every real friend
> of our civil and sacred privileges.[77]

'We are informed from different Parts of the Kingdom,' declared
a Dublin Patriot organ in early 1779,

> that the several Associations who have formed themselves into
> military Corps, are determined never to be deluded to join in
> any Cause but in the mere support of the Constitution; and
> that no Motive shall incite them to engage in any Measure,
> where an insidious Set of evil Counsellors may be tempted to
> act against the Blessings of the glorious Revolution.[78]

The objective fact was that 'the Blessings of the glorious Revolu-

tion' had simply never been conferred upon Ireland. The Bill of
Rights applied only to England, and although the Scottish
parliament had been able in 1689 to capitalise on the events in
England to enhance its constitutional position, the governing
classes in Ireland had been in no position to extract significant
constitutional concessions from William.[79] What Patriots meant
by 'the Constitution' in the 1770s had no objective existence
except in the pages of Molyneux and the minds of his readers, a
fact which one of their spokesmen was, perhaps inadvertently,
recognizing when he wrote, 'Let Irishmen resolve to support their
Constitution, and they will have a Constitution.'[80] Yet this
mythical constitution provided Irish Protestants with both a
rationale for threatening non-compliance with the basic political
laws of the regime under which they lived and a goal to be
attained by that behaviour.

The threat of French invasion never materialised, and the
Volunteers soon found themselves acting as an armed auxiliary
to the Patriot Party in its constitutional struggle with the ministry.
In the autumn of 1779 the Irish parliament almost unanimously
passed a resolution against the mercantilist restrictions which
Britain had imposed on Ireland's external trade over the preceding century, and the celebration of William III's birthday in
Dublin was marked by a Volunteer parade outside the Parliament House around the equestrian statue of William which was
decorated with such slogans as '. . . A Free Trade—Or Else ! ! !'[81]
Although the Volunteer demonstration was peaceful, a few days
later Dublin weavers and other workmen whose interests were
prejudiced by the commercial restrictions rioted, compelling
several MPs to swear that they would vote 'for the good of
Ireland, free trade, and a short Money Bill'.[82] We get a good
example of Patriot rationalisation of their political behaviour
from the response of 'A Lawyer Volunteer' to a suggestion that
the Dublin Volunteers offer to keep order in the capital during
parliamentary debate of 'any Constitutional Question' :

> You are associated, my Friends in the Defence of the
> *Constitution,* or in order to *restore* it. It has been the invariable
> Custom of Formalists and Hirelings to confound the *Constitu-*
> *tion* and the *Law,* and to call that the *only* support of the
> Constitution which is but *one* Support, and is, at certain

Times, insufficient;—I mean perfect Obedience to *positive Law*. Though this Law should, on some particular Occasion be infringed by an exasperated People, yet a Friend to Constitutional Liberty will be cautious how far he interferes. He may destroy that Spirit on which Liberty subsists.[83]

This is a clear articulation of what Rose would call an 'ultra' position : the Patriots were willing to break laws in the interests of their own definition of 'the Constitution'.

In the event, the British government granted 'free trade', but since the concession could still be revoked by the British parliament at any time, and Henry Grattan, the Patriot leader in the Irish Commons, turned his considerable oratorical gifts to obtaining British recognition of Irish legislative autonomy. In the ensuing two years, the government found not only that its ability to command a majority in the Irish parliament was increasingly uncertain, but, more important, that it could not rely upon the ascendancy, in their role as magistrates and jurymen, to execute 'English' laws. Though the real military efficiency of the Volunteers might be questioned, the government, in the wake of defeat in America, was unwilling to challenge their power. In February 1782, a Convention of delegates from Volunteer corps throughout Ulster meeting at Dungannon passed resolutions drafted by Grattan, Henry Flood, his rival for the Patriot leadership, and Charlemont, the commander of the Volunteers in Ulster, which called, in effect, for the repeal of the Sixth of George I and Poynings' Law. Soon Volunteer corps throughout the country were adopting the 'Dungannon Resolutions'.

The viceroy in Lord Rockingham's Whig ministry, which took office in the spring of 1782, was astonished to learn that in Ireland they were not considered 'better friends to the constitution' than their predecessors.[84] In Ireland, Whig principles were being taken with a seriousness unknown in England for two generations. Grattan described the Dungannon Convention as 'an *original transaction*', comparable to the Revolution and to Magna Carta, which 'was not attained in parliament, but by the *Barons armed in the field*'.[85] The Patriots pressed their case with undiminished zeal, and in May the government conceded. The Sixth of George I and the relevant parts of Poynings' Law were repealed, the independence and autonomy of the Irish judiciary

was established, and the right of the Irish parliament to exercise
a check upon the ministry through biennial, rather than perpetual, Mutiny Acts was affirmed. Flood continued to press for
explicit renunciation by the British parliament of the right ever
again to legislate for Ireland—a demand which was conceded in
1783. The Patriot victory might be represented as the recovery
of a constitution, as the 'restoration of the Rights of Ireland'[86]
whose prior existence had been 'placed out of the reach of
controversy, by the work of a great scholar and philosopher',[87] i.e,.
Molyneux, or as a new 'compact' between Ireland and England.[88]
It redressed essentially all the grievances of those who were effectively represented in the Irish parliament.

The fact that the landed elite of Ireland should strive to place
their relationship with authority on a contractual footing analogous to the arrangement their English counterparts believed themselves to have achieved in 1689 is wholly unremarkable. The
eighteenth century was an age in which educated men throughout the Atlantic world thought about political authority in terms
of original contracts, of which the Irish 'Constitution of 1782'
might be called a textbook example. Whereas in England the
contractarian myth rested upon the social reality of the gentry's
special role in maintaining public order, however, and really
defined only *their* political obligation, in Ulster it rested on a
different reality. In Ulster each Protestant irrespective of social
position was assumed to have a special role in the maintenance
of order in a special situation where massive disorder was traditionally expected from one source: the Catholics. The public
band was the *ad hoc* community defined by that role and while
the community was not a claimant to sovereignty, banding did
have the character of a primeval social contract seeking to place
its relationship with the sovereign power on a contractual basis
or, perhaps more exactly, to get the sovereign power to acknowledge the terms of its trusteeship of authority. The community's
essence was that its members could *trust* one another, and no one
else. It stood uneasily between those who could never be trusted
(the Catholics) and a sovereign power which might be trusted only
within limits. The sovereign power—in the seventeenth century
the king, in the eighteenth the Westminster regime—should be
compelled to agree to very explicit terms.

But was it true that the Catholics could never be trusted?

The very fact that the ascendancy was prepared to press its advantage against the government much further in the 1780s than would have been conceivable on any of the earlier occasions of public banding in the eighteenth century suggests that the Catholic threat was perceived to have declined. This was the first widespread banding after the death of the old Pretender in 1766. Until that date Irish Catholicism was formally, if un-enthusiastically Jacobite,[89] the bishops being appointed on the nomination of the Pretender. Important sections of the hierarchy and the Catholic community were anxious for a way out of the anachronistic role in which they had been cast by events in their great-grandfathers' time. In 1774, when parliament provided a procedure for Catholics to profess allegiance to the Hanoverians, deny the pope's temporal jurisdiction in the British realms, and repudiate the notions that excommunicated sovereigns might be lawfully killed and that no faith need be kept with heretics, the Munster bishops incurred Rome's displeasure by sanctioning the oath without even consulting the Holy See.[90] In 1778, when the benefits of an act relieving Catholics of certain civil disabilities were made conditional upon the taking of such an oath, the arch-bishop of Dublin, seventy of his clergy, and several laymen appeared at the King's Bench and took it—a gesture which was noted as particularly auspicious coming at a time when 'a Storm from the united Powers of the Family of Bourbon seemed ready to burst upon our Heads'.[91] Indeed, throughout the alarms which provoked the Volunteer movement, there was not the slightest hint of Catholic disloyalty. On the contrary, when a rumour (false, as it turned out) reached Cork in June, 1779, that a French fleet was in Bantry Bay 'a Number of very respectable Roman Catholic Gentlemen' offered to march with the local Volunteers.[92] Technically it was an offence for Catholics to carry arms, but a few volunteer units nevertheless enlisted them and others accepted their financial support.[93]

Furthermore, this was an auspicious moment for a decline in Protestant fears of the Catholic menace. Within international Catholicism the authority of the pope—whose machinations were supposed to render Catholics incapable of undivided civil allegiance—was at its lowest ebb in modern history. A Protestant advocate of Catholic relief in 1775 could make the plausible, albeit novel, suggestion that should the pope ever attempt to interfere with the British Protestant establishment it would be easy enough to send naval forces to overawe him in his little citadel on the Tiber.[94] It was even possible for some Protestants to hold the optimistic belief that 'Popery' was withering away and that Catholicism would evolve into simply another dissenting sect. This belief was probably encouraged by the fact that at this date Irish Catholicism, albeit somewhat fortuitously, did give an impression of nonconformist simplicity. Many Catholic chapels built as the penal laws were relaxed resembled the austere Presbyterian meeting-houses—some even to the point of locating the altar at a side wall and arranging the seating around it so that the congregation faced one another,[95] a ground-plan which for Presbyterians symbolised rejection of the 'popish' separation of priest and people. Moreover, the native Irish devotional tradition was characterised by genuine simplicity, which was enhanced at this time by a prudential avoidance of any display which might give offence to the civil authorities. Not until what Professor Larkin has termed the 'devotional revolution' of 1850–75 did many of the more sensuous elements of continental Catholic worship—statuary, stained glass, incense and music—make much headway in Irish Catholicism.[96] Thus, in 1784, when the Belfast Volunteers demonstrated their goodwill towards the Catholics by marching to Mass at St Mary's chapel,[97] what they witnessed may have looked, sounded and smelled much like what they were accustomed to experience in their own meeting-houses.

One must not read too much into gestures like this one : though the Volunteer movement showed some sympathy for the extension of civil liberties to Catholics, only a minority of Irish Protestants were prepared to countenance Catholic influence in the making of state policy. Nevertheless, the mere willingness of elements in the landed elite to use the Volunteers so boldly for their constitutional ends was evidence of a salutary capacity to assess the Catholic threat realistically. The age of religio-dynastic politics was over; a new wholesale forfeiture of Irish land like that enacted by the Jacobite parliament of 1689 was now outside the realm of realistic possibility. No doubt some dispossessed Catholic gentry families would have taken advantage, through litigation, of any legal loophole in the land settlement,[98] and perhaps if Catholics had instantly been granted rights to full political participation they would have used their power to create such loopholes. Once Catholics were permitted to purchase land, by the 1778 Relief Act, it was certain that within a generation the land settlement would be secure even against that possibility. When the land settlement finally came to be undone, in 1903, it was not for the purpose of reinstating the heirs of the O'Neill and the O'Donnell.

Yet if the realism with which propertied Irish Protestants were able to assess the Catholic threat accounts for their willingness to turn the band against the government, ought it not also to have undermined the whole *raison d'être* of public banding within a generation or so? Indeed, if all Irish Protestants had been landed gentry it might have done so. We shall see, in Chapter Two, why for several succeeding generations after 1800, banding was more relevant to the needs of the Protestant lower orders than to their betters. In Chapter Three we shall examine how the tradition of banding, kept alive largely by the men of little or no property, once again was appropriated by the elite of the Ulster Protestant community.

The events of the Volunteer period not only called into question the reality of the Catholic threat which was the justification for banding, but also highlighted the difficulties of applying contractarian ideas in a society with broadening political participation. Social contract ideas were probably never intended to define the allegiance of an entire population participating in the politics of a modern mass society. Contractarian thinkers resort to various devices to impute to each individual his own consent to an original compact. The impracticability of such reasoning, however, in a society larger than a city-state or governed by more than a small homogeneous elite (like those which dominated both the British and Irish parliaments in the eighteenth century) is highlighted by Rousseau's device, the general will, which must somehow be unanimous even if individuals perceive their wills to differ radically. It soon became evident that the 'Constitution of 1782' did not fully express the general will even of that limited community constituting the public band. The Irish parliament, whose powers were so enhanced by that transaction, was still controlled by landlords who, because of anomalies in the system of representation and the economic dependency of their tenants, could return their nominees with little concern for the desires of ordinary Protestants.

On 1 July 1783—the Boyne anniversary—a group of Volunteer delegates meeting at Lisburn called for another Dungannon assembly representative of Volunteer units throughout Ulster 'to deliberate on the most constitutional means of procuring a more equal representation of the people in the parliament of Ireland'. Such a reform would restore 'the balance of the constitution' by enabling 'the constituent body' to 'regain its constitutional control over its trustees'. 'Venal majorities' acting against 'the true intent of the institution of parliaments' would thereby be abolished.[99] The Dungannon assembly picked up the logic of this declaration, resolving unanimously, 'That by the ancient constitution of parliaments, elections of representatives were for centuries annual, and in many instances more frequent; and the exercise of suffrage, among freemen, universal.' Reform along the lines they proposed would tend 'to a renovation of, not an innovation in, the constitution'.[100] A 'Grand National Convention' met in Dublin in November to take up the issue, and although it had the menacing appearance of an alternative parliament, its proposals, predictably, were supported by only a derisory minority in the real parliament on College Green. Though the Volunteers did receive half-hearted support from two of the Patriot leaders, Flood and Charlemont, and the enthusiastic backing of the eccentric Anglican Bishop of Derry, the Earl of Bristol, their former ally, Grattan, repudiated their reform project.

The project went into eclipse partly because both the government, now relieved of American entanglements, and the landed elite were ranged against it and partly because the reformers themselves were soon split by the introduction of the question of admitting Catholics to the franchise. Nevertheless, in the excitement generated a few years later by the French Revolution, it was revived in Belfast, Dublin and elsewhere by 'Societies of United Irishmen', whose agitation led to an abortive rebellion in 1798. Ironically, a principal aim of the reformers was in fact attained in 1800 when the government cajoled and bribed the Irish parliament into voting its own extinction, for the Act of Union disenfranchised the rottenest of the old borough constituencies. The county constituencies, which were acknowledged to be the least venal ones but had returned only 21.3 per cent of the 300 members of the Irish House of Commons, returned 64 per cent of the 100 Irish members in united House of Commons.

The reform episode illustrates, however, how risky contract-arian politics are in an environment of widening political aware-ness. The reformers were playing exactly the same game as their Patriot leaders had played before 1782. They were conjuring up a mythical 'constitution' which had somehow been agreed to in the dim recesses of the past and which supposedly called for government according to their present aims. The Patriot leaders had thought they could safely behave this way in an environment in which the fundamentally common interests of all those who effectively participated in 'politics' provided a discernible general will. By accepting the support of the public band, however, they introduced into active politics persons whose interests were by no means identical with their own. Members of a democratic society of any complexity simply possess too few common interests to make the general will obvious. No modern regime could achieve stability if groups of its citizens were continually threatening to withdraw their consent from its institutions in the name of con-tracts supposedly entered into by their ancestors. Thus, while the Whiggish contractarianism of the Irish landed elite in the eighteenth century was fully consonant with the spirit of that age, the parliamentary reform episode of 1783–1800 demonstrates how inappropriate that spirit would be to the needs of societies of near-universal political participation. Such societies would become the norm in nineteenth-century Europe.

2

Freedom, Religion and Laws
1760-1886

'Two Nations', Once Again

Social contract thinking, with its emphasis on fundamental
rights of the citizen *vis-à-vis* his government made important and
lasting contributions to the framework of law in Western
societies. However, as a mode of rationalising the political obligation of the subject, it was a rather brief challenge to what we
might call primitive allegiance, which is often as strong in modern
democratic societies as it was under pre-modern monarchies.
In a sense, only the object of primitive allegiance has altered. As
one American southern historian has written, 'modern democratic
thought, by adopting the view that the ultimate authority lies in
the people, has brought us to the point where the nature of the
association which constitutes a people takes on almost as mystical
a quality as once pertained to the nature of the anointment which
a crowned king received from God.'[1] This 'association', the
'nation', can command the loyalty of its citizens as effectively as
the most revered monarch of earlier times. While perhaps few
modern men consciously adopt the slogan 'my country, right or
wrong', citizens of most modern democratic states are prepared
to put up with a great many measures which they abhor on the
part of their governments, provided they perceive the government to be in the hands of their co-nationals.

It might be argued that nationalism simply constitutes an
effective general will, thereby rendering the basic social contract
myth viable in a democratic society. Actually, nationalism vitiates
that myth, for it makes little pretence of authority taking its rise
in a bargain freely entered into. Groups may in some sense
'choose' whether to consider themselves nations, but no one
pretends that individuals have much choice over their nationality
within the framework thus established (except, of course, by
migrating from one national territory to another). Indeed, the

ardent nationalist would deny even that groups exercise choice over their nationality. Nationalism has fostered a new myth that nations are 'natural', that each is associated with a foreordained national territory, and that each individual inherently possesses a 'nationality' which disposes him to want to be ruled by persons of that nationality. While these assumptions are preposterous when taken in the absolute sense in which they are put forward by nationalists, it is quite true that the vast majority of citizens of modern states do generally accept the myth of nationality. Furthermore, it is probably, on balance, a salutary myth : it is hard to imagine how complex and democratic societies could achieve cohesion and their states attain stability in the absence of some such myth to overrule the contradictory promptings of self-interest on the part of their members. The nation, one student has written, 'has in fact become the body which legitimises the state'.[2]

If, therefore, we are to understand Ulster Protestants' sense of political obligation since the end of the eighteenth century we must consider how they have fitted into a world of 'nations'. In general, two answers have been proposed to the problem by what may be called respectively the 'one-nation' and the 'two-nations' schools of thought. The one-nation school starts from the pre-supposition that Ireland is a nation and that a sense of common nationality on the part of the inhabitants of this 'natural' geographic unit possessing a common history and culture is inevitable and right. Brushing aside the protests of northern Protestants that Ireland had no national history and no distinctive culture shared by themselves, partisans of this school tended to attribute northern particularism to the malevolent influence of the English in fomenting sectarian division or (a Marxist refinement) a conspiracy on the part of the ruling classes to divide the working class. The manifest willingness of the English in recent years not to obstruct Irish unity by consent, and the abundant evidence provided by the media that Protestant working-class opposition to Irish unity has not abated since the days when it was just plausible that they were being duped by Tory squires, have dealt the one-nation school a blow from which it will probably not recover. Its exponents in the historical profession are reduced to the unpromising activity of trying to prove that the seventeenth-century settlers were Gaelic-speaking.

The two-nation theory must be taken more seriously. In a pamphlet published by the Workers' Association for a Democratic Settlement of the National Conflict in Ireland, its exponents argue that the northern Protestants are 'a distinct nation, or at least part of one', and that Unionism is a species of 'nationalist ideology'.[3] A prime cause of the division of the working class along sectarian lines has been not British imperialism but the separate Catholic nation's imperialistic designs on the North. Only when members of the Catholic nation recognise that the northern Protestants are a separate nation entitled to separate self-determination can an effective working-class political movement on lines satisfactory to the authors be created.

Now it is unexceptionable that the northern Protestants are a distinct community and do not consider themselves part of the Irish nation. Unfortunately the assumptions of the contemporary world do very generally compel a group to assert that it is a 'nation' or part of one, to earn the right to self-determination, and the two-nation theorists accept those assumptions. I intend no derogation from the North's claim to separate self-determination when I suggest that what it may be necessary to assert in a public forum to gain public acceptance for a valid claim may obscure matters if carried over into serious academic discourse. The two-nation theorists conceive of nationhood primarily as a mode of social solidarity whose demands must be fulfilled in order that politics may take its form from another mode of solidarity : social class. In their view the North passed 'the crucial test' of nationality when 'the ability of its ruling class to rally all its members into a common alliance ready if necessary to fight for a national objective'[4] was demonstrated in 1912. Now a sense of solidarity across class lines certainly is one attribute of nationalism, and this feature of Ulster Unionism perhaps justifies Peter Gibbon, the author of the most sophisticated analysis yet to issue from the two-nation school, in calling it a 'quasi-nationalist' movement.[5] Considered as a phenomenon in modern western—latterly world—history, however, nationalism is a good deal more than an inconvenient obstacle to working-class solidarity.

When the two-nation theorists call the Ulster Protestants 'a distinct nation', and then hedge their bet by adding 'or at least part of one', they are, perhaps unwittingly, confessing the difficulty with their theory. Are they saying that Protestant Ulster is a distinct nation like Scotland and Wales within a multi-national community, the United Kingdom? Or are they saying that the human community embraced by the United Kingdom is a 'nation', of which Ulster Protestants consider themselves members? Actually neither of these propositions is quite satisfactory. The Ulster Protestant community is like Scotland (before the recent rise of national separatism in Scotland) in that it has exhibited no clear determination to be politically separated from the United Kingdom. On the other hand, it is unlike Scotland in that whereas Scottish national feeling has until recently been fully compatible with a sense of 'British' nationality legitimising the Westminster regime, the Ulster Protestant community has evoked a kind of group loyalty incompatible with acceptance of the full implications of British nationality.

The difficulty with both the one-nation and the two-nation schools is that neither possesses a clear idea of why nationality came to be the normal mode of political association in the nineteenth century. The one-nation school assumes that nationality is built into the order of nature and its emergence in the nineteenth century requires no explanation. The two-nation school assumes that the natural mode of social aggregation is social class and that national solidarity requires to be explained basically as an abnormal obstacle to the attainment of that end. Actually there is nothing 'natural' about national sentiment—millions of people who lived before the nineteenth century got along quite happily without it. It became normal in most parts of Europe and eventually the rest of the world thereafter in consequence of certain specific social changes. Once we recognise these facts, it becomes possible to suggest a third alternative: that Ireland embraces one (Catholic) nation and one (Protestant) community upon which, for certain specific reasons, the general causes of nationalism did not take effect so fully as elsewhere.

A number of social scientists have advanced theories to account for the rise of nationalism in societies undergoing modernisation[6]—that complex of social changes which accompany the transformation of an agricultural society into one dominated by, or in the shadow of, factory industry. These changes include not only a transformation of the individual's external environment under the impact of scientific and technological advance—a transition to self-sustained economic growth and therefore the prospect of affluence for a vastly increased segment of society, the advent of mass education and mass communications, the rise of participatory forms of politics—but also, characteristically, an internal transformation of his personality. Persons who have undergone modernisation are more likely than their predecessors to be open to innovation, to be able to imagine themselves in situations outside their immediate experience, to be oriented towards the present and future rather than the past, to believe in planning and the possibility of man's learning to dominate his environment, to view the world as calculable rather than determined by fate, and to believe in distributive justice.[7]

One theory of the relationship of modernisation to the rise of nationalism, that of Ernest Gellner,[8] is particularly useful. Gellner focuses upon two features of the modernisation process: (1) the fact that it erodes accepted structures of traditional societies, and (2) the fact that its effects are uneven, hitting different territories at different times. To deal with the first feature, Gellner draws the anthropologist's distinction between 'structure' and 'culture' in a society. He postulates an inverse relationship between the degree of structure in a society and its need for culture. 'Primitive' societies generally have highly developed structures in which each individual has a clearly ascribed role regulating his relationships with every other member. They may also have a rich culture of ritual, dress, modes of conduct, etc., but, Gellner asserts, this shared culture is not indispensable for the effective functioning of the society. Everyone knows what everyone else expects of him and what responses are available in the small number of repetitive social situations, simply from the pattern of stable role relationships. He cites the example of two small South American Indian groups which fused into a single roving band despite the fact that they spoke two mutually unintelligible languages. Because the total group was so small, and role relationships so clearly understood, the band could successfully cope with the relatively simple problems facing it without even the bare minimum of common culture represented by language. According to his theory, this kind of accommodation is inconceivable in a complex, modern society where relationships are typically 'ephemeral, non-repetitive, and optional.' In consequence, communication, the symbols, language (in the literal or in the extended sense) that is employed, become crucial. The burden of comprehension is shifted from the context to the communication itself : when interlocutors and contexts are all unfamiliar, the message itself must become intelligible—it is no longer understood, as was the case in traditional societies, before it was even articulated—and those who communicate must speak the same language, in some sense or other.[9]

The erosion of traditional social structures means that the individual's essence is no longer simply his social position. He must carry his identity with him in his manner of conducting himself, his 'style'. Moreover, Gellner argues, literacy is the minimal requirement for 'effective moral membership of a modern community', and only a 'nation-size' educational system can command the resources to produce universal literacy. Hence, 'something roughly of the size of a "nation" is the minimal political unit in the modern world'. Furthermore, the products of such an educational machine are generally mobile within the linguistic frontiers corresponding to it, but not across them.

To understand the effects of the unevenness of modernisation, Gellner asks us to imagine it moving, like a 'tidal wave', through territories A and B, initially under the same sovereignty. Just as the people of A are approaching affluence, the B-landers undergo the worst initial dislocations of modernisation. The lot of most B-landers will be to fill the lower ranks of the proletariat of the total A + B society. The solidarity of the working class being, in Gellner's view, a myth, the men of A will try to exclude those of B from whatever share of affluence they are winning. If the men of B are 'fairly radically differentiated from those of A', i.e., if 'they can easily be picked out in the street— in virtue of pigmentation, or deeply rooted and religiously sanctioned customs', then their lot will be even worse and 'their discontent can find "national" expressions'. Their own small intellectual class will probably resist the temptation to pass into A, realizing that 'if it succeeds in detaching B-land, by the rules of the new national game, in which intellectuals are not substitutable across frontiers, it will have a virtual monopoly on the desirable posts in the newly independent B-land'.[10] What makes the 'nation' different from lesser and earlier 'loyalty-evoking groups', according to Gellner, is its 'non-intimate, mass nature . . . and the definition of membership by (in effect) "culture", in the sense of a *kind* of schooling, and the fact that membership is direct, and not mediated by intervening subgroups.'[11]

While Gellner's theory does not account for all aspects of nationalism, the two features of modernisation he identifies provide a useful framework for examining the problem of nationality-formation—or the lack of it—in Ulster. The theory separates the issue of how modernising peoples, *in general*, come to conceptualise their political experience in terms of nationality from the issue of which *particular* nation such a people will come to regard as their own. In the next section, we shall investigate the extent to which modernisation actually did erode traditional social structures in Ulster, in hopes of understanding how far Ulster Protestants may have developed a need for nationalism in general. We shall try, in the subsequent section, to understand the Protestant community's stance towards the particular nationalisms which were active candidates for its adherence, by considering its position with respect to the 'tidal wave' of modernisation. In the final section of this chapter, we shall use a different theory to explore an aspect of the problem of nationality-formation in Ulster for which Gellner's theory is less useful.

The Lower Orders and the Highest Sphere

What was the social structure of the Ulster colony on the eve of modernisation, around 1760? It was an agricultural society in which land was generally held on fairly long leases from the heirs of the grantees in possession at the end of the seventeenth century. Only two of the towns erected as strong points in the plantation, Belfast and Derry, were more than local market centres. Many of the country folk supplemented their income by linen weaving, but this activity had not yet seriously disrupted role relationships, as it was primarily carried out independently of any complex industrial organization, weavers obtaining materials and selling cloth in a free market. The colony was divided ethnically into Scottish settlers concentrated in north and east Ulster and English settlers inhabiting mid and south Ulster. The two groups could be distinguished by dialect, customs, dress, and, of course, religion, the Scots being generally Presbyterians, as we have seen, and the English members of the established Church of Ireland. Both groups were 'Protestants', though the term 'Protestant' was often reserved for members of the established church in contemporary usage.

Both groups understood themselves to stand in a special relationship to the largely Anglican landlord minority. Although James I's intention that Catholics be prevented from taking leases except on designated reservations had not been realised, landlords were willing to offer rather favourable terms in order to get Protestant tenants, who were presumed to be better risks from the standpoint of physical security and perhaps more attuned to 'English' farming practices. Protestants had been able to drive hard bargains with landowners, as most of the land in question was not particularly attractive—except to the descendants of its original occupiers. The Protestant tenantry thus imbibed the notion that they were especially important to their landlords and entitled to privileged treatment. The fact that rents were remarkably stable for several decades in the early eighteenth century[12] probably contributed to a feeling that Ulster Protestant society was a kind of idealised feudal arrangement in which economic relations were regulated more by the paternalism of landlords than by capitalist economic forces.

By the late eighteenth century, several forces were at work to disrupt this happy relationship. The land, after several generations of tillage on an 'English' basis, was becoming a much more marketable commodity, and, at the same time, as the Catholic-Jacobite threat receded, security considerations no longer impelled landlords to set artificially low rents and refrain from demanding other exactions simply to be sure of keeping a Protestant tenantry. A more complex development was the growth of textile manufacture. In mid and south Ulster, especially in north Armagh, whose soil was not especially fertile, linen weaving was beginning to become the primary, rather than a supplementary, activity of tenants, who subdivided their holdings into tiny patches on which only a limited sort of agriculture was possible, to augment the diet the weaver would purchase with hard cash.[13] In some areas population density soared, and we may speculate that the younger age-groups grew disproportionately as weavers found that income could be increased by more hands to work the looms.[14] At the same time, any necessity of maintaining an original holding intact having been abandoned, a traditional bond of social control within the family must have been weakened. Even outside the area of most rapid demographic change, weavers began to find themselves in new relationships of dependence to other weavers and/or to yarn jobbers who supplied material and disposed of cloth in a market of increasing complexity. Complicating all these changes was the fact that Catholics, who before 1740 had woven only the coarse, narrow, 'bandle linens' intended for local consumption, were now moving into production of fine linens just like the Protestants.[15] Even such stability as might have been achieved within a society which now included virtual rural cities of weavers was under threat by the mid-1780s from the introduction of power-spun cotton fibre in Belfast, which would draw many of the weavers off the land entirely and into a real city.

There is no reason to assume that northern Protestants had an easier time adjusting to the psychic traumas of modernisation than did southern Catholics when their society went through a somewhat different process of modernising almost a century later. At the time in question, each population was being deprived through emigration of those members who would presumably have been readiest to accept change with alacrity. In a sense, linen was the Protestant's potato, allowing population to grow to fantastic densities because of a common tendency in traditional societies to value attachment to the soil as a good in itself rather than look upon the soil as an exchangeable commodity which might well be traded off for other benefits. The fact that many weavers, even in the hinterland of Belfast, were willing well into the nineteenth century to continue a rural existence at incomes well below those obtainable in the factories[16] was a relic of such traditional values. By the late eighteenth century, however, landlords were increasingly treating land as an exchangeable commodity, the tenancy of which was no longer constrained by security considerations, and this fact, together with the evolution of textile manufacture, was forcing social change upon the Protestant tenantry.

As we might expect, the dislocations which modernisation brought, between 1760 and 1800, prompted a good deal of unrest. There were three potential targets of protest: (1) the emerging elite of textile manufacture, (2) the old landlord elite and (3) Catholics. Apart from a 'turn-out' at Lisburn in 1762[17]

C

there was remarkably little protest focused upon the textile elite. Moreover, up to 1795 there is little evidence, despite the fact that Catholic willingness to pay higher rents for Protestant-held land was articulated as a grievance, that Catholics actually suffered from Protestant agrarian violence, except in North Armagh. There a bitter sectarian conflict between Protestant 'Peep-of-Day Boys' and Catholic 'Defenders' raged intermittently from 1784 to 1795. This was the area where division of labour and subdivision of holdings had gone the farthest, and at least on the Protestant side the unrest seems to have been aggravated by conditions which did not obtain elsewhere in Ulster. Prominent in Peep-of-Day Boy ranks were a class of 'journeymen',[18] young, unmarried weavers in the workshops of more substantial weavers. A local Catholic described the peculiar problems of social control in this area in these words,

> the great influx of cash and plentiful markets of provisions among the lower orders of the people, and so many young boys taken at a short apprenticeship to the linen-business, they get the handling of cash before they know its real value, prompts them to intoxication and riot before they have well digested their mother's milk.[19]

The Armagh sectarian troubles were of great significance for the future, but at the time, they were geographically very confined.

Much more widespread, in the 1760s and 1770s, had been Protestant agrarian violence directed against landlords and objects associated with landlord power, such as clergymen of the established church and county grand juries through which the landlords collectively exacted cesses and labour service to build roads sited to serve their own convenience. Major outbreaks in 1763 and 1770–72 were both triggered by specific localised issues, but spread rapidly over several counties. Though the character of the violence was quite similar to that committed by the contemporary Catholic Whiteboys in the South—cattle-maiming, arson of corn, destruction or theft of timber, breaking of fences—the objectives of its perpetrators reflected the peculiar needs of northern Protestants. In 1763 one of the principal activities of the 'Hearts of Oak' was to administer 'illegal oaths'—not, as one might suppose, to other peasants as they joined the conspiracy, but to any gentlemen they could manage to waylay.[20] Such gentry were forced to sign solemn undertakings not to be parties to innovations such as recently levied county cesses.[21] The 'Hearts of Steel' made plain their objective of 'obtaining perpetual leases of lands at their valuations',[22] and their spokesmen stressed the basis of their claim : 'That we are all Protestants and Protestant Dissenters and bear unfeigned loyalty to his present majesty and the Hanoverian succession'[23] and that 'not one Roman Catholic is ever suffered to appear amongst us'.[24] It is noteworthy that one of the pre-1780 agrarian bands bore the ominous name, 'Peep-of-Day Boys'.[25] One of the rioters' complaints was 'That some of us refusing to pay the extravagant rent demanded by our landlords have been turned out, and our lands given to Papists, who will pay any rent.' Nevertheless, the course of the agitation demonstrates that it was the landlords, not the Papists, who were regarded as having erred.

Protestant agrarian violence thus constituted a plea to the landlord class to restore the traditional order. If their grievances were redressed, one group of rioters promised, the landlords would 'as heretofore live in the affection of their tenants'.[26] Of course, the traditional order could not be restored : modernisation was inevitable and landlords were capable of only temporary gestures to prevent it. Apparently there was an effort in the mid-1770s by landlords, led by Lord Hillsborough, 'to discourage all monopolizers of land, to portion out their estates in smaller parcels, and to lett those parcels at such moderate rents as will establish an interest to the tenant in the leases'.[27] Rents on one of Hillsborough's own estates, however, demonstrate that this policy was short-lived.[28] Sustained economic growth was beginning to occur in Ulster, and it would have been most peculiar if the landlords had not appropriated a share of that growth. It does not follow from the inevitability of modernisation, however, that every feature of the traditional order was doomed. This was a very peculiar traditional order whose structure embodied a special relationship between the Protestant lower orders and the landlord elite. It might be possible to reaffirm that special relationship by means other than granting demands which would have forestalled economic growth, staved off geographic mobility and ossified social relationships.

Indeed it was possible, and in effect, if not in intention, the first such reaffirmation was the Irish Volunteer movement, whose role in politics was discussed in Chapter One. A prominent volunteer activity was to put down local unrest.[29] More important, the movement visibly acted out the special relationship of Protestant tenantry to gentry. 'It is a notorious truth', wrote a Dublin correspondent of the *Belfast Mercury*,

> that nothing has civilized the lower orders of people throughout the kingdom so much as their being enlisted under the Volunteer standard; those riotous assemblies, which disgraced the nation, and defiled the Sabbath, are now changed into decent tranquil meetings, when a connection with their superiors begets affection; and a general subordination renders the whole peaceable and virtuous—no *Houghers, White Boys, Hearts of Oak, Hearts of Steel*, now infest the land; the laws are executed without delay or danger....[30]

The north Armagh troubles may have been the exception that proves the rule: it is possible that the Peep-of-Day Boys occupied too low a rung in the complex social hierarchy of that district to be considered fit material for Volunteer corps.

The Volunteer movement, however, also revealed that there were now two distinct elites in the North: the landlord elite, represented in the Irish parliament whose autonomous powers were increased with Volunteer assistance in 1782, and the Presbyterian textile (and mercantile) elite which politically had gained nothing by that 'revolution'. The mercantile elite had been prominently involved in volunteering from the start, and they stood to gain from parliamentary reform, which the volunteer movement unsuccessfully advocated in the mid-1780s. In 1791, under the stimulus of the French Revolution, the mercantile elite again took up the cause of parliamentary reform, together with that of removal of Catholic disabilities, in newly-formed 'societies of United Irishmen'. The continued existence of Volunteer units being too risky, they were suppressed by the government in 1793. Both elites were thus deprived of potential organised Protestant mass support in the countryside, and in the political turbulence of the ensuing five years each fell back upon more primitive sorts of popular agitation: the Presbyterian elite upon rural folk still motivated by agrarian grievances, the gentry upon those motivated by sectarian animosity.

Though the immediate issue was in fact decided by the

government's determination to repress the United Irishmen in 1797 and 1798, the relative abilities of the two elites to attract support was of long-term significance. At first glance it would seem that the Presbyterian elite had a broader base of support than the gentry. They could rely upon widespread agrarian grievance among Protestant tenants (especially Presbyterians remote from concentrations of Catholic population) in several counties, not to mention the Defender cells which had spread south from County Armagh and now resembled the Whiteboys of the previous generation. The Protestant sectarianism upon which the gentry fell back had remained largely confined to County Armagh for a decade. However, the Belfast United Irishmen were offering their followers a programme for radically recasting a political order which, at best, was remote from the latter's concerns. Assurances from Belfast merchants that, of course, the new order would redress peasant grievances were a poor alternative to what the gentry could offer—the re-establishment of the special relationship for which Protestant tenants had been pleading in the 1760s and 1770s and which had been temporarily restored in the form of the Volunteers.

The fact that the first gentry initiative was to take the atypical Armagh Protestant rioters under their protection under the newly-coined name of 'Orangemen' in 1795 is misleading. Orangeism is significant for more than the history of the 1790s because it quickly spread to Protestants beyond County Armagh and even made recruits among United Irish supporters.[31] In the years after the suppression of the rebellion, Protestant attachment to 'the ideals of '98' dwindled to a few Belfast families, whereas an Orange spokesman could claim in 1835, in a forum where he had every reason not to exaggerate, that the Order had around 200,000 members, i.e., more than half the adult male Protestants in Ireland.[32] The rural 'old light' Presbyterians, whose adherence to the United Irish cause may have owed more to surviving pre-modern readiness to believe that a kind of apocalyptic deliverance was at hand, than to any genuine affinity for the radical enlightenment views of Belfast merchants,[33] clearly provided many early recruits to the Orange system.[34] Furthermore, although the population of Belfast as it existed in the 1790s may have been uncongenial soil for the growth of Orangeism, that population was rapidly being augmented by immigrants who brought their Orangeism with them from the countryside.

Modernisation was not halted. Ulster did complete its 'take-off' into sustained economic growth. Political power was gradually transferred from a small landed elite to the whole adult population—Catholics included. Geographic and social mobility within their own society—not just the option of leaving it permanently through emigration—did become a normal experience for Ulster Protestants. They did adopt a scientific world-view and, I shall argue, adapt their religious ideas to it. But while the social structure of Ulster was being drastically altered by these changes, Orangeism sustained for Protestant workers in town and country the sense that the most important feature of the old structure—a special relationship between them and their Protestant betters—still obtained. When the Orange gentry framed the rules of the institution, they insured that 'the higher orders' would 'mingle with their humbler brethren', by requiring that each member of the elite 'grand lodge' also join a 'private', i.e., local, lodge.[35] When the government banned public Orange processions, an Orange gentleman might offer his own property as a site for an alternative demonstration. Most important, the Orange Order had the trappings of secrecy. Secrecy was important not as a cloak for some sort of dark conspiratorial machinations, but as a pointed affirmation of the special relationship. Although the 'intelligent orangeman' might not even remember the secret sign after his initiation, this aspect of Orangeism was peculiarly attractive to 'the lower orders, who are pleased with the idea of sharing the same secret with so many of those moving in the highest sphere of society'.[36]

Recent writers are quite correct in minimising the direct involvement of the Order in politics, especially in the mid nineteenth century. The true significance of Orangeism has always lain not in what it *does*, but in what it *is*. It was a new public band, different from the earlier ones primarily in that a permanent institution was created. Its permanence derived not from the dangers it met at its inception, however, but from the fact that it met needs which the further course of modernisation would increase rather than diminish. Many Ulster Protestants seized an opportunity to preserve the shadow, though not the substance, of stable role relationships at the onset of those changes which characteristically erode them. It was, I believe, the kind of opportunity which at least a segment of any population under-going the initial dislocations of modernisation would have grasped, but the pre-existing habit of emigration may have made such a segment bulk especially large in this particular population. The ostensible purpose for which the special relationship was sustained—the maintenance of public order—could be pursued without arresting the much more substantial changes associated with modernisation. One of these changes, increasing geographic mobility, facilitated the growth of Belfast to a position of domin-ance over the entire life of the province. The widening of political participation offered new reasons for maintenance of a special relationship in the northern metropolis, albeit in an altered form and not bounded by the Orange institution itself.

The introduction of machine-spun cotton transformed Belfast from a little port of some 13,000 inhabitants in 1782, to an industrial city of over 50,000 by 1831, when its textile industry was reverting to linen with the advent of machine-spun flax. By 1861 the population stood at 122,000, and the newly-established shipbuilding industry was beginning to diversify the city's econo-mic base. By the end of the century the population had grown to nearly 350,000, or 30% of the population of the province. Throughout the eighteenth century, the city's inhabitants had been principally Presbyterian, but rapid immigration from the countryside drastically altered the denominational balance. Catholics, who were about 8% of the population in the late eighteenth century, constituted about one-third of the much larger population by the middle years of the nineteenth, after which their proportion of the population began to decline, though their absolute numbers continued to rise.[37] Furthermore, many of the immigrants were, at least nominally, Church of Ireland members drawn down the Lagan valley from the overpopulated linen country of mid and south Ulster. The diversity within Belfast Protestantism was further enhanced by the growth of Methodism (many of whose adherents still regarded themselves as Church of Ireland members well into the nineteenth century) and, from the middle of the century, a variety of smaller conver-sionist sects. Though Presbyterians continued to dominate the city's elite, they were reduced to a mere 35% of the total population by 1861.

It is easy to see how this changing ethnic balance in the city

might be productive of sectarian conflict, as indeed it was. It is
perhaps less easy to see how the sense of a special relationship
between the Protestant lower orders and their betters could
survive. The Protestant weaver or tenant farmer's son who
moved to Sandy Row might well now find himself working for
one of the few wealthy Protestants in Ireland who deplored the
special relationship, for many of the Presbyterian factory owners
still spurned the Orange system and cherished the ideal of legal
equality, though with none of the revolutionary zeal that had
animated a few of their fathers. Indeed, the absence of a readily
visible Protestant elite anxious to act out the special relationship
with them probably accounts for the relatively slow growth of
the Orange institution among Belfast workers during the early
decades of the century. Orange lodges had existed in Belfast
since 1797, and as early as 1813 an Orange procession in the
town precipitated a sectarian riot resulting in two deaths.[38]
Protestant participants in what became endemic sectarian conflict
were often misleadingly described as 'Orange' irrespective of
whether they were actually members of the Order. Reliable
membership, figures for the Order in any period are difficult to
obtain, but we do know that in 1851 the Belfast lodges had
1,335 members,[39] or only about one in every ten of the adult
male Protestants in the town. For Ireland as a whole the comparable proportion was probably more like one-quarter.[40]

There were, of course, a few Orange gentlemen in Belfast:
Thomas Verner, the Sovereign (i.e. mayor) of Belfast in the
years 1812–15, 1819–23 and 1841–42, was related to one of the
leading Armagh Orange gentry families and belonged to the
Order.[41] The mere fact that he was Sovereign, however, indicates
that he was isolated from the most influential circles in the local
elite. The Belfast Corporation was widely regarded as a mere tool
of the town's debt-ridden absentee landlords, the Donegall
family, and it had been superseded as the effective local government since 1800 by 'Police Boards' more representative of the
town's real leadership. One thing that facilitated the development of vertical ties of dependency between Protestant immigrants from the countryside and at least a segment of the Belfast
elite was, ironically, the demise of the old, apparently irrelevant,
town corporation and the emergence of something like democratic electoral politics.

Until 1832 the Corporation had faithfully returned the
Donegall family's nominees to parliament, but under the first
Reform Act the franchise was extended to perhaps 2,000 house-
holders. In 1842 the Corporation itself was finally abolished in
favour of an elected Council. In the new era of electoral politics,
leading members of the mercantile and manufacturing elite took
the field with high hopes as a Reform or 'Liberal' Party. Their
opposition seemed to be merely the nominees of the politically,
and almost financially, bankrupt Donegall interest. From the first
quasi-popular election in 1832, however, in which the two
'Conservative' candidates won comfortable majorities over their
Liberal opponents, it was clear that electoral politics in the new,
industrialising Belfast would be very different from the politics of
acclamation which the Liberals' fathers had played in the
Belfast of the 1790s. Between 1832 and 1870 the Liberals won
only an occasional victory in either parliamentary or municipal
elections, usually through a fluke or through arrangements with
the Conservatives to minimise the latter's embarrassment over
their manifold sharp practices.[42]

Undeniably the Conservatives were better at playing the game
by its new rules (and outside those rules) than the Liberals:
while the Liberals were looking after the balance sheets in their
linen mills, the Conservatives were attending to the electoral
register. The fundamental reality of Belfast politics, however, was
already sectarianism. The Liberals commanded the Catholic
vote and the Tories the Anglican (and Methodist) vote. While the
Liberal elite was predominantly Presbyterian, more Presbyterian
electors voted for the 'Protestant' (i.e. Tory) candidates than for
the Reformers, who because they would not eschew Catholic
votes were painted as at least covert supporters of Daniel
O'Connell and the Catholic ascendancy which his programme
for Repeal of the Union was presumed to intend. The Tory
margin which this ethnic arithmetic produced was narrow enough
that until the second Reform Act in 1867 the Liberals could hope
for an occasional victory. The large number of working-class
Protestants enfranchised in that year simply swamped the small
number of more prosperous Protestant voters whom the Liberals
could hope occasionally to seduce away from the Tories. The
one seat which the Liberals won in 1868 by taking advantage
of a temporary split in Conservative ranks was their last victory

in Belfast parliamentary elections, though they were still able to win a few seats in other parts of Ulster until 1880.

As Conservative colours were clearly the safest ones to sail under, the Tories had no difficulty in attracting politically ambitious members of the mercantile and manufacturing elite, and the socially irrelevant Donegall interest perished with the impecunious second Marquis in 1844. A system of patronage developed in which the new Tory elite distributed to Protestant workers favours in the gift of the municipality they controlled, as well as what Dr Gibbon has called 'nepotistic' access to employment in the private sector.[43] It was a system familiar to students of ethnic politics in American cities. Two components of modernisation—geographic mobility and increasing political participation—had reacted with one another to recreate in the Belfast setting something which looks remarkably like the special relationship preserved in the countryside two generations earlier first by the Volunteers and then by the Orange Order. Indeed, the Orange lodges in Belfast did constitute an element, alongside others, in this patronage system.

By around 1870 the Orange Order as an institution had declined very considerably. Its membership in the Ulster countryside consisted principally of Anglican small farmers and labourers and some of the landlords, who generally played only a marginal role in its proceedings,[44] though in Belfast and the smaller towns it did attract some artisans and tradesmen as well as general labourers.[45] The Orange lodges remained important as an exemplar of the public band and the bearers of a particular attitude toward authority which will be discussed below. Their activities were important in that they could easily trigger sectarian strife in which the idea of public banding would be propagated to other parts of the Protestant community. For these reasons, they are significant antecedents to the Ulster Unionism which emerged in 1886. It is probably a mistake, however, to regard the special relationship embodied in Orangeism—even in the more extended form it assumed to meet the exigencies of Tory politics in Belfast—as in itself the source of the inter-class alliance which characterised Ulster Unionism after 1886. A patronage system is not a public band. The managers of Tory politics in Belfast were not consciously endorsing a special security role for Protestant workingmen, except perhaps in one marginal respect. Until its abolition following the 1864 riots, places on the town police force, which were in the gift of the Corporation, went almost exclusively to Protestants.

But what did these developments have to do with Ulstermen's perceived relationship to public authority? An early feature of Orangeism was its formal sanction of conditional allegiance. Opponents of the Order were quick to point out that Orangemen bound themselves to support George III and his successors 'so long as he or they support the Protestant ascendancy, the constitution and laws of these kingdoms'.[46] Actually the Order's gentry sponsors came to be somewhat embarrassed at the conditional oath, and when challenged at official inquiries a generation later were anxious to explain it away as absolving them of their allegiance only in the most extraordinary circumstances, such as an attempt by the king to disestablish Protestantism against the wishes of parliament.[47] No doubt they were quite sincere in this profession, and when oath-bound societies were outlawed in 1823 they were probably relieved to be able to direct lodges to abandon the administering of oaths and admit members on the strength of the official oaths of allegiance, supremacy and abjuration taken before a qualified magistrate.[48]

The conditional oath is significant because it reflects the popular conception that the proper relationship between the public band and the constituted authority is a contractual one. According to an Orange clergyman, the oath had been drafted not by the gentry, but

> by persons in very low life, and who, I believe, meant in the doing so to enforce the original oath of allegiance as taken by the people, and the coronation oath taken by His Majesty, as established at the Revolution; and their object was, if possible, by any influence of theirs, to keep the present constitution as far from being altered in any way as they could.[49]

Now on the face of it, the oath's emphasis on the 'constitution' as the contract defining the loyalty of Orangemen might seem to portend the same difficulties which bedevilled the last previous public band, the Irish Volunteers. Once the immediate crisis of the rebellion was over, what was to prevent the divergent social groups in the Order from conjuring up different versions of the 'constitution', as did their predecessors in the 1780s, to fit their different political interest? Ironically, the Act of Union had solved this problem at a stroke. The dominant source of 'constitutional' controversy in England in the next generation, the system of representation, was settled in principle for Ireland by that Act's disenfranchisement of the Irish rotten boroughs. At the same time, with the extinction of the Irish parliament it was no longer necessary for the gentry to frame their conception of 'the constitution' in such a way as to justify enlarged powers for that institution. The awkward problem that the same historical events which had assured the establishment of Protestantism had also restricted the Irish parliament's authority now became irrelevant. 'The constitution', which Orangemen were determined to transmit 'unimpaired and unaltered'[50] to posterity, came to be implicitly defined as whatever it was that King William had established.

The purpose of the Orange processions, according to one Orange gentleman, was 'to commemorate great national events, such as the establishment of the British Constitution by the Bill of Rights in 1688'.[51] Implicit in this statement is a definition of the constitution at variance with the more English conception of the constitution as a slowly evolving body of law and convention. It is understood as a once-for-all transaction—a contract undertaken with King William. The Union, which was initially opposed by many Orangemen, came to be accepted as a new solemn compact undertaken for the purpose of maintaining the basic 1688–1690 bargain under changed conditions. The system of representation was simply not part of the 'constitution' as Orangemen understood that term. Indeed, once Catholic emancipation had been enacted the surviving content of this constitution was very slender. Of course, given the readmission of Catholics to full political rights in 1829, the restoration of an Irish parliament would be understood as a breach of this constitution, but after the collapse of Daniel O'Connell's movement for repeal of the Union this was hardly a real threat. By the 1850s, almost the only element of this 'constitution' remaining to be defended was the legal establishment of the Anglican Church. In 1869, when parliament disestablished the Church of Ireland, whose position had been guaranteed by the Act of Union, some Orangemen took a short-lived interest in Home Rule[52]—the proposal for a separate Irish parliament within the United Kingdom. The prospect of disestablishment had been depicted as 'a gross violation of solemn oaths, compacts and engagements'.[53] Shortly after disestablishment was enacted, it was noted at a Conservative election meeting attended by 4,000 to 5,000 Belfast workingmen, three cheers given for the Queen were not taken up with enthusiasm because 'they have had it put in their heads that H.M. forfeited her coronation oath'.[54] Actually, any disposition to act upon this reasoning quickly died out, partly because few of the Presbyterians were prepared to make an issue of the fact that disestablishment abrogated part of the Act of Union, and, more important, because the Home Rule issue quickly became associated with the national aspirations of Catholics.

In a formal sense, then, Orangeism gave to its humbler members a sense of having a more direct relationship to authority, in the person of the monarch, than they had enjoyed in the public bandings of the eighteenth century when that relationship was mediated through a constitution to which their landlords were more truly parties than they were. The monarch's person, however, was of steadily diminishing importance as a locus of authority anyway—a fact which perhaps their landlords appreciated better than they did. The formal condition Orangemen still attach to their allegiance to the crown—that its wearer be a Protestant—is objectively trivial, and loyalty to the monarch's person is simply not a problem for most Ulster Protestants, nor has it been for nearly three centuries. The problem is that Englishmen insist on confounding loyalty to the Queen with acceptance of the political system which she symbolically heads. For them, the monarch is a symbol of the English (or British) nation, and loyalty to her entails compliance with the national consensus expressed in the decisions of national institutions. This idea is an English version of the normal assumption of the modern world, that man's highest temporal loyalty is evoked by a community rather than a person—in particular, the national community in which, according to Gellner, membership is 'direct, and not mediated by intervening subgroups'.

The specific rationale developed by the Orange institution for conditional allegiance in the early nineteenth century was not of lasting importance: indeed the institution's dilemma at the time of disestablishment was the *reductio ad absurdum* of that rationale. Its significance is as an illustration that the public

band naturally conceives itself bound to the sovereign authority
not by national identification but by a contractual bond. The
special relationship embodied in Orangeism, and in other aspects
of Ulster society, had helped many Ulster Protestants to avoid
the full consequences of the erosion of traditional role relationships which is supposed to create the need to identify strongly
with the national culture and community. To be sure, as
modernisation proceeded it did generate new and changing role
relationships defined in terms of social class, much as in other
industrial societies. Catholics benefited and suffered much as did
Protestants from such changes. Orangeism sustained within this
modernising society, however, the core of a community which
cut across social classes, in which all were in some sense equal in
their common Protestantism. Social change might put one's class
in jeopardy—one might cease to be an independent weaver or a
strong farmer and become instead a factory operative or a ship-
yard worker—but one could never lose the status which attached
to being a Protestant, except by some unthinkable act, such as
marrying a Catholic. Although legally Ulstermen's membership
in the putatively national community, the United Kingdom, was
direct, many an Ulster Protestant was not forced so completely
as members of other modernising societies to identify with a
national culture. In many situations his essence was still his
social position, i.e., his Protestantism.

Citizenship and Nationality

On the face of it, the second part of Gellner's theory offers a
plausible, if highly simplified, account of how there came to be
two, and only two, nation-states, in the British Isles, divided
roughly by the present border. In the latter half of the eighteenth
century industrialisation got underway not only in England,
but also in the two parts of Great Britain whose inhabitants were
'fairly radically differentiated' from the English : Scotland and
Wales. Just as Gellner's theory would predict, the Scots and the
Welsh, sharing in the rising affluence modernisation brings, were
not tempted to erect their particularisms into 'national' differences. Scottishness and Welshness were valued as subordinate
identities, but while the espousal of these identities may have
occasionally reflected irritation at the actions of the Westminster
regime, they did not represent the profound discontent of a people

who view a neighbour across the yawning chasm which divides development from underdevelopment. A sense of 'British' nationality overrode these local identities and legitimated the Westminster regime in those parts (until very recent years when the capacity of British society to sustain rising affluence has been called into serious question). It is significant that although there was widespread discontent in Scotland with the 1707 Act of Union in the early eighteenth century, such discontent was practically non-existent between 1750 and 1850 when the fundamental social transformation took place.[55]

Conversely, when most of Ireland modernised, nearly a century later than Britain, its inhabitants did perceive themselves as excluded from the affluence of their more advanced neighbour for approximately the reasons Gellner delineates. Their distinguishing marks—principally their Catholicism—allowed their discontent to find 'national' expression. Unlike the rest of Ireland, however, Belfast and its hinterland modernised simultaneously with Britain. Our problem in this section is to assess where the Ulster Protestant community came to fit in the world of 'nations' being created by the geographically uneven effects of modernisation. Our consideration of the 'erosive' effects of modernisation in the preceding section gave us reason to suspect that, for significant segments of that community, nationality might have been somewhat irrelevant. Nevertheless, those segments, notably the Orange Order, did not constitute the whole of the Ulster Protestant community, and if we are to understand the position of that community as a whole, we must attend to the signals it was receiving from the two claimants to its 'national' allegiance; the 'United Kingdom of Great Britain and Ireland' on the one hand, and 'Ireland' on the other. To what extent did Ulster Protestants come to consider either of these entities their 'nation'?

Now it is incontrovertible that after the first decade or so of the Union the overwhelming majority of Ulster Protestants were happy to remain members of the United Kingdom state: the timing of their local industrial revolution simply never gave them reason to feel excluded from the prosperity of industrialising Britain, and therefore never prompted them to erect any distinguishing mark of their community into an argument for separation. The issue, however, is whether they considered their membership in the United Kingdom state to derive from a 'nationality' shared with the other members of that state. Here it is useful to reflect on two further attempts to define the nation, as a phenomenon in the modern world. Karl Deutsch observes that one of the tests by which we know a group to be 'a people'— at least potentially a 'nation'—is whether it is 'a community of *predictability by introspection*' in which one can anticipate the behaviour of other members by putting oneself in their place. This characteristic, Deutsch suggests, is 'one of the most important bases for the notion of a people for that "consciousness of kind" of familiarity and *trust*, which we have for people whom we understand, and whom we even understand to be like such excellent people as ourselves'.[56] It is also, I would argue, the aspect of nationality which musters diffuse support for a democratic state which is coterminous with such a people : one assumes that even if one disagrees strongly with the government of the day, it will not invade one's most basic rights if it is composed of persons 'like' oneself. Did Ulster Protestants come to trust the whole people of the United Kingdom, as represented in its democratic regime, as a satisfactory guarantor of their civil rights? And did such trust derive from a feeling that they were 'like' the other members of that putative nation? Moreover, did the United Kingdom, for them, meet Rupert Emerson's definition of the nation as the 'terminal community' within which 'there is the assumption of peaceful settlement of disagreement, based on the supreme value of national unity, whereas in conflict between it and other communities there is an assumption of the possibility of violence'?[57]

If Ulster Protestants were to perceive the United Kingdom as a people whose democratic institutions they could trust (because its other members were 'like' themselves) it was essential that the regime established in 1800 succeed in providing them equal rights of citizenship alongside the other communities in the United Kingdom. But if they were to perceive the United Kingdom as a people within which they could assume that disagreements could be settled peacefully, it was equally essential that the other communities—in particular, the Irish Catholics—also gain and accept equal citizenship. The regime's task of attaining both these aims simultaneously was particularly complex because while the Ulster Protestant community was rapidly becoming a bustling little industrial society, much of the Catholic population of the South lived, until the Great Famine, in a stagnant and impoverished economy.

The admission of Catholics to parliament in 1829, although prised out of a Tory government by a menacing Catholic agitation, committed the Westminster regime irrevocably to the principle of equal citizenship for Catholics within the United Kingdom. Actually Sir Robert Peel had made a more significant, though less dramatic application of this principle some fifteen years earlier when he created a constabulary for which Catholics, as well as Protestants, were recruited.[58] Indeed, the formation of a centrally-controlled constabulary and the creation of a system of paid resident magistrates were part of process by which, throughout Ireland, the regime freed itself from dependence upon the local gentry and their Protestant retainers for the crucial function of maintaining public order.[59] These steps— though principally a response to the fact that in most parts of the country Protestants, gentry or otherwise, were too thin on the ground to be relied upon—were in the direction of making the United Kingdom a nation which might command the allegiance of its most radically differentiated component community, the Irish Catholics.

Nevertheless, governments soon recognized that Ireland posed distinct problems from those of Great Britain, requiring radically different remedies. Nowhere was this truer than in the area of public order. In Ireland, an agrarian society, still racked by primitive and sometimes horrific forms of protest, seemed to be in continual need of extraordinary measures. The industrialised North posed problems of order which, while different from those of the agrarian South, could not be altogether separated from them in state policy if the goal of at least apparent equality of citizenship for Catholics was to be pursued. In the early and mid nineteenth century the Irish gentry were surrendering their special role in maintaining public order as gracefully as have their English counterparts in the twentieth. Lower-class Protestants did not surrender this role so gracefully, however, for the regime which ceased to sanction that role failed, when the chips were down, to evoke trust that it would guarantee the rights which Protestants had hitherto believed themselves authorised to defend on their own initiative. The state's drift toward neutrality between the religions would lead not to equality of citizenship for both islands, but, ironically, to a second-class citizenship for both Catholics and Protestants in Ireland.

For purposes of this analysis, the crucial right of the citizen was the right of free expression throughout his state's territory. In eighteenth-century Ireland, as well as England, whole boroughs and counties—both the private property and the supposedly public space therein—had been, for political purposes, the 'territory' of particular local magnates. As virtually all Irish property was in Protestant hands, only Protestants enjoyed freedom of expression—to the extent that anyone did—throughout Ireland. Ordinarily the fact of Protestant dominance was uncontested : as late as the first two decades of the Union, Orange parades up and down the country seem to have usually passed off without serious incident, Catholic onlookers sometimes joining in the festive spirit of the occasion. With the movement for Catholic emancipation, however, Protestants became acutely aware that numbers would soon count for more than property. In this context, Irish localities become not so much arenas for the free competition of political parties and ideas as the 'territory' of whichever religion, Catholic or Protestant, was dominant in numbers.

Thus Orange parades assumed the function of marking out Protestant territory. A recent historian has translated the message of the drums as, 'We are your superiors : we know you hate this demonstration of that fact : we dare you to do something about it : if you don't, you ratify your own inferior status.'[60] Perhaps an equally accurate translation would be, 'We are the majority here. If you disagree, come out and try to stop us and we will prove to you that there are more of us than there are of you.' Catholic/nationalist demonstrations were understood to convey the same message. As the official historians of Orangeism have put it, 'Where you could "walk" you were dominant, and the other things followed.'[61] Virtually every part of Ireland was understood to be either Catholic or Protestant territory. When a promoter of the cooperative movement tried to enlist both communities in a common endeavour in one southern town he was told, 'Rathkeale is a Nationalist town—Nationalist to the backbone—and every pound of butter made in this town must be made on Nationalist principles, or it shan't be made at all.'[62]

In 'normal' times both sides tended to confine their rituals to accepted territorial boundaries: in a provincial town, for example, Orange and Green arches to celebrate the ethnic festivals would be erected only in areas traditionally recognised to be Protestant and Catholic respectively.[63] Rioting characteristically followed an escalating series of gestures by which each side overstepped the accepted physical boundaries or committed some novel 'aggressive' act.[64] In Belfast, where sharply segregated residential patterns developed as immigrants poured in from the countryside, the sense of territoriality was extremely keen, and rioting of major proportions broke out in 1857, 1864, 1872 and 1886. Examples of behaviour which helped to trigger widespread disorder include the burning of an effigy of O'Connell on the perimeter of a Catholic district (1864), an attempt to hold a Catholic 'Lady Day' procession past the Church of a leading Presbyterian controversialist (1872) and a series of open-air sermons by Protestant clergy in ethnically neutral territory, the Custom House steps (1857).

Commenting on the 'party processions' which were the commonest immediate occasion for rioting, the *Saturday Review* delineated the choices faced by the state:

> ... there are only two ways in which they can rationally be dealt with. The simplest course is to prohibit them by law, and to suppress them by force; but if they are tolerated, they ought, according to the American practice, to be protected by the whole force of the Government.[65]

These choices represented two distinct ways in which the authorities might have diagnosed the problem of disorder in the North. On the one hand they might deem the problem to be 'provocation' and attempt to prevent acts which might anger the opposite party. On the other hand, they might deem the problem to be interference, by the side which chose to be offended by these gestures, with the rights of assembly, free speech and freedom of movement on public streets. Many of the 'provocative' acts were in bad taste—for example, a mock funeral for Daniel O'Connell complete with a mock 'priest' which marched to a Catholic cemetery in 1864—but, in themselves, few did actual harm to the other side.

Though it is difficult to generalise about the government response to a wide variety of explosive situations in Belfast and the Ulster countryside over several decades, characteristically the government chose to diagnose the problem as one of provocation. It took, in other words, what the *Saturday Review* called 'the simplest course'. It was usually easier to identify 'provocative' acts or classes of such acts and put a stop to them by legislation such as the Party Processions Act of 1850, by persuasion, or by *ad hoc* proceedings under common law, than to provide the force necessary to protect all those who chose to exercise free speech and to assemble and march in public places. This course was made even simpler by the fact that in British constitutional practice such rights exist only in a rather ethereal form; the government of the day can override them so long as it enjoys the consent of the legislature in so doing. The legislature was accustomed to going along with even more sweeping suspensions of civil liberties in areas of Ireland disturbed by agrarian violence—policies which would have been unthinkable if applied to England—and it was no doubt easy for MPs to regard the northern disorders as one more case in which 'the Irish' had to be treated differently from Englishmen.

The attention of contemporaries was focused on the fact that it proved legally and politically impractical to deem Catholic processions in overwhelmingly Catholic southern districts 'provocative'. The resentment of northern Protestants at the apparent inequity in the banning of their processions when quite similar activities were allowed in the South, did lead to repeal of the Party Processions Act in 1872. The repeal of that act, however, did not reflect a new government determination to enforce everyone's right to march. The speech of the government spokesman in the Lords on the second reading of the repeal bill reflects rather a hope—soon to be proved false—that both sides would 'forebear from exercising' the 'privileges Parliament was . . . willing to restore to them' wherever 'they were likely to give offence or likely to lead to breaches of the peace'.[66] The state persisted in diagnosing the basic problem as 'provocation'.

A correspondent of *The Times* in 1857 had called open-air preaching, which was that year's fashion in 'provocation',

> one of those peculiar demonstrations which partake of the nature of a challenge to the world at large. It is an assertion of manorial rights, a proclamation that you are lord of the

soil, that you are at home on the ground, and that all around you—earth, air, and sky is your own.[67]

This was true enough as an analysis of the psychology of the street-preachers and their most enthusiastic well-wishers, but only because their right of free speech was not incontestably maintained against the attacks of Catholic mobs by the forces of the state. If the government had routinely extended sufficient protection to anyone who wanted to parade, preach or otherwise demonstrate in a public place, these activities would probably have ceased to be perceived as assertions of 'manorial rights'. Such exercises would no longer have been evidence that the side which successfully promoted them could muster enough of its partisans locally to prevent their being interfered with by the other side. Rather the files of police alongside the marchers or the ring of soldiers around the preacher would have been visible proof that, at least in public places, public order did in fact derive from the sovereign power.

This of course is not a (somewhat belated) policy suggestion, but a way of illustrating the historical problem with which we are confronted. No doubt any attempt to make all public places in Ulster truly public would have been very costly in funds and probably in the lives of security forces. Governments do not characteristically make that sort of commitment to defend civil liberties unless they are responsible to a justiciable bill of individual rights, rather than to a representative assembly most of whose members regard the particular exercise of liberties in question as rather silly. Naturally, the two communities who wanted to conduct these exercises regarded them not as silly but as assertions of fundamental human rights. In the absence of state protections of such rights, their defence devolved upon the communities themselves.

Working-class Protestants in Belfast, and no doubt many of their co-religionists in country districts, diagnosed the problem of public order very differently from the government. In the view of successive governments, the problem was the rioting and its cause was provocation by both sides. In the view of Protestant participants and their sympathisers, the riots were not the problem but the solution. The problem was that their rights were being violated by the Catholics—first in attacks upon their demonstrations and, as incidents escalated, in invasions of their territory with murderous intent. Like the Peep-of-Day Boys of the 1780s, who conceptualised their actions as attempts to enforce the penal laws against possession of arms by Catholics,[68] the Protestant rioters regarded their actions not as violations of public order, but as measures to defend and restore it where the government was unwilling to do so.[69] Moreover, their concept of order was not completely out of step with contemporary standards in the outside world : they were asserting rights to free expression which were thoroughly up-to-date, even if the content of that expression was not, and their spokesmen were even willing at times to concede similar rights to Catholics.

In an important sense the loyalty of the Shankill or Sandy Row resident to the United Kingdom was that of the proconsul rather than of the citizen. Westminster, by treating him, together with his Catholic fellow-countryman, as 'different' from Englishmen in point of rights, forfeited the chance to convince him that he could trust a 'nation' corresponding to the United Kingdom, and composed of persons 'like' him, to secure his rights. The modernising state, in an effort to promote equal citizenship for all Irishmen, willy-nilly made them all inferior to their prospective co-nationals in Great Britain. The public band thus retained its relevance not only for Orangemen, but also for many working-class Protestants who were not inducted into Orange mysteries— in the case of those women and adolescents prominent in certain phases of the Belfast rioting,[70] Protestants who were not even eligible for induction.

There was, however, one element in the Protestant community which genuinely believed it possible for the United Kingdom to become a nation. The Ulster Liberal party, by appealing for the votes of Catholics as well as Protestants, was implicitly affirming that within the United Kingdom context the two Irish communities need not be enemies. Moreover, its programme explicitly called for a liquidation of those vestiges of Protestant dominance which compromised equality of citizenship. The party, as such, was a small segment of the province's elite, but it did manage to attract the votes not only of a significant share of Catholics, but also of some Protestant tenant farmers. In the 1870s it was actually making some modest electoral gains. The number of Protestants willing to make the leap of faith in the possibility of the United Kingdom becoming a nation, by voting Liberal, was never large. Nevertheless, the fact that such a group existed at all is significant.

The Ulster Liberal party succumbed in the 1880s, when the Home Rule movement siphoned off the Catholic vote without which it was not electorally viable. By examining the genesis of Irish nationalism and the response of the Protestant community to it, we shall discover that the Protestant constituency of the Ulster Liberals, while apparently affirming a United Kingdom nationalism, was really acting on a myth which, while distinct from that of the public band, was at bottom contractarian.

The Great Famine of the 1840s set in motion the process of modernisation in southern Irish society. It virtually wiped out the subsistence sector of the southern economy and starkly demonstrated the danger of subdivision to the point where one holding could produce only enough potatoes to keep a family alive. Hitherto, the extraordinary nutritional value which could be extracted from an acre of ground by raising potatoes, together with the lack of effective legal or customary barriers against subdivision, had insulated peasants in many areas from the full social consequences of Europe's population explosion since the mid-eighteenth century. In England (and the North of Ireland) the 'surplus' population, which improved hygiene and a decline in epidemic disease had permitted to survive, was moving to industrial towns or adopting new occupational roles in the countryside, and in either case developing new patterns of social relationships. In southern Ireland, however, peasants had often been able to remain within a familiar peasant society, albeit on patches of land which diminished in each generation. They were, of course, living on borrowed time, and when the cataclysm came in the 1840s, they were forced to make fundamental adjustments.

One of these adjustments was, in effect, to control fertility by postponement of marriage until an intact and agriculturally viable holding could be provided through death or 'retirement' in the older generation. The second adjustment was emigration, which, after the initial panic flight of the famine and immediate post-famine years, probably involved mainly those young people who did not want to accept the new demographic regimen. The net effect was a steady decline in population which has continued almost to the present day. In this context a good deal of rationalisation of the agricultural economy was possible. Aided by legislation for disembarrassing landed estates encumbered by debt and previously almost unbreakable entails, new groups, often moderately well-off Catholics, bought land and managed it in more economically productive ways. In many cases this involved substitution of grazing for more labour-intensive tillage. The three decades after the Famine were a generation of modestly-rising prosperity for rural Ireland. It was in these years that southern Catholic society as a whole began the modernisation process, albeit in an atypical way, as an agricultural province of an industrialising society rather than as the locus of industrialisation.[71]

Gellner's theory predicts that a people undergoing the 'worst initial dislocations of modernisation' at a time when their neighbours within the same sovereignty are already enjoying the full benefits of modernisation, will be tempted to erect some identifiable trait of their group into a 'national' difference. Among the elite of the Irish Catholic population one can find antecedents of such a process of self-definition as early as the 1640s, when Old English and Gaelic Irish found themselves classed together as 'Irish Papists'.[72] Even in the early nineteenth century, however, local and personal allegiances probably mattered more to the typical peasant than any such abstraction as 'Ireland'.[73] Daniel O'Connell's successful movement for Catholic emancipation and his futile agitation for repeal of the Union gave many peasants their first practical experience of modern democratic politics. O'Connell's contribution to the involvement of Catholicism as an *institution* in nationalism was immense, but in assessing the responsiveness of individual peasants to his message, it is difficult to sort out the national theme from the charismatic force of his personality.[74] The fact that such proto-nationalism as his movement represented actually seemed to recede in the two decades after his death and the collapse of the little Young Ireland rebellion of 1848 suggests that his personal charisma loomed larger.

To understand how religious affiliation came to be erected into a genuine 'national' difference by the vast majority of Irish Catholics, one must appreciate the peculiar course of modernisation in southern Ireland. Its 'worst initial dislocations' were suffered by those who were removed altogether from the society by death or emigration. For those who remained in the society,

modernising entailed frustration—e.g., postponed marriage—
more than dislocation. Significant dislocation came in the late
1870s, when the competition of overseas, primarily American,
extensive farming rather suddenly depressed European agricultural economies, and in Ireland this long-term problem was
compounded by a run of bad harvests. Many tenants found
themselves unable to pay their rents—or unable to pay them and
maintain the standard of living to which they had become accustomed in the previous generation—and a widespread agitation
for abatement of the rent burden ensued. Significantly, the agitation of the Land League became linked to the parliamentary
movement for 'home rule' which had been started by a Dublin
Protestant barrister, Isaac Butt, a decade earlier and captured by
the more charismatic Wicklow Protestant landlord Charles Stewart
Parnell in 1880. The practical amalgamation of the two causes,
land reform and home rule, reflects more than the undoubted
political skill of Parnell. Parnell's movement was the beneficiary,
not the creator, of a genuine popular nationalism based on the
enormous sense of deprivation of the 'underdeveloped' *vis-à-vis*
the 'developed' which was catalysed in the late 1870s by a massive
disappointment of rising expectations.[75]

Of course, national separatist ideas had been in circulation for
decades and had inspired pathetic little rebellions in 1848 and
1867. It was only in the 1880s, however, that virtually all
Catholics came to subordinate all other political objectives to the
goal of self-government. To say this is not to contradict the
importance of the 'land question'. The land agitation was not
limited to tenant farmers, but captured the enthusiasm of a
disproportionate share of shopkeepers, innkeepers, publicans,
teachers and journalists[76]—what Gellner would call B-land's
'own small intellectual class'. More fundamentally, in symbolic
terms—in the reverberations they sent through both the Catholic
and the Protestant unconscious—the national question and the
land question as posed by the Land League were one. 'Land for
the people' was, of course, in a literal sense a claim concerning
property, not sovereignty. 'Landlordism', however, was the most
visible manifestation of British sovereignty in the Irish countryside, and the line between 'land for the people' and 'Ireland for
the Irish' was a hazy one.

The visible sign of Ireland's underdevelopment was continued emigration. Now in strict economic terms, the depopulation of the Irish countryside was no different from the inevitable migration of population out of agricultural regions of any industrialising state. If, however, the Irish defined Ireland rather than the United Kingdom as their 'country', then migration to employment was tantamount to expatriation, for all the industrial cities to which displaced peasants might go were 'foreign' except Belfast, the one such city in which they would most surely meet, in practical form, the discrimination which in a more general sense is inevitably perceived by the underdeveloped community on the part of its developed neighbours. The practical content of the attack on rent was a demand by Irish Catholics for the right to live in 'their own country'—a right which, it was confidently assumed, would be even more effectively guaranteed by the establishment of a native parliament under which industry would flourish as it was believed to have done under 'Grattan's Parliament' of 1782–1800. The land campaign was therefore at the heart of the national consciousness forged in the years 1878–86.

That the Protestants of Belfast and its industrial hinterland would not identify with this Irish nation was foreordained by the fact that they were already sharing in the affluence of industrial Britain and simply did not have—indeed could not even empathise with—the sense of deprivation felt by southern Catholic farmers. There were also, however, tens of thousands of Protestant tenant farmers in Ulster, who did have agrarian grievances quite similar to those of Catholics. Indeed, Presbyterian tenants had taken the lead in land reform agitation since the 1850s and had been quite willing to join forces with Catholic agitation for similar purposes in the South. With the advent of the Land League, however, the different connotations of land reform in the two communities became apparent.

The goal of the Presbyterian land agitation had been to defend, consolidate and extend the 'Ulster custom' of tenant right. It was argued that James I had granted certain proprietary rights not only to the undertakers, but also to their tenants.[77] The most commonly asserted such right was fixity of tenure, but exponents of the concept often extended the argument to embrace other privileges as well, such as 'easy rents'.[78] One enthusiastic young Presbyterian minister went so far as to assert that Ulster landlords had no right to charge more than the original plantation rents of roughly one shilling per acre.[79]

The idea that the Ulster custom rested upon an original contract between crown and tenants was a myth devised in the nineteenth century to explain and exploit an objective fact—that something called 'tenant right' was indeed bought and sold by incoming and outgoing tenants, respectively, in most parts of Ulster (as it was also in a few parts of the other three provinces). The origins of this 'custom' as W. H. Crawford has shown, lay in the fact that long leases, which had simply been more common in Ulster than in the other provinces, tended to become inconvenient for both landlord and tenant with the fluctuations of food prices in the wake of the Napoleonic Wars and were in many cases replaced by yearly tenancies.[80] Ulster tenants had come to expect and demand relatively secure tenure, and lawyers devised the concept of the 'Ulster custom', which the law could envisage only as 'payment for improvements', to rationalise the realities of landlord-tenant relationships in the province.

Catholic as well as Protestant tenants benefited from the Ulster custom, and spokesmen for Protestant tenants were quite willing to call for the extension of the custom to the southern provinces so that it could benefit southern Catholic tenants as well. To be sure, there was some discontent among Ulster tenants when the 1870 Land Act, which attempted to do just that, actually rendered their own position less favourable in some cases by trying to codify the custom's provisions and thereby depriving them of the legal advantages to be gained from vagueness. Nevertheless, we should not underestimate the disposition on the part of Protestant, especially Presbyterian, tenants to agitate for reforms of benefit to Catholics as well as themselves in the period 1850–1880. This disposition, however, emphatically did not entail any feelings of separate Irish nationality. The slogan 'Tenant right' or, as it was sometimes expressed, 'Tenant right and no surrender',[81] had radically different implications from 'Land for the people'. Protestant tenants were, at bottom, making a claim for something they believed the crown had *given to* their ancestors in the seventeenth century; Catholic tenants, under Land League auspices, were claiming something they believed the crown had *taken away from* their ancestors in the seventeenth century. If we conceive the two claims as narrowly confined to issues of property, the projected outcome of the agitations might be remarkably similar : a recognised proprietary interest in the soil on the tenant's part to protect him not only from eviction in the short term but also, to a greater or lesser extent, from the rent burden. Underlying the two movements, however, were diametrically opposed conceptions of legitimate sovereignty. 'Land for the people' contained the germ of the idea that the Irish people, rather than the British crown, were the proper locus of sovereignty in Ireland; the claim for 'tenant right' was a reaffirmation of the Crown's sovereignty and a call for it to honour certain obligations it had undertaken in order to make that sovereignty effective in Ireland. Not surprisingly, in the early 1880s, when Presbyterian tenants found that they could not join the Land League agitation without at least implicitly sanctioning the national claim, they simply disappeared from its ranks and sought redress of their grievances in isolation from their Catholic counterparts.

While Protestant tenant farmers rejected Irish nationality despite some apparent identity of their economic interests with those of Catholic tenants who were the backbone of the national movement, Belfast Catholics enthusiastically embraced Irish nationality despite the irrelevance of the national movement's principal social programme to their actual needs. Their efforts to rationalise their position could be amusing and revealing. In December, 1884, and January, 1885, the *Belfast Morning News*, the principal Catholic organ in the city, published two reports from their 'Special Commissioner' to investigate the linen industry, which were afterwards much-cited by Unionists because they quoted, with apparent approval, suggestions that Irish linen ought to be boycotted in America as 'Orange'. Naturally, suggestions such as this, which may have been useful in consolidating Catholic support for Nationalism before 1886, were a severe embarrassment to Nationalist spokesmen thereafter when the task at hand was to convince English opinion of their good intentions toward Ulster. Actually the articles are a naïve blend of hostility toward the 'linenites' and confidence that the programme of the Land League (by this time styled the 'National League') held the key to the 'linenites' own emancipation from supposed oppression. The linen trade, the 'Special Commissioner' argued, had been 'a scourge and not a blessing to Ulster'.

'Up the heathery mountain, down the rustling glen', the fair linen has laid its foul mark in impossible rents; for lint and loom and linen, not the land, paid the rent. But for the stone of flax, the hank of yarn, the web of linen, the grinding land-lord exactions which have kept Ulster poor could never have been put in force.... That's the reward Ulster gained by its unswerving blind devotion to linen, loyalty, and landlordism.[82]

This analysis reflects not only the sectarian animosity of northern Catholics, but also a fundamental divergence in social values between Protestant Ulster and Catholic/Nationalist Ireland. For the latter, attachment to the soil was of supreme value, and insofar as industrialisation undermines such attachment, its evils outweigh whatever benefits the 'linenites' have been deluded into perceiving in it. Needless to say, northern Protestants themselves, who rightly regarded the linen industry as the origin of the North's prosperity even if its rural manifestation was now a dwindling anachronism, did not share these values.

In the years 1878 to 1886, therefore, an Irish nation, com-posed, for all practical purposes, of the Catholic population of the island—and *only* the Catholics, bar a few cranks and politi-cians—crystallised as a self-conscious entity. Its existence and boundaries were reflected in the fact that from 1885 onwards some 85 of the 103 Irish parliamentary constituencies—i.e., those with Catholic majorities—regularly returned Nationalist mem-bers. Moreover, the fundamentally Catholic character of the nation was confirmed in 1884–85 when the Roman Catholic hierarchy concluded what Professor Larkin has described as a 'concordat' with the national movement[83] by which it was tacitly understood that Catholic educational interests would be defended by the Nationalist Party, that the movement would eschew 'unconstitutional' methods and, in return, the national claim would be sanctioned as legitimate by the Church. The effects of this 'concordat' were evident in the increasingly prominent role played by clergymen in Nationalist organization —a phenomenon which did not pass unnoticed in the North.

Out of long habit, not out of any feeling of exclusion from the prosperity of industrialising Britain, Ulster Protestants gener-ally continued to think of themselves as Irish. For them—a point which Irish nationalists could never grasp—Irishness, like Scottishness and Welshness, was fully compatible with continued membership in the British state. For a few—a very few—members of the Protestant elite the United Kingdom indeed became the nation: the community within which they were prepared to assume that peaceful settlement of disagreement was, or ought to be, normal. The United Kingdom failed, however, to transform a residuary attachment on the part of urban working-class Protestants and Orangemen throughout the countryside into an active sense of incorporation into itself as a 'nation'. To the extent that the Tory segment of the elite patronised Orangeism it abetted the forces working against making the United Kingdom a nation. However, those forces—crucially, the three-generation lag between the onset of modernisation in the North and in the South—were so overwhelming that the erection of an Irish nation was inevitable. The Irish nation failed to attract the allegiance even of that Protestant group, the tenant farmers, whose socio-economic circumstances most closely resembled those out of which Irish nationalism arose among Catholics. Indeed, the specific issue which gave Irish nationalism its driving force— land reform—highlights the fundamentally contractarian character of the political thinking of even some Protestants who had ceased to regard Catholics as the natural enemy. The only segment of the Ulster Protestant community which genuinely embraced a nationalist myth—the Liberal elite—was about to be politically decimated by the defection of the bulk of their followers, the Ulster Catholics, to a different nationalist myth, and by the subsequent abandonment by their political allies in Britain, of the futile effort to make the United Kingdom a nation.

Myths Sacred and Secular

Thus modernisation worked in such a way as to produce two nations in the British Isles but to leave, in the North of Ireland, a community many of whose members did not feel fully incorporated into either. Provided that one is alert to the possibility that Gellner's explicit and implicit premises may not have been realised in particular modernising communities, and admits the possibility of the odd exception to the apparent universality of nationalism in the modern world, then Gellner's theory does help us to understand this process. A shortcoming of the theory, however, is its failure to tell us much about the capacity of nationalism to evoke emotional commitment and thereby generate diffuse support for modern states. Gellner sees his theory as a refutation of the simplistic view that national sentiment is an atavism representing the victory of man's irrational 'dark gods' over his 'cold Reason'.[84] I believe he is right to discard the dark gods of unreason as a means of explaining how nationalism arises, in favour of 'genuine, objective, practical necessity, however obscurely recognised'. Nevertheless, the dark gods remain a defining characteristic of the thing to be explained : nations do evoke feelings capable of overriding cold, rational calculations of self-interest.

An alternative theory which better accounts for this aspect of nationalism asserts that nationalism is the 'religion' of modernisation,[85] in the sense that it performs for a modern society that function of 'reaffirming the group' which Durkheim identified as the most important function of those systems of belief and practice which are usually described as religions. As traditional religions decline under the impact of modernisation, it is argued, something else is required to sanction society's norms and justify its authority relationships. The most important new authority relationship in the modern world is majority rule. Nationalism can justify the individual's submission to the majority by reassuring him that the population within which the majority was reckoned is indeed the 'natural' unit to which he belongs, (or, of course, it can justify erecting such an entity into a new arena of majority rule).

To apply these concepts in the Irish case, however, one must first come to terms with the fact that both Irish communities continue to practice their conventional religions with a regularity which astounds observers from other modern societies. I have suggested elsewhere that the strength of Catholicism in modern Ireland derives in large measure from the Church's successful adaptation to modernisation. One way to understand that adaptation is to consider religion's function of helping believers to cope with stress. Where customary, sometimes extra-canonical, practices before the 1840s had helped peasants to cope with the primary source of stress in that age—the threat of starvation—a reformed and revivified canonical Catholicism helped them thereafter to cope with the new source of stress entailed by southern Ireland's peculiar style of modernisation—the threat of rootlessness.[86] In this process of sanctioning and legitimating popular desires for a secure attachment to the land, however, the Church was also lending her authority to Irish nationalism, for, as we have seen, it was on the land question that the socio-economic forces making for nationalism became focused. Thus the Church transferred the main burden of reaffirming the group from her own shoulders to those of a new secular myth. Undoubtedly the Church enhanced her own authority and reinforced the devotion of her flock by this alignment with popular forces. In reality, Irish nationalism was deeply and unavoidably sectarian, but in the minds of most of its ideologues it was secular. It is easy to find statements by Irish nationalists implying that Protestants were mere alien settlers, but the strain of nationalism which asserted that they were properly part of the Nation was of crucial importance. This latter strain was possible, moreover, because despite the obvious interpenetration of the sacred and the secular, nationalism did have an integrity distinct from canonical religion.

The success of the Protestant churches in retaining the active adherence of their flocks can also be understood in terms of those institutions' adaptation to modernisation.[87] That adaptation, however, produced a different configuration of the sacred and the secular in the community's total myth-structure, and it must be analysed within a different frame of reference dictated by differences in the prior historical experience of Protestants and Catholics. At the Reformation, Protestant churches had generally been more successful than Roman Catholicism in transmuting anxiety over the uncertainty of physical survival into anxiety over the uncertainty beyond death. This latter uncertainty could be particularly acute for those who took seriously the theological system of John Calvin.

Two emphases within reformed Protestantism served to soften Calvin's terrible dictum that one could neither know nor affect God's eternal decrees that one was either saved or damned. One of these emphases, which I call 'conversionist' is familiar to students of Anglo-American Protestantism : while there is nothing one can do to affect God's awful determination, still one can have an inner experience of assurance that one is among the elect. Presbyterianism in Scotland and Ulster before the nineteenth century was reluctant to make this overt compromise with

Calvin's awful logic. Peter Gibbon has rightly described this religious system as 'intellectualist';[88] it enjoined a strict, rational performance of one's moral duties, as adjudicated by a system of church courts: kirk sessions, presbyteries, synods, etc. It was not this intellectualism, however, which enabled the system to meet popular needs, but an emphasis compatible with it which I call 'prophetic', using that term in its Old Testament sense to connote both prediction of providential intervention in the world and an element of social criticism, even social protest.

The system of Presbyterian polity was important in itself— a point which baffled conversionist evangelicals—because the goal was the conversion not of individuals but of the whole secular order. The Presbyterian enthusiast hoped to impose godly discipline upon both the elect and the unelect, who could not be empirically distinguished in this world. The system could function to alleviate his own anxieties over his ultimate end not because any amount of righteousness would win salvation, but because the society could still believe that God was really and literally active in the physical world and the political order. By standing firm for Presbyterian ideals, one became an instrument of divine purposes and potentially of dramatic providential intervention in the external world. If Providence was a bit slow in bringing about his kingdom—a Presbyterian kingdom—on earth, still one's task was clear: to keep the reformed church true to her standards within the community which nominally accepted them, not to have conversion experiences and still less to promote such illusory experiences in others. Thus, in the eighteenth century, in contrast with England and America, where popular religion took on a decidedly conversionist character under the leadership of John Wesley and his disciples, the cutting edge of popular religion among Scots and Ulster Scots was represented by the Seceders, Burgher and Antiburgher, and a sect of 'strict Covenanters', which tried to outbid each other in fidelity to seventeenth-century Presbyterian standards in doctrine and polity.

It was inevitable that the conversionist emphasis would have to supplant the prophetic in the course of modernisation if reformed Protestantism was to retain widespread popular appeal. The prophetic emphasis had been able to confer popular appeal upon an austerely intellectualist tradition only by virtue of a premodern capacity to believe in the possibility of supernatural

D

intervention in the external world. The conversionist emphasis confined the 'magic' to the internal world of the individual's psyche. As late as the political excitement of the 1790s there were enough remnants of the old world-view to render those events amenable to millenarian interpretation in Presbyterian country districts. During the first two-thirds of the nineteenth century, however, Ulster Presbyterianism was decisively transformed into a fundamentally conversionist religious system. Ulster Anglicanism also took on a conversionist complexion, and to the extent that it failed to do so it began to lose adherents to Methodism and other conversionist sects. The prophetic emphasis had thrived upon doctrinal disputation within Presbyterianism, and the real significance of the General Synod's decision to enforce subscription to orthodox doctrinal standards after 1829, which incidentally forced out the little 'new light' party who preached Enlightenment theology, was to lay aside all such controversy in favour of active evangelical endeavour. When the Rev. Henry Cooke proclaimed 'the banns of a sacred marriage'[89] between the Presbyterian Church and the Church of Ireland at a huge Loyalist demonstration at Hillsborough in 1834, he probably did not accurately express the political sentiments of all his Presbyterian colleagues. There was, however, if not a marriage, at least a growing consensus within Protestantism that denominational differences over doctrine and polity were secondary to the great business of saving souls.

There was a built-in ambiguity in the word 'conversion' : most evangelicals conceived of conversion as a process which anyone, presumably already a nominal church member, might undergo. No change in denominational affiliation need follow. In the Irish context, however, it was probably inevitable that an attempt would be made to 'convert' the Roman Catholics in the very different sense of getting them to prove the genuineness of their inward conversion by changing their outward church membership. The shift in meaning was not immediate; as late as 1820, when the General Synod established a committee 'for promoting the cause of Presbyterianism in the south and west of Ireland', its agents were forbidden to proselytise and instructed 'to confine their attentions to those areas where it was known for certain that Presbyterian families lived'.[90] Nevertheless, by the 1830s both the Presbyterian Church and the Church of Ireland were caught up in the quixotic enterprise of trying to convert the Catholics.[91]

Within Protestantism the conversionist emphasis could sustain popular religion precisely because it was a successful adaptation to the empiricism of a modern scientific world-view. It allowed the individual to verify his salvation through his own experience, but the experience in question, being internal, was incapable of corroboration or disproof by any other observer. The matter was far different in relation to the Catholics. Under eighteenth-century conditions it had been quite possible for, say, a Presbyterian to believe that perhaps a few of the Catholics were among the elect. Catholics were viewed, however, not as individuals, but as a collectivity under the evil dominion of the pope. There was no point in trying to promote conversion experiences by which elect Catholics might verify their election (though it would be most worthwhile for the civil magistrate to take more seriously the task assigned him by the Westminster Confession of suppressing Popish 'heresies and blasphemies'). Now, however, Catholics were being treated as individuals. Not surprisingly, few were converted, and the refusal of the vast majority left them individually responsible for their contumacy. Though no theologian would have put it this way, in effect Catholics were offered the opportunity to demonstrate their election, and, virtually to a man, they turned it down. The conversionist emphasis provided for the first time 'empirical' verification that the Catholics were not among the elect.

These developments, combined with the Ulster Protestant community's need, in default of any genuine nationalism, for an integrative myth, led to the erection of an exaggerated version of traditional Protestant views of Catholicism into a myth which Mr Frank Wright has ably analysed in his study of Ulster Protestant ideology.[92] Liberty, according to this myth, is a defining characteristic of Protestantism. This liberty, not just the right of private judgment, but a freedom of the soul deriving from the saving truth of the Bible, long rejected by Catholicism, was now rejected by Catholics. Therefore Catholic attacks upon, say, street preachers, and Catholic resistance to required Bible-reading in the primary schools, seemed to prove that they would use the power of their numbers to destroy that liberty which mattered most. The myth tended, therefore, to reinforce the basic assumption of the public band and contradict any assumption that

Ireland or the United Kingdom might be an arena for the 'peaceful settlement of disagreement'. The Presbyterian street-preacher, Rev. Hugh Hanna, giving evidence before the Commission to investigate the 1857 Belfast riots, was asked whether he would consider it his duty to preach when he believed riot would ensue. 'I would, sir', he replied. 'Our most valuable rights have been obtained by conflict; and if we cannot maintain them without that, we must submit to the necessity.'[93]

Conversionist evangelicalism generated in the Ulster Protestant community an enthusiasm—most dramatically manifested in the frenetic revival of 1859—comparable to that generated among Irish Catholics by nationalism. Each of these phenomena was in practice confined to one community, but each catalysed certain attitudes toward the other side. Nationalists were capable of conceiving of a kind of secular salvation for the other side without compassing their religious conversion. The expectation that Protestants would eventually come to recognise their 'true' nationality was an apocalyptic hope which defied the lessons of actual experience. Intelligent people have been able to cling to that hope because nationalist myths are a common and generally unchallenged currency of modern political discussion. A very few conversionist evangelicals were perhaps able to conceive of salvation for members of the other side without the latter forsaking the church of their fathers. To most Protestants, however, such a salvation was at best unlikely, at worst inconceivable. In the course of modernisation, Protestants had discarded a heritage of apocalyptic thinking, but Catholics were acquiring a new, secular capacity for apocalyptic vision.

Thus Irish nationalism was capable of reaffirming the group not only as it was—a sectarian nationality—but also as it 'ought' to be—an Irish nation transcending the sectarian division of Irish society in this present age. In this latter respect, it resembled the prophetic myths of pre-industrial Presbyterianism. The supplanting of such prophetic myths left Ulster Protestants with a myth which, once it was clear that the Catholics, as individuals, would not be converted, could reaffirm the group only as it really was— a community deeply divided from its neighbours. Moreover, this division would only become sharper as Irish nationalism consolidated its hold on those neighbours.

3

'Here we Stand, a Loyal Band'
1883-1920

The Stakes of the Game

During the years from the 1880s to 1920 Irish Protestants sank their political differences in common opposition to the Home Rule threat. There is, as we have seen, no mystery over why they rejected Irish nationalism and, almost to a man, gave 'unionism' priority over all other political objectives. Until the Third Reform Act (1884) lowered the franchise qualification and dis-enfranchised several anachronistic parliamentary boroughs, it had still been possible for a few Conservatives, appealing basically for Protestant votes, to be returned for southern constituencies. Moreover, as late as the 1880 general election Ulster had remained an arena for the more-or-less gentlemanly contention of Liberals and Conservatives. Informed people knew, of course, that Ulster was not solidly Protestant, but only Cavan, with an overwhelmingly Catholic electorate, returned Home Rulers. In several other Ulster constituencies Catholics were a majority in the population but still a minority in the electorate, albeit an important minority on which the electoral survival of the Liberals depended.

With the 1885 election, electoral results came to reflect demo-graphic realities with tolerable precision. Home Rulers routed Conservatives and Liberals from every constituency in the three southern provinces except for the two Dublin University seats. These results were repeated with only trivial variations, at every general election until 1918. Despite the fact that Unionists could only win about half the Ulster seats, there was clearly a difference between the situation of Unionists in Ulster and in the rest of Ireland. In Ulster they could at least make a showing in the game of democratic politics, and it was soon evident that *Ulster* Unionism would develop its own character, identity, organisation and, ultimately, goals. Indeed as the Home Rule threat was emerging in the early 1880s, 'Ulster' as a distinct entity came to take on a heightened significance. In 1883 a by-election in Mona-ghan was won by a Home Ruler, T. M. Healy, and Nationalists, raising the cry 'All Ulster is ours', began organising a series of public meetings throughout the province. This action was at once regarded as an 'invasion', and Orange counter-demonstrations were systematically organised to resist the threat. Though Healy himself may have been the first to use the term 'invasion of Ulster', the phrase captured exactly the way many Protestants viewed the action.[1] To be sure, there had long been a sense in which Ulster was considered Protestant territory to be defended. When 'the Repealer' (O'Connell) visited Belfast in 1841, he did not simply receive a disappointing reception; he was 'repulsed'.[2] During the Fenian agitation of the 1860s, the agent of a County Tyrone landlord wrote to reassure his employer, 'Baa say I, for the black North will take care of itself. . . .'[3] Now, however, the dwindling fortunes of Loyalists outside the province made it clear that in electoral terms Ulster would be the last redoubt. The province as a whole was invested with the sense of territoriality which the Orange Order and Protestant ghetto-dwellers had kept alive in the middle years of the century on the level of much smaller, more discrete, geographical units. Ironically, 'Ulster' acquired this territorial significance just at the moment when rationalisation of the franchise and system of representation was to make clear that only about half of the nine-county province was 'really' Protestant territory.

In addition to demonstrating Catholic dominance throughout the three southern provinces and half of Ulster, the 1885 election created a situation in which neither Conservatives nor Liberals held an overall majority in the House of Commons. The 86 Irish nationalists would be able to prevent either party from govern-ing without their consent, which would be conditional upon a commitment to enact Home Rule. Such a commitment was given by the Liberal leader, William Ewart Gladstone, in 1886. A remarkable feature of northern response to the impending legisla-tive crisis was a widespread assumption on the part of Protestant farmers and workers that their own right to continue living in Ireland was literally at stake. Nationalist flights of rhetoric, calling for the 'extermination' of landlords and the banishing of 'colonists', on platforms in Catholic districts during the early

1880s had not passed unnoticed in the North, where they were
taken literally and perceived as a practical programme of which
recurrent agrarian outrage in the West and South were the
precursors.[4] Late in 1885 rumours began to sweep the North to
the effect that in remote Catholic chapels 'raffles', 'lotteries' or
'auctions' of Protestant property were already taking place against
the day when Home Rule would be established and its presumed
object, dispossession of the Protestants, could take place in an
orderly fashion.[5] Intelligent Unionists looking back on this period
were inclined to view these rumours with scepticism or jocularity,[6]
and indeed they had their comic side. In one case the priest who
supposedly auctioned off a certain Presbyterian manse for a few
shillings was reported to have thrown the adjacent meeting-house
into the bargain gratis for use as a barn.[7] Nevertheless, these
rumours were seriously believed. During the Commons debates
on Home Rule in June, 1886, serious rioting was touched off in
Belfast by a quarrel between a Protestant and a Catholic construc-
tion labourer in which the Protestant understood the Catholic to
say that 'neither me nor any of my sort should get leave to work
there or earn a loaf there or any other place'.[8]

This assumption that Home Rule would inevitably mean
Catholic dominance in the starkest and most literal sense has
puzzled and bemused southern nationalists ever since the 1880s.
Both the assumption and the southern inability to comprehend it
can perhaps best be understood in terms of what Alvin Gouldner,
in his brilliant analysis of ancient Greek society, has called the
'contest system'.[9] Politics so conceived is necessarily a zero-sum
game, for the point of engaging in it is not to achieve anything
tangible, but, as in an athletic contest, to experience the pleasure
of victory over one's antagonist. It is axiomatic in, say, a wrestling
match, that one athlete must win and the other lose : both cannot
win. The humiliation of the loser is inseparable from the exalta-
tion of the winner. The 'territorial' obsession of Irish Catholics
and Protestants in the nineteenth century lent a zero-sum
character to politics as perceived by the lower classes, for there
was only so much territory to be divided. Moreover, the fact that
the leading tangible goals of the Catholic side—first 'Repeal' and
then 'Home Rule'—long seemed unobtainable also helped make
the contest system seem the normal mode of politics throughout
Ireland. On the Protestant side a leading goal of political activity

had been the maintenance of Protestant ascendancy, which really did imply dominance of one side over the other. Though that goal had diminished in importance with disestablishment in 1869, and though it had never fully captured Presbyterian affections, the notion that politics was basically about the dominance of one side or the other had survived the demise of the former symbol of Protestant dominance, the established church. In 1886, Robert Lynd asserted, most Presbyterians believed that Home Rule would put them 'under the heel of a majority that hates them and would do everything in its power to humiliate and dispossess them'.[10]

The events of 1885–86, however, made possible a crucial change in southern Catholic attitudes. Gladstone's conversion to Home Rule suddenly placed that object within the realm of realistic possibility : something tangible might indeed be attained by politics. At the same time Catholic electoral dominance in the three southern provinces was established firmly, finally and irrevocably. Consequently, southern politics gradually ceased to resemble a zero-sum game.[11] In nearly all constituencies the Protestants had been decisively beaten and simply retired from the field. Nationalists emphasised the fact that their own leader, Parnell, was a Protestant, and welcomed the odd Protestant who offered to stand for parliament under the Nationalist banner, proudly exhibiting him as evidence of the falsehood of northern allegations that they sought dominance over the Protestants. Over the generation after 1886 many southern Catholics began to forget the contest system in which their fathers had been involved, and found it increasingly hard to grasp why northern Protestants refused to regard Home Rule as a gain for all Irishmen rather than a defeat, humiliation and unparalleled disaster for their side in a zero-sum game.

Northern Catholics probably found it easier to understand. For both them and the northern Protestants, politics remained a zero-sum game. 'Our turn is coming now', a Belfast Catholic dealer in used furniture cried to a Protestant customer in 1886, 'and, by God, we'll learn you what we can do.'[12] Small wonder that when this same middle-class Protestant walked through Sandy Row on the day Home Rule was thrown out by the House of Commons, Protestant working men enquired after the fate of the Bill in the words, 'Is them 'uns bate'?[13]

In the six months between Gladstone's conversion and the defeat of the first Home Rule Bill, preparations for armed resistance to an Irish Parliament seem to have been made at a few places in Ulster, mainly under Orange auspices. These preparations lacked central coordination, partly because Ulster Liberals and Conservatives, and indeed Orange and non-Orange factions within Conservatism, had not had time to sort out issues of leadership in the new political situation which was being created and partly, no doubt, because informed people realised[14] that even if the government managed to get the Bill through the Commons, the Lords would overwhelmingly reject it. In fact, Gladstone split the Liberal Party in Great Britain, and after the ensuing general election the Conservatives returned to office with the support of a bloc of 'Liberal Unionist' defectors from Gladstone's party.

The Ulster Liberals could only interpret the conversion of their erstwhile hero as treachery of the most cynical order, and though they maintained a skeletal Liberal Unionist organisation in Belfast, they ceased after 1886 to be an independent force in Ulster politics. One of their most articulate spokesmen, Thomas MacKnight, editor of the *Northern Whig* expressed their sense of betrayal when he argued that

> When the Ulster settlements were made, there was an implied compact that they who crossed the Irish Sea on what was believed to be a great colonising and civilising mission should not in themselves, nor in their descendants, be abandoned to those who regarded them as intruders, and as enemies.[15]

This contractarian interpretation of the past was MacKnight's rationale for Ulstermen taking their stand on the 'foundations' of 'the English Constitution, as hitherto understood, with its leading principle, the protection of the individual rights of the citizen'. He would have emphatically repudiated the conception of the constitution preserved into the nineteenth century by the Orange Order: that its leading principle was Protestantism. Unionist orators, especially but not exclusively former Liberals, frequently reiterated that their opposition to Home Rule arose out of no desire to reimpose Protestant ascendancy. In this sense, MacKnight's 'implied compact' was different from the traditional Orange understanding of a contractual relationship with the crown. Moreover, whatever may have been understood in the darker recesses of the Shankill Road, the view represented by MacKnight set the tone for public Unionist rhetoric over the next generation. It was thus possible for even the Liberals in Ulster's elite to resume leadership roles in the public band which, for several generations, had been kept alive mainly by their social inferiors. From about 1885 it seems to have become socially acceptable for well-to-do Presbyterians to join the Orange Order.[16] But while the Order did certainly grow stronger in this period, the public band would assume new forms more in keeping with the demands of the political situation.

By 1892, when another general election seemed likely to return Gladstone to power—as indeed it did, with sufficient strength including the Irish Nationalists to carry Home Rule in the Commons—Unionist forces in Ulster had recovered from whatever disarray had impaired their unity in 1886. In June of that year they mounted a superbly orchestrated demonstration, a specifically *Ulster* Unionist Convention of 11,879 picked delegates from throughout the province in a specially-constructed pavilion near the Botanic Gardens, Belfast. Speaker after speaker voiced their fixed determination to repudiate the authority of any parliament which might be set up in Dublin and to resist its decrees. Though passive resistance was the general theme, there were frequent suggestions of armed opposition. The Convention was a demonstration by, as one speaker put it, 'men who know what is at stake and mean to stand by their engagement'. (Cheers.) The delegates were urged to 'look to Ulster as the Marathon where the invaded stand and conquer'. (Loud cheers.)[17] The demonstration was the latest embodiment of the public band—as the *Northern Whig* correspondent rather awkwardly described it, 'a "bund", the homogeneity of which nothing now can shake'.[18] Preparations for active resistance went so far as the formation of an Ulster Defence Union in March 1893, and the importation of a few rifles,[19] but the Lords' rejection of Home Rule in September, the retirement of Gladstone, and the return in 1895 of a Conservative/Liberal Unionist majority, removed the issue from practical politics for, as it turned out, nearly a decade.

The need for vigilance waned, though Ulster Unionism could still be galvanised into action at the merest hint of Home Rule as happened in 1904–05 when the Under Secretary, Sir Antony MacDonnell, a Roman Catholic with proconsular experience in

India, was discovered to be entertaining ideas, put forward by certain southern landlords, for a very limited devolution of governmental powers to a representative body. Ulster Unionist pressure forced Balfour, the Conservative Prime Minister, to sack the Chief Secretary, George Wyndham, who had, perhaps more out of neglect than design, allowed his senior civil servant to stray into such heresy.[20] In 1907, the first Liberal government since 1885 to enjoy a secure majority independent of the Irish Nationalist MPs, brought forward a similar devolution scheme. No doubt Ulster Unionism would have raised an even louder clamour than they had two years earlier if the Nationalists' own supporters had not resoundingly spurned the scheme at a Convention in Dublin within a few weeks of its introduction. Conservative efforts to 'kill Home Rule by kindness', culminating in Wyndham's Land Purchase Act of 1903, had indeed helped to reduce the violence and intimidation which had seemed central to the Home Rule movement in the 1880s. Once a genuine national consciousness is formed, however, the removal of the original causes for its formation will not instantly dissolve it. A fundamental postulate of nationality is that good government is no substitute for native government. Though nearly three decades experience at Westminster had mellowed the fiery young lieutenants of Parnell who were now the Irish Party's middle-aged leaders, they were responsible to a constituency which was still committed, with a single-mindedness difficult to appreciate in England, to the attainment of national self-government. That constituency was now much more willing than a generation earlier to put away all thoughts of physical force and wait patiently for 'constitutional' methods to work. It was prepared to accept a settlement considerably short of total independence. But it would have instantly repudiated its leaders if they did not seize the first opportunity which presented itself to extort Home Rule out of the English. Such an opportunity did present itself in 1910.

Since the Liberals won their overwhelming Commons majority in 1906, the Conservatives had been systematically using their permanent majority in the Lords to wreck controversial government legislation. Though the Lords had an undoubted right to veto general legislation, in 1909 they made the great strategic error of rejecting the Budget—a violation of what had come to be regarded as a fixed convention of the constitution, that the

Commons were supreme in finance. The government went to the country on the issue of the 'People's Budget' and the powers of the second chamber; Asquith, the Prime Minister, also publicly reserved the right to bring in Home Rule. The result of the election was an almost equal division of Liberals (275) and Unionists (273) with the 82 Irish Nationalists (together with 40 Labour members) holding the balance. Redmond, the Nationalist leader, did his duty. He extracted guarantees from Asquith that if the Irish Party supported the government over the Budget, the government would indeed curb the Lords' powers in such a way as to prevent a veto of Home Rule. After an abortive constitutional conference and another general election producing virtually the same result, Asquith proceeded in 1911 with a bill to provide that legislation passed by the Commons in three successive sessions would become law even without the Lords' consent. The Lords, faced with the possibility of a mass creation of Liberal peers to swamp their opposition, acquiesced in the Bill and the way was clear for the introduction of Home Rule, which was of course Redmond's price for keeping the government in office.

Time of Threatened Calamity

Naturally these events were viewed with alarm in Ulster. The Irish Unionists at Westminster, i.e., the Ulster Unionists plus the two members for Dublin University, had recently chosen as their leader one of the University members, Sir Edward Carson, a Dublin barrister having, ironically, no previous connection with the North. While Carson masterminded party strategy at Westminster and provided charismatic leadership for Ulster resistance, that resistance was effectively organised by his lieutenant, Captain James Craig, a Belfast distiller and MP for East Down. Shortly after the Parliament Act received the royal assent the Ulster Protestant community initiated its campaign against Home Rule with a demonstration of 50,000 Orangemen and Unionist club members in the grounds of Craig's home, Craigavon, overlooking Belfast Lough. The tone of the occasion, as of the movement it initiated, was set by Lord Erne who quoted a letter from the Governor of Enniskillen in 1689 declaring, 'We stand upon our guard and do resolve by the blessing of God to meet our danger rather than to await it.'[21] They met their danger by authorising

steps, which were formally initiated by a 'Special Commission'
two days later, to establish a 'Provisional Government of Ulster'
which would come into operation the day Home Rule was enacted
and be maintained 'until Ulster shall again resume unimpaired
her citizenship in the United Kingdom'.[22] Moreover, at the
demonstration one Orange contingent from Co. Tyrone was
observed to march with special precision. It turned out that
they had already been practicing military drill and their example
was quickly taken up by other lodges.[23] It was ascertained that
the law permitted any two Justices of the Peace to authorise
drilling in their neighbourhood, provided that its object was to
make citizens more efficient 'for the purpose of maintaining the
constitution of the United Kingdom as now established and
protecting their rights and liberties thereunder'.[24] That was
precisely what the Ulster Unionists believed themselves to be
doing, though their leaders might have denied that the Parliament Act was part of the constitution 'as now established': in
that respect, the constitution was 'in suspense'.

As significant as these local preparations was the attitude of
the Conservative Party in Great Britain. Late in 1911 the witty,
sophisticated Arthur James Balfour retired from the Tory leadership and was succeeded by the dour, unimaginative Andrew
Bonar Law. The new leader was a Canadian of Scottish origin
with strong family connections in Ulster. He instinctively sym-
pathised not only with the abstract arguments against Home
Rule, but with the Ulster Protestants' own perceptions of their
plight. Under his leadership the Conservative Party in Britain,
smarting from the humiliation they had suffered at the hands of
British democracy, recklessly threw in their lot with the counter-
revolutionary forces of Ulster democracy. On the eve of the
Bill's introduction, in April of 1912, Bonar Law, accompanied by
seventy British Unionist MPs, travelled to Belfast to join in
another massive demonstration at the Balmoral Show Grounds.
The British Tory leader told the assembled crowd that they held
'the pass for the Empire',[25] and though he stated that they must
trust in themselves the clear implication of his presence was
that the measures they took would have British Tory backing.
That implication was borne out by the events of the next two
years.

The public band as a body of men bound together in mutual

trust for the purpose of community defence—the implicit social contract—had already shaped the character of Ulster resistance to Home Rule. It was now to be perfected, for the first time since the seventeenth century, by the promulgation of an explicit contract of government. At the Craigavon demonstration Carson had verbally entered into 'a compact with you, and every one of you', adding that 'with the help of God you and I joined together —I giving you the best I can, and you giving me all your strength behind me—we will yet defeat the most nefarious conspiracy that has ever been hatched against a free people'.[26] According to the principal apologist for Ulster Unionism, the 'most dramatic moment' of the Balmoral demonstration six months later was when Carson and Bonar Law clasped hands 'as though formally ratifying a compact made thus publicly on the eve of battle', but its 'most impressive moment' was when 'the vast assemblage, with uncovered heads, raised their hands and repeated after Sir Edward Carson words abjuring Home Rule'.[27] This ceremony gave rise to the idea in the mind of local Unionist leaders of a more formal bond of mutual obligation among Ulster Protestants. Craig undertook the task of drafting an oath to be administered to the Unionist populace, and a Belfast businessman, B. W. D. Montgomery suggested to him that he take as a model 'the old Scotch Covenant. It is a fine old document, full of grand phrases, and thoroughly characteristic of the Ulster tone of mind at this day.'[28] Perhaps the 1581 Covenant, with its unabashed abuse of popery, was a bit too characteristic of the Ulster tone of mind for use by leaders with any sensitivity to English opinion. In the end a simpler document was produced:

ULSTER'S SOLEMN LEAGUE AND COVENANT

Being convinced in our consciences that Home Rule would be disastrous to the material well-being of Ulster as well as of the whole of Ireland, subversive of our civil and religious freedom, destructive of our citizenship and perilous to the unity of the Empire, we, whose names are underwritten, men of Ulster, loyal subjects of His Gracious Majesty King George V., humbly relying on the God whom our fathers in days of stress and trial confidently trusted, do hereby pledge ourselves in solemn Covenant throughout this our time of threatened calamity to stand by one another in defending for ourselves and our

children our cherished position of equal citizenship in the
United Kingdom, and in using all means which may be found
necessary to defeat the present conspiracy to set up a Home
Rule Parliament in Ireland. And in the event of such a Parliament being forced upon us we further solemnly and mutually
pledge ourselves to refuse to recognise its authority. In sure
confidence that God will defend the right we hereto subscribe
our names. And further, we individually declare that we have
not already signed this Covenant. . . . God save the King.

Though the specific phraseology of the Scottish Covenants was
rejected, one should not minimise the extent to which the community was aware of the precedents of its action. Before publication the covenant was submitted to the main Protestant Churches,
and, significantly, the words 'throughout this our time of threatened calamity' were added at the suggestion of Presbyterian
spokesmen,[29] who remembered the embarrassment caused for
their Church as late as the nineteenth century by those who held
that the original Scottish Covenants were perpetually binding
upon posterity. The author of a work of local history published
in 1912, in describing a public band entered into by the Protestants of his parish in 1745, commented, 'Times and movements
have changed, but the temper of the Kilrea men in times of
national danger seems unalterable.'[30]

The 23rd of September was appointed as the day for signing
the covenant throughout the province, and the arrangements for
the event were another of the magnificent feats of organisational
skill on which the Unionist leadership so prided itself. The day
began with religious services and climaxed with the orderly
affixing of signatures—a few of them in blood—along a third
of a mile of tables in the Belfast city hall and in smaller towns
throughout Ulster. A total of 218,206 men signed the covenant.
Their womenfolk were not permitted to sign it—the covenant
was an undertaking to fight if necessary, and that was man's work
—but a separate 'Declaration' attracted the signatures of 228,991
women.[31] The social contract implicit in the community's traditional self-understanding had been made explicit. The covenant,
Carson declared at Coleraine, 'was a contract between them as
Ulstermen, and Ulstermen were not in the habit of breaking
their contracts'.[32] It affirmed the community's allegiance to the

king, but a declaratory preamble adopted by the Ulster Unionist Council confirmed 'the steps so far taken by the Special Commission',[33] i.e., the establishment of a Provisional Government. No one, apparently, suggested this time that the king himself be called upon to sign the covenant, but it was probably assumed that he was in sympathy with it : a proposition which the conventions of the constitution now happily prevented him from confirming or denying. Such an assumption is reflected in the leaders' concept of the Provisional Government as a device for holding Ulster 'in trust' for the King, pending the repeal of Home Rule.[34]

Ulster Protestants were embarked upon a course which, in ordinary commonsense terms, was plainly illegal. They proposed to defy an act of the United Kingdom parliament as soon as it should be passed in what was now due and proper form. To understand their moral justification for their action, we should begin with the covenant's assertion of their conscientious conviction that Home Rule would be 'subversive of our civil and religious freedom' and 'destructive of our citizenship'. Upon these assertions rested the argument that although loyal citizens are bound to obey all ordinary laws, Home Rule would be no ordinary law for it would in itself negate their citizenship. In fact, the Irish government proposed in the Bill would have been very similar to an American state government. Ireland would have continued to be represented in the Westminster parliament, though in reduced numbers, which in fact would have more closely reflected her actual proportion of the total United Kingdom population than the swollen representation she still enjoyed in deference to a now anachronistic provision of the Act of Union. The Westminster parliament would retain power over defence, foreign affairs, new customs duties, and, to a large extent, the level of internal taxation. Even police would be reserved to Westminster control for six years. There was an appeal in law to the privy council and the Westminster parliament retained 'supreme power and authority' over all 'persons, matters and things' in Ireland. Elaborate restrictions were devised to prevent the Irish parliament from interfering with religious freedom or practicing sectarian discrimination. Indeed, these 'safeguards' gave rise to private, partly well-founded, fears in the Catholic hierarchy that education, especially on the secondary level, would be pushed 'in the direction of secularisation'.[35]

Though the government, with the acquiescence of the Nationalists, was willing to accept any reasonable proposals for safeguards to religious freedom, as far as Ulster Unionists were concerned such provisions would be mere 'paper safeguards'. One rationale for this attitude was articulated by a convention of Presbyterians, which alluded to recent papal decrees on the subjects of mixed marriages and the jurisdiction of civil courts over ecclesiastics : 'Under Home Rule . . . the Parliament and the Executive are certain to be controlled by a majority subject to the direction of the authors of the *Ne Temere* and *Motu Proprio* Decrees, against whose domination all safeguards would be wholly valueless.'[36] But even if one accepts that Catholic legislators would wantonly disregard the safeguards at a mere jerk on their leading-strings by their presumed Roman masters,[37] why could not the Protestants rely on Westminster to reverse judicially or legislatively any such transgression by the Irish parliament? In their eyes, Westminster's sovereignty under the Home Rule Bill would be a mere sham which the Irish parliament would dispose of at the earliest possible opportunity. Statements by Nationalist leaders that the present bill would satisfy Irish national aspirations were treated not as naïve (which perhaps they were) but as deliberately deceptive. Certainly, it was possible to find statements, even recent statements, by these same leaders, particularly on American platforms, expressing an Irish demand for complete sovereignty or at least Dominion status. Such discrepancies, which in the political life of other societies might have been treated as simply politicians' understandable adjustment of their rhetoric to their audiences, took on great importance in the minds of Irish Loyalists because they corroborated their own image of the Nationalist movement as devoid of moral scruple and, conversely, their own self-image as the only people in Ireland who could be trusted. Probably when Nationalist spokesmen in this period contemplated expansion of the proposed Irish parliament's powers, for example in finance, they genuinely, albeit naïvely, expected this to happen with the consent of Irish Protestants. It was an article of Nationalist faith that if the Protestants would once give self-government a try, they would soon come to like it and become its most enthusiastic advocates.

Protestant fears turned on a similar article of Loyalist faith— that Irish nationalism was an insatiable beast which could never be satisfied short of total independence: when Redmond said just that in America he was speaking the truth; when he purported to accept less at Westminster he was lying. In actual fact, Republicanism was moribund in Edwardian Ireland. Even if the increasingly moderate tone of the Irish Party leaders was nothing but a politic course adopted to avoid alienating British opinion, those leaders represented a constituency whose adult generation, at any rate, was genuinely averse to absolute and total separation. 'Home Rule' represented just about the right amount of self-government—neither too little ('devolution') nor too much (a republic). What 'Home Rule' might be was negotiable, so long as it included an institution clearly labelled 'Irish parliament'.

In Ulster Protestant minds, the objective fact of moderation in nationalist goals and methods over the preceding generation was simply overridden by their *a priori* assumption that the essence of Irish nationalism was a revolutionary separatism founded on unalloyed hatred of the English and themselves, unconstrained by anything but the need to deceive the English. The resurgence of revolutionary nationalism during World War I, the 1916 Easter Rising, the escalation of the national demand as a new generation of national leadership sought to differentiate itself from the Parliamentary Party, and the progressive cutting of links with Britain over the next three decades by the Irish state established in 1922 seemed to corroborate the beliefs about Irish nationalism held by Loyalists in 1912. Actually, those beliefs and the actions founded upon them had something of the character of a self-fulfilling prophecy. The Irish demand for institutions of self-government had remained intense despite the moderation of its goals and methods. The Ulster agitation frustrated the national demand at a point when expectations of its attainment had reached a fever pitch by, in the eyes of nationalists, changing the rules of the 'constitutional' game after play had begun. The gun was given a new credibility in politics, and a new generation of leaders, willing to use or at least tolerate physical force, captured the imagination of Catholic Ireland not so much because the Home Rule which the old generation promised was not enough, but because the latter could not deliver on their promise.

Nevertheless, we must take the assumptions of Ulster Loyalists in 1912 at face value if we are to understand their actions. In their minds, they faced a threat unchanged from the days of the Land League, and many of them fully expected all the terrors which undoubtedly had accompanied the nineteenth-century agrarian struggle to be visited upon them under the authority of the state if they submitted to Home Rule. It is fair to add that their image of the disposition of nationalist Ireland towards them was unavoidably coloured by the attitudes of northern Catholics who were indeed prone to think in terms of the inevitable dominance of one side or the other by any means at its disposal.[38] At bottom, therefore, the Ulster Loyalist justification for the 'technical' illegality of their action was, paradoxically, that they were the only law-abiding people in Ireland and that they were defending themselves against an enemy with no respect for law, order or decency.

The covenant spoke of 'using all means which may be found necessary to defeat the present conspiracy to set up a Home Rule Parliament in Ireland', and implicit in this use of the term 'conspiracy' was another, related, line of justification for the resistance. Ulster Unionists and English Tories argued that by introducing Home Rule in the 1912 session the government was playing a cynical trick upon the electorate. The Liberals, it was argued, had failed to make Home Rule a leading issue in the two 1910 general elections, but had concentrated their campaign rhetoric upon the powers of the peers and the tariff reform issue.[39] The peers had long recognised that they could not successfully oppose a government which manifestly enjoyed the support of the electorate on a given issue, and Tory ideologues had erected this negative reality into a positive argument for the continued existence of the anomalous second chamber in a democratic age. The function of the peers was to protect the electorate against a government which tried to legislate on controversial matters for which it had no mandate. In such a case the government had the option of going to the country, and if it was returned with a decisive majority, the peers, so the theory ran, would give way. Of course, it was only in respect of Liberal legislation that the peers performed this kindly office for the electorate: controversial Tory measures—such as the 1902 Education Bill—for which no 'mandate' had been obtained sailed through the upper chamber with scarcely a flutter. Though the Tory conception of the peers' role in a democratic age was scarcely a recognised convention of the constitution, it did have a rough-and-ready plausibility. The introduction of the Home Rule Bill in 1912 led Tory spokesmen to accuse the government of using the Parliament Act to deprive the electorate of its right to express itself on the subject, though it could be argued that in not one but two general elections the electorate had surrendered that 'right' by decisively endorsing radical alteration in the peers' powers. Treating the government as a 'revolutionary committee', the Tories argued that it had deliberately concealed its Home Rule policy from the electorate in 1910. Hence the notion of a 'conspiracy' to enact Home Rule. If Home Rule had been submitted to the electorate, Bonar Law declared in 1912, 'there would be a difference between the Unionists in England and the Unionists in Ireland. Now there is none. We can imagine nothing which the Unionists in Ireland can do which will not be justified against a trick of this kind.'[40]

It is reasonable to question how far Bonar Law actually spoke for his English colleagues. As far as many English Conservatives were concerned, this line of argument was probably a mere ploy in the game of trying to force an election which, through the ordinary operations of the political pendulum, they might finally have a chance to win. In the minds of Ulster Unionists, however, the 'conspiracy' interpretation represented a more deep-seated and sincere sentiment.[41] Their radical distrust of the Irish Catholics had been, since Gladstone's conversion in 1886, almost matched by their distrust of the English party which was prepared to 'sell' them to their 'enemies'. For them, an arrangement between the Liberals and the Irish Nationalists to bring in Home Rule would probably have still constituted a 'conspiracy' even if it had been placarded in every parish in England, rather than simply acknowledged quietly by Liberal spokesmen upon inquiry at the 1910 elections.[42] The Ulster Unionist Council had declared 'that it is incompetent for any authority, party, *or people* to appoint as our rulers a government dominated by men disloyal to the Empire and to whom our faith and traditions are hateful.'[43] While they were prepared to go along with the English Tory argument that the British people had not properly been consulted, ultimately they were not prepared to submit the issue to the arbitrament of that people. This was the plain meaning of their formation of paramilitary units, the Ulster Volunteer Force (UVF), to resist any attempt to implement Home Rule in the North.

The dilemma of the Ulster Protestant community derived from their conception of both their political obligation and their rights of citizenship in contractual terms. Lacking a genuine feeling of co-nationality with the British people, they could not entrust their fate to 'safeguards' which depended on the willingness of that people to intervene in Irish affairs to rectify abuses. Just as the guarantee of Ulster Protestant allegiance was their own fidelity to the contract of government, so the guarantee of their rights, as they saw the matter, was the reciprocal faithfulness of the sovereign authority. But the sovereign authority was effectively no longer a single person, the monarch, but a parliament responsible to the people. The people are fickle, and it is a fundamental feature of the British constitution that parliament is incapable of giving binding promises : any law enacted by one parliament can be repealed by the next. That constitutional system simply lacks a concept of entrenched rights beyond the reach of the current Commons majority. However capriciously and hypocritically the Lords may have exercised their veto, the fact that they exercised it in a uniformly conservative direction had forestalled for a time the stark reality of modern British politics that the citizen's sense of security in his fundamental rights depends totally on his sense of co-nationality with the whole people who constitute the polity. That the system has worked so well within Great Britain itself is a testimony to the self-perceived homogeneity of the people of that island. The Parliament Act forced upon the consciousness of Ulster Protestants the fact that they could find reassurance of their fundamental rights neither in a felt sense of co-nationality with any people—British or Irish—nor in the capacity of British institutions to give promises which came up to their own exacting standards of honesty.

Though the Ulster Unionists paid lip-service from the beginning to the protection of the interests of the southern Protestants, and though they and their British allies continued to hope that somehow they could prevent Home Rule from being enacted for any part of Ireland, they were prepared, realistically, to make separate terms for Ulster. They supported an amendment offered by a Liberal private member to exclude the four counties with clear Protestant majorities from the bill, making clear that they

could not be content with only those four counties, and late in
the 1912–13 session they themselves offered an amendment to
exclude the entire province. These amendments were defeated
by the Liberal-Nationalist-Labour majority, and the entire bill
was passed by the Commons on 15 January 1913, and rejected
by the Lords two weeks later. It now seemed certain that the
bill would become law under the operations of the Parliament
Act sometime in the summer of 1914, after the Commons had
twice more passed it 'without altering a comma'.

Mounting preparations for resistance in Ulster gave parliament itself an air of apparent irrelevancy during the 1913 session.
The government had no stomach for coercing Ulster and was
certain to offer some sort of compromise, but for strategic
reasons was not prepared to do so until the 1914 session when
they were about to clear the last hurdle of the new parliamentary
procedure. Redmond preferred to offer 'Home Rule within
Home Rule'—a large degree of local autonomy for the North
under a Dublin parliament.[44] The Cabinet, however, opted for a
plan to allow individual counties to opt out of Home Rule
altogether for six years. The scheme was designed to meet, so far
as the four counties with Protestant majorities[45] were concerned,
the Tory objection that the electorate had not been properly
consulted. Within the six years there would presumably be two
general elections (though the unforeseeable European War meant
that in the event there was only one) and if the electorate really
objected to Ulster's inclusion in Home Rule it could elect a
Unionist majority which would make the temporary exclusion
permanent. The scheme was a serious attempt to meet reasonable
objections to the bill, and, in keeping with their refusal to be
bound by the United Kingdom majority in this matter, the Ulster
Unionists rejected it.[46]

The government was left with no honourable alternative to
pressing on with the bill for the third and final time. At the out-
set of this proceeding, however, it committed a set of blunders
which gravely compromised the very limited room for manoeuvre
which it enjoyed. Plans were laid for a show of military force in
Ulster with the overt purpose of guarding key installations from
raids for arms, presumably by the UVF. The two ministers with
most direct responsibility, Winston Churchill at the Admiralty
and Col. John Seely at the War Office, went about their task

in a way which suggested to those disposed to believe the worst of the government that the real aim was to provoke open conflict with the UVF. Certain senior military officers propagated this view of the matter and precipitated the decision of a number of officers at the Curragh army camp, Co. Kildare, to resign their commissions rather than take part in the exercise. The government's credibility was further damaged when Seely yielded to the demand of one of the ringleaders for written assurances—subsequently repudiated by Asquith—that the army would not be used to impose Home Rule on Ulster. A month later the government appeared even more helpless when the UVF managed to smuggle some 20,000 rifles into Larne and efficiently distributed them throughout the province.[47]

Acutely aware, therefore, of the dangers of trying to coerce Ulster, Asquith introduced his offer of a plebiscite by counties on six-year exclusion as an Amending Bill, which was promptly amended by the Lords to provide permanent exclusion for the whole nine counties. At this point, the king intervened to invite representatives of the two British and two Irish parties to Buckingham Palace to try to work out a compromise. The conference worked within the framework of the Amending Bill—how much of Ulster was to be excluded and for how long? At Redmond's insistence, the question of temporary or permanent exclusion was deferred until agreement could be reached on the territory affected—which in fact never happened. The conference quickly reached an impasse poring over maps of Counties Tyrone and Fermanagh.

Nevertheless, the Ulster Unionists had essentially won the argument for self-determination for the area with a Protestant majority, though they may not have realised it at the time. The issue of 'temporary' versus 'permanent' exclusion was really beside the point. Once Unionist Ulster was excluded beyond the life of the Parliament then sitting, it was highly unlikely that the Nationalists at Westminster would be able to force her subsequent inclusion. Parliamentary situations in which the Nationalists could exert decisive leverage occurred only once or twice a generation and would become much less frequent when southern Irish representation was reduced with the implementation of Home Rule. The suggestion that exclusion might be temporary may have fooled some of the Nationalists' supporters, who liked to believe that once Ulster Protestants saw Home Rule working they would like it and want to come under its jurisdiction, but Nationalist leaders were under no such illusions. At the Buckingham Palace conference Redmond and Dillon faced a strategic choice between pressing for excluding a large area which, because of its large Catholic minority might offer a greater 'prospect of an early desire by that area for inclusion under an Irish Parliament'[48] and pressing for exclusion of an area containing as few Catholics as possible. In opting for the latter course, the Nationalist leaders were tacitly acknowledging that whatever they might tell their followers, exclusion was, in the nature of things, permanent.

Within days after the conference broke up, the outbreak of World War I suddenly transformed the entire situation. The war came almost as a relief to the protagonists at Westminster, for it provided an opportunity to lay aside the Irish problem. The Home Rule Bill was placed 'on the statute book' together with an Act suspending its operation for the duration of the war; it was understood that some arrangement for Ulster would have to be made before it actually took effect. The Unionists protested bitterly against it being enacted at all, but they backed the government in the war effort. Redmond made impressive gestures of loyalty, and once Home Rule was enacted, called upon Irishmen to enlist in the forces. He, at least, actively hoped that by demonstrating their loyalty in Britain's hour of crisis Irish Catholics could radically transform the realities which had led to the impasse on the eve of the war. In the event, despite a significant, if not overwhelming, response to his call for troops, developments in nationalist Ireland during the war only confirmed Ulster Unionists in their prewar convictions. Late in 1913 a nationalist paramilitary body had been formed in the South in response to the UVF. Although Redmond had managed to assert his control over these 'Irish Volunteers' in the spring of 1914, shortly after war broke out their most active and enthusiastic units repudiated his leadership and fell under the influence of the tiny, secret Irish Republican Brotherhood. At Easter, 1916, some of these units mounted a brief insurrection in Dublin which their leaders knew would be futile, but which they hoped would awaken the 'national soul' of Ireland. Though the Catholic populace initially responded to the rebellion with detestation, as soon as the British military authorities began executing the leaders there was a great wave of sympathy for them. Asquith, who now headed a wartime coalition government, deputed Lloyd George to try to reach a settlement with Carson and Redmond, which, by bringing Home Rule visibly into operation, might stem the tide of disaffection. Agreement was reached for the immediate operation of Home Rule in the twenty-six southern counties. Carson undertook the task of persuading the Unionist minority in three Ulster counties—Cavan, Donegal and Monaghan—to forego their claims upon their fellow-covenanters. Redmond and his colleagues undertook to persuade the Catholic majorities in Tyrone and Fermanagh to accept exclusion on the assurance that this settlement really would be temporary (for the duration of the war) with full Irish representation at Westminster being retained until resolution of the issue as a safeguard of this assurance. After Redmond and Carson had laid their prestige thus on the line, Unionist members of the coalition forced the Cabinet to alter the terms in a way which undercut Redmond. The settlement was to be openly presented as permanent, and the safeguard, however, insubstantial, of continued full Irish representation at Westminster was to be dropped. Redmond thereupon repudiated the agreement.

It is doubtful that Redmond genuinely hoped to prevent permanent exclusion of the four Unionist counties, but he probably sincerely thought he could recover Tyrone and Fermanagh after the War, provided he and his party could survive politically that long. A prerequisite for their survival was to get Home Rule into immediate operation for at least the area of undisputed Catholic dominance. But before long, the Irish Party began to lose by-elections to candidates adopting the label 'Sinn Féin' (Irish for 'we ourselves'), the name of a hitherto insignificant Dublin political movement which between 1905 and 1910 had advocated a programme of absention from Westminster and passive non-co-operation with British rule as an alternative to the Irish Party's methods for obtaining Home Rule. Journalists had affixed the name 'Sinn Féin' to the 1916 rebels, though no actual organization answering to that name now effectively existed. During 1917 and 1918 such an organization was created, virtually *de novo*, upon very hazy principles. Essentially a vote for Sinn Féin was a vote to repudiate the Irish Party in favour of a new generation of national leadership and to honour the memory of the 1916 rebels. Its partisans were prepared to use the word 'republic' openly, though they did not close the door against some settlement short of a republic (e.g. dominion status) so long as it was more than the Irish Party had been willing to accept. They used 'partition' as a stick to beat the Irish Party but offered no alternative except the ludicrously impractical notion of submitting Ireland's claim to the post-war peace conference. In the area of strategy, however, their proposals were crystal clear : upon election they would refuse to take their seats at Westminster. In consequence, when they decimated the Irish Party in the 1918 general election, they guaranteed that the Ulster Unionists would be the principal Irish voice in the Parliament which would, at least with respect to the North, settle the future constitutional framework.

The Honest Ulsterman

Thus, the Ulster Protestant community did successfully assert a claim to self-determination. Does this fact make their movement a species of nationalism? To deal with this question, we must first recognise that the Ulster Unionists consistently opposed any form of Home Rule for any part of Ireland. To be sure, from the time of the 1911 Craigavon demonstration, the leaders understood that they might have to make separate terms for Ulster, and their promise that in framing the constitution for a Provisional Government of Ulster they would have 'due regard to the interests of the Loyalists in other parts of Ireland'[49] was little more than an exercise in face-saving. Furthermore, their commitment in 1912–14 to wreck the Bill *in toto* was partly dictated by their alliance with the English Tories for whom Ulster was a useful pawn in the game of trying to bring down a government they could not outvote. Nevertheless, even after the war, when most British Unionists had accepted the necessity of Home Rule for southern Ireland, the Ulster Unionists continued to vote against *any* Home Rule, at least 'for the record'. It is not too great an oversimplification to say that they would *vote* against Home Rule for Ireland to the end of time, but they would only *fight* for the exclusion of Ulster. Their acceptance of the 1920 Act was a choice of the lesser of two evils, and it is difficult to argue with Dr Buckland's judgment that 'the creation of

Northern Ireland was not the product of the demand of a local Ulster nationalism *à la Basque*.'[50]

Nevertheless, Dr Gibbon has recently maintained that 'in so far as they laid claim to an identity which was territorially based, the Unionists were creating a form of nationalism'. The 1892 Ulster Unionist Convention, he argues, signalled 'the birth of a new being, the "Ulsterman". His birth was greeted with the provision for him, by an array of publicists, of a unique "character", "heritage" and destiny.'[51] Indeed, a modest literature celebrating Ulster did appear between 1913 and 1923. It was obviously stimulated partly by the widespread popular interest in the Ulster problem, but those items which flowed from Ulster Protestant pens do indeed bear a superficial resemblance to the rhapsodies on national heritage and character which characteristically accompany a nationalist movement. However, the scarcity of examples before 1913 should make us suspicious of the claim that 'the Ulsterman' as a self-conscious 'national' identity was 'born' in 1892. Insofar as it does advance arguments for an Ulster nationality, the concentration of this literature in the decade 1913–23 may indicate not that a nationalism spontaneously arose in Ulster society, but that that society's spokesmen adopted the language of nationality when it was necessary to achieve their political goal.

More to the point, however, when one actually examines this literature in detail, it turns out to be less than a ringing affirmation of an Ulster nationality. One of the works Gibbon cites, Rev. James Barkley Woodburn's *The Ulster Scot: His History and Religion*,[52] for example, is really a history of the Presbyterians. If Woodburn's purpose is to assure the Ulster Protestant community that it is a nation, he chooses an unlikely means for attaining that end : he celebrates the achievements of only half of that community. Several writers take great pains to affirm that Ulster folk are genuinely Irish. One of the authors adopts the pseudonym, 'An Irishman'.[53] Another, the Rev. T. M. Johnstone of Belfast, develops an elaborate argument that Ulstermen are the most 'typically Irish' of the inhabitants of the island : that they preserve characteristics which have been lost in the other provinces.[54] In part, these assertions reflect resentment at the nationalist jibe that Ulster Protestants were 'only Scotch' and the implied derogation from their right to live in Ireland. James

Logan tells a pointed anecdote about an Ulster Protestant clergyman who replied to such a charge from an Irish-American who claimed to be 'American' after only twelve years residence in the United States by pointing out that his own ancestors had lived in Ireland for over 300 years.[55] Despite the adversary context which heightened their self-image as Irishmen, however, Ulster Protestants genuinely and spontaneously thought of themselves as 'Irish'. The fact that, like most contemporary Scots and Welshmen, they did not erect this ethnic identity into an argument for political separation from England does not detract from the sincerity of their feelings. To be sure, there was an element of affectation in such gestures as blazoning 'Erin-go-Bragh' across the façade of the pavilion of the 1892 Ulster Unionist Convention[56] or presenting Carson with a copy of the covenant 'illuminated on vellum, with a rich Celtic design',[57] but the same charge could be levelled against the Gaelic pretensions of contemporary Irish nationalism. When Ulster Protestants in this period spoke of 'our country', 'our common country' or 'our native land'[58] they almost invariably meant *Ireland*.

Of course, Ulster Unionists recognised a difference between themselves and the Catholic majority of the island, but they did not spontaneously think of this as a distinction between two 'nations'. Major Edward Saunderson, for two decades the leader of the Ulster Unionists in the Commons, gave the classic pre-1912 formulation of their perception when he wrote, in 1884,

> There are now two classes—Two Irelands—both professing to have the welfare of their country as their dearest wish, but seeking to secure it by entirely different means. The one—Disloyal Ireland—by intimidation, by murder, by threats of revolt and separation, seek to extort by force from English fear that which England's reason refuses to concede; the other—Loyal Ireland—strive for their country's welfare by every lawful method within the lines of the Constitution of the Empire.[59]

The distinctiveness of the loyalists is defined by this 'Two Ireland' theory not in terms of nationality, but in terms of moral virtue. The issue is not one of 'Ulster' versus 'Ireland' or even of

Protestant versus Catholic, but of 'Loyalty versus Treason'. Implicit in this formulation was the assertion that England's task was not to arbitrate between two nationalities in Ireland, each of which might have some portion of right behind its claims, but rather to listen to one of the two Irelands which had all the right on its side. Only when 'England's reason' was clearly conceding that what Saunderson called 'Disloyal Ireland' was a nation, around 1912, was the 'two Irelands' formulation supplanted by a 'two nations' theory.

To understand the two nations theory as Ulster Unionists did after 1912, we should attend to their greatest apologist, Ronald McNeill, who wrote in 1922, 'To the Nationalist claim that Ireland was a nation [Ulster] replied that it was either two nations or none, and that if one of the two had a right to "self-determination", the other had it equally.'[60] The idea that Ireland consisted of two nations was a second-best alternative to the assertion that she was not a nation at all. Unionists' first impulse was to deny that Ireland was a nation, primarily by debunking the nationalist myth that Ireland had been a unified, independent polity sometime before the Anglo-Norman invasion. 'An Irishman', for example, does adopt the two nations argument when he comes to discuss the Home Rule Bills,[61] but an important theme of his narrative of Irish history before that point is 'that Ireland never was a nation in the political sense, with the possible exception of the few years between 1782 and 1800'.[62] As late as the debates on the 1920 Government of Ireland Bill, Carson, in offering to extend the hand of friendship to nationalists as 'members of the same country' with himself, he could not bring himself to say 'nation', because 'Ireland was never a nation'.[63] At the heart of the Unionist position was a denial that Ireland was a natural claimant to sovereignty. Their own claim to self-determination was not absolute, but conditional upon the prior acceptance by England of what they regarded as a manifest untruth: that Ireland is a nation. Once that condition was met, and to the extent necessary to claim separate treatment, they were prepared not to quarrel with the description of themselves as a second 'nation', but they were more comfortable with terms like 'distinct community'[64] or 'separate entity', which, unlike 'nation', did not connote an absolute claim to sovereignty. The 1920 Bill, a Belfast MP told a meeting at Dromara, 'recognised that Ulster was an entity, and as an entity entitled to its parliament just as fully as the rest of Ireland'.[65]

Significantly, the 'two nations' argument as an explicit theory to counter Home Rule seems to have been introduced by British, rather than Ulster, Unionists. Early in 1912 *The Times* carried a series of special articles on Home Rule by W. F. Monypenny, one of which was entitled 'The Two Nations in Ireland', and the concept was picked up by Bonar Law in his speech at the Balmoral demonstration a few weeks later. Monypenny's articles were republished in 1913 as a book entitled *The Two Irish Nations*. Although several of the Ulster apologias published in the succeeding decade note the two nations concept with approval, only one by an Ulster author is actually organised around an argument that Ulster is a nation. That one, *Unconquerable Ulster*, is the exception which proves the rule, for its author, H. M. Pim, was one of those rare Belfast Protestants who had become an Irish nationalist for a time. He was interned briefly after the Easter Rising because of his connections with advanced nationalist politics and journalism. By his own account, he was active in Sinn Féin until the popular support given to de Valera's leadership and inflammatory rhetoric after the latter's release from prison in 1917 convinced him 'that I had been devoting myself to the support of a people who ... were unfit for self-government'.[66] His argument in *Unconquerable Ulster*, that Ulster has a better claim than Ireland to be a nation,[67] is an application to his new-found cause of the principles of the one he had now forsaken.

One of the apologias for the Ulster movement, *The Soul of Ulster* by Lord Ernest Hamilton, former MP for North Tyrone, and a serious amateur historian, does advance a theory that Ireland consists of two 'races', as distinct in the twentieth as in the seventeenth century : the Irish natives and the British settlers. Unlike several of the other writers we have noted, he has no hesitancy in agreeing with some Irish nationalists that the settlers 'are not Irish at all'—'they have not a drop of Irish blood in their veins'.[68] The Ulster planters, he is at pains to stress, resisted 'the allurements of the native girls' and did not merge into a 'hybrid mass' like the Anglo-Norman-Irish of the late middle ages. Their determination to abstain from intermarriage, he implies, was reinforced by the Catholic Church's insistence on children of mixed marriages being raised as Catholics.[69] Within this framework, the Home Rule issue is devastatingly simple: 'The only attraction of Home Rule to the inner soul of the Irish (especially in Ulster) is the hope that it will provide the machinery by which the British colonists can be got rid of and Irish soil revert once more to the Irish.'[70] In his highly-coloured description of the 1641 'massacre', he remarks that 'the elimination of aliens has always been the first item on the official Nationalist programme. They take up room.'[71] He freely admits that the original dispossession of the Irish involved injustice, but the injustice was committed by the British government, not by the colonists themselves or their descendants: 'A man is not responsible for the back history of every Chippendale chair he buys.'[72]

Though it would certainly have been easy for Hamilton to depict his 'race' of British colonists as a 'nation' entitled to self-determination, he does not do so. He takes his stand firmly on the ethics of colonisation and the prescriptive rights of the colonists to protect their property. Moreover, precisely because his account is the most uncompromising of all Ulster apologias in its insistence on a radical distinction between the Catholic and Protestant communities, it provides in a curious way a clue to the difficulties Ulster Protestants had in wholeheartedly constructing a self-image as a second 'nation' in Ireland. It is an axiom of nationalist thought that nations are somehow 'natural', and explicitly racial ideas like those of Hamilton would seem well-adapted to the creation of a national myth. Yet when Hamilton comes to consider the situation at the time when he is writing (1917) his argument takes a curious turn based on his (no doubt honest) misapprehension that Sinn Féin was fundamentally areligious and anti-clerical. If Sinn Féin should spread, he expected the offspring of its adherents to 'be brought up free of allegiance to any fixed creed' and therefore indifferent to the Catholic Church's rule that children of mixed marriages be raised as Catholics, which had 'always' hitherto prevented intermarriage. In consequence, within a generation 'the bridgeless chasm between the native and the colonist will be a thing of the past'.[73] Though he fears that mixing of the races will not be 'elevating' and expects that 'the true Ulsterman will relinquish his birthright reluctantly, and only by the pressure of very gradual processes',[74] he is optimistic that 'Ireland will become of one mind' and that 'the verdict will be against Home Rule'. 'When the priests can no longer cherish their dream of seeing the surface of Ireland peopled with Irish Roman Catholics, who pay dues, in place of British Protestants who do not', he writes, 'all the driving force will be out of the Home Rule crusade.'[75]

This surely must be one of the most remarkable applications of racial ideas in an age which abounded in racist theories, for it welcomes miscegenation rather than deploring it. Though its author certainly attributes inferior characteristics to Catholics, he is unable to resist the non-racist conclusion that the root of the problem is not their inborn traits, but their manipulation by malevolent forces, namely, the Catholic Church. While it is impossible to assess how representative Hamilton was of Ulster Protestant opinion in his own day, recent social research has revealed a very similar stance among a broad spectrum of contemporary Ulster Protestants. Beliefs about Catholics which appear at first glance to be classic racist attitudes turn out upon examination to be quite different : such beliefs 'are not, for the vast majority, based on the notion that Catholics are inherently endowed with unfavourable characteristics, but on the view that the malignant influence of other forces (notably the Catholic Church) works to produce these [characteristics].'[76] Hamilton's argument, however idiosyncratic it may have been in detail, does seem to reflect a genuine reluctance among Ulster Protestants to see the difference between themselves and Irish Catholics as natural, inevitable, immutable. 'The present barrier to the merge-ment of the two races, which alone can solve the Ulster question', Hamilton concludes, 'is the Roman Catholic Church, which interposes impassable barriers of moral barbed-wire between the native population and the Protestant colonists.' If only Sinn Féin can remove that barrier, 'hatred of England . . . will die a natural death. It is a manufactured article, and the driving-power of the factory will give out.'[77]

Though the apologists for Ulster Unionism are, thus, extremely reluctant to put their case in terms of an Ulster nationalism, they do, undeniably, invest the 'Ulsterman' with distinctive character-istics. James Logan, devoting one chapter to 'the Ulsterman' and a second to the more specialised variety, 'the Belfast Man', sums up the latter's characteristics with a sort of scorecard: 'Determina-tion 98, business capacity 94, courage 91, trustworthiness 90, self-esteem 84, mental vigour 78, hospitality 70, general culture 55, artistic tastes 48, social graces 44.'[78] If we discount 'business capacity', which Logan represents as more dominant in Belfast than in the countryside,[79] the qualities on which Logan gives the Belfast man scores of 90 per cent or better are ones which justify the Ulster Protestant community's recent political behaviour. 'Trustworthiness' is the virtue of keeping bargains, while 'determination' and 'courage' are qualities essential for the success of the public band. Logan is not asserting that Ulstermen have *a* collection of characteristics which entitle them to be considered a separate nation. Rather, he is endowing them with *the* characteristics which were appropriate to the original purpose of their ancestors' settlement in Ireland, which had ensured their survival and enabled them now to enforce a claim for separate treatment, and which should have entitled them—though it was too late for this by the time Logan wrote—to be listened to in preference to the Irish nationalists as to the future of the whole of Ireland.

The 'honest Ulsterman' was a central motif in the loyalist myth-structure which emerged from about 1885. The guiding principle of Irish nationalism, as represented by the Land League, was perceived to be 'the repudiation of contracts', motivated by 'the tenants' greed and dishonesty'.[80] Protestant farmers who refused to go along with the League, it was argued, were being abused for their willingness 'to discharge their obligations like honest men'.[81] If expressions like these occurred only in public they might perhaps be dismissed as mere attempts by landlord interests to flatter Protestant farmers into deferential politics. In a private letter to a substantial landlord in 1892, however, a Unionist MP argued, 'If something is not done the Judicial Rents will not be paid and we shall have an agitation amongst the best & most Honest Farmers in Ulster.'[82] 'Honesty' came to be understood as a defining characteristic of Ulster Protestants even when they threatened to behave just like the Catholics.

While there was a strain in Irish Protestant thinking which denied that Catholics were capable of true honesty[83]—except, of course, when they candidly acknowledged intentions which Protestants regarded as wicked or foolish[84]—another strain was the hope that they would follow Protestant example and forsake dishonesty. A poem celebrating the 1892 Ulster Unionist Convention pleads,

E

Wake, Erin! wake to thy disgrace!
   'Tis as thy children thus we ask;
   Fling off, tear up, the hideous mask
That thus conceals our mother's face.
   Despise, denounce, the sordid art
That bribes to guilt by lure of gain,
With falsehood warps the simple brain,
   With falsehood steels the tender heart.

Be honest and humane again!
   Take counsel of the wise and good,
   And make thy sons one brotherhood
Of patriotic Irishmen!...[85]

Over the next generation, however, it became clear that the Catholics had permanently rejected the counsel of 'the wise and good' and would continue to vote, election after election, for nationalist candidates.

Honesty was supremely important in a community which defined its own cohesion and its relationship to authority contractually, for honesty is the virtue associated with the keeping of bargains. 'The Southerner will perhaps secure more orders as a commercial traveller by his charming manner and gift of words', James Logan writes, 'but the Northman will outdistance him in persistence, punctuality in delivery and in *keeping his promise*.'[86] And a few lines later he draws the moral of this homely contrast: the Belfast man 'being loyal to England . . . naturally expects England to be loyal to him'. Indeed, an emphasis on the bargain-keeping virtues was, in part, appropriated by Ulster Unionism from the pre-existing popular culture of Irish Loyalism. The hero celebrated in that culture, the 'Protestant boy', is noteworthy for being 'trusted' and 'true': he is a man who keeps his bargains. He is conceptualised in a fundamentally different way from the hero celebrated in the ballad tradition of Irish nationalism. The nationalist hero's prime virtue is his willingness to die for his country. While Ulster Protestant culture does value courage and mourn its dead, it tends not to glorify martyrdom for one's country as a good in itself.[87] The 'sash my father wore' is not a prospective 'winding sheet' like the green flag the archetypal Irish hero wants wrapped round him.

This kind of asymmetry *vis-à-vis* the nationalist culture nearest at hand reflects the fact that the community consciousness created between 1885 and 1920 was not in essence an Ulster nationalism.

It might be suggested, however, that that consciousness was a peculiarly intense sense of British (or perhaps 'United Kingdom-ish') nationality. If we take 'nationality' in the narrow, legal sense in which it is sometimes used—as a synonym for 'citizenship'—this proposition is incontrovertible. Citizenship, however, is the modern term for full membership in a *state*, and to use the term 'nationality' in place of it is to introduce the same confusion that arises from the popular usage of 'nation' when 'state' is intended. Of Ulster Protestant determination to remain part of the British state there can be no doubt. The question is whether they con-sidered their relationship to that state to flow from their member-ship in a British nation. Now insofar as the nationality principle in modern politics assumes that all members of a given nation will recognise the whole body of the nation as the ultimate repository of sovereignty, Ulster Protestant determination to resist Home Rule even if Home Rule were the settled determination of the British nation does call into question the extent to which they felt truly co-national with the people of Great Britain. Yet nationality cannot be wholly disentangled from citizen-ship. Though we may question whether their British citizen-ship was really at risk under the 1912 Bill, their plea that it was, while not proving that they felt co-national with the British, does perhaps answer the *prima facie* case that they did not.

To understand this issue, however, we should ask in what sense Ulster—indeed Irish—Protestants asserted themselves to be British. We have seen how anxious their spokesmen were to assert that they were truly Irish, but they clearly felt some ambivalence which the Rev. Thomas Johnstone articulated by saying, 'If in one sense, Ulstermen are Irishmen first and Britishers afterwards, in another sense they are Ulstermen first and Irishmen after-wards.'[88] No doubt, depending on the context and circumstances, various Ulstermen would have different priorities. Perhaps the best way to understand their attitude toward the designation 'British' is to say that they denied being 'merely' British. In one sense, to be merely British would contradict their own self-image as being more than British. The 'British' entity which most truly commanded their enthusiastic attachment was not Great Britain or the British Isles but the Empire.

What the Protestant Archbishop of Dublin called 'Imperial nationality'[89] could be an attractive concept for a variety of reasons. By identifying with the Empire one could be British in one sense without ceasing to be Irish—or Canadian, Australian, etc. Moreover, the late nineteenth-century myths of empire glorified precisely the proconsular virtues which many Irish Protestants had traditionally regarded as the basis of their relationship to authority. The idea of a little band of brave men with a mission to maintain order and civilisation among a more numerous and recalcitrant population of ungrateful natives for the latter's own good struck a responsive chord in Ulster. Unionists sometimes referred to Ulster as the 'Imperial Province' of Ireland, an expression which carried overtones of a civilising mission to the rest of Ireland.[90] Moreover, the Irish Protestant gentry were especially prominent in Imperial affairs, particularly on the military side, while many ordinary Ulster Protestants had family ties with the dominions, particularly Canada.

'Imperial nationality' is, on the face of it, a contradiction in terms : an empire is, by definition, a multinational affair. The position of the white dominions, no less than that of the non-white colonial dependencies, was, or would eventually become, anomalous in the world of 'nations'. The subsequent history of the British Commonwealth/Empire has made plain that ultimately sovereignty would in practice derive from national consensus within the dominion in question, and where the crown has been retained it is, as in Britain, as a mere convenient symbol and a necessary cog in the machinery of government built on a Westminster model. The rise of Ulster Unionism, however, coincided roughly with the period in which it was just possible to believe in the viability of a group of self-conscious communities autonomous with respect to their internal affairs but acknowledging a common sovereignty which was more than symbolic. Though the Westminster Parliament was sometimes called the 'Imperial Parliament', its constituency was in fact Great Britain and Ireland, not the Empire.[91] If the Empire (or, what was really meant, the white Empire) constituted a nation, no representative institution existed deriving its authority from the democratically ascertained consensus of that 'nation'. One could identify with the Empire, therefore, without having to face the awkward question of one's political obligation if one radically dissented from the 'national' will.

Ulster Protestants, therefore, in the period from 1885 to 1920, identified with several overlapping groups which have the appearance of nationalities. They certainly all thought of themselves as Irish, which for them was no more in conflict with also being British than being a Texan is with being an American. They were also being driven to think of themselves as Ulstermen, a designation which they were reluctantly prepared to put forward as a 'nationality' if that was a necessary ploy in the game of self-determination they were, perforce, playing. Moreover, to be an Ulsterman was in a sense to be not just British, but more than British : to avoid the implications of nationality altogether by identifying with a community, the Empire, to which no actual nation-state corresponded. Their ambivalence on the issue of nationality is really a symptom of the irrelevance of nationality to their claim, as they understood it. They demanded first the rejection of Home Rule, and ultimately self-determination separate from the rest of Ireland not on the ground that they were British, but on the ground that they were loyal.

Loyalty is quite different from nationality. Everyone, according to the myth of nationality by which our world is ordered, possesses a nationality. Not everyone, according to Irish loyalist thinking is loyal. Members of a nationality can be distinguished by certain attributes, according to the myth of nationality, and a prime task of statesmanship is to erect state boundaries enclosing homogeneous peoples so defined. Loyalty is not such an attribute in Ulster Protestant thinking. Their claim was not equivalent to one they might make if instead of being loyal they were merely French-speaking or dark-skinned or hot-blooded or even anti-Popish. The question for statesmen was not how to meet national aspirations, but, in the words of a Belfast Methodist minister, 'Shall the loyal be deserted and the disloyal set over them?'[92] Loyalty is a moral principle translated from the realm of personal relationships into politics; it ought to override any pleas of nationality. It carries the connotations of lawfulness, which Protestants understood to be what distinguished them from their Catholic fellow-countrymen. Obviously there was a problem in sustaining the self-image of lawfulness when the community undertook preparations for the massive defiance of a statute, and this is precisely why those preparations were organised, both in 1892 and in the 1912–14 agitation, with such obsessive regard to discipline, order and solemnity. Law meant less the actual statutes which lawyers contest in the courts, than the public order which they are intended to maintain. It was crucially important to Unionist leaders to depict massive illegality on their part as, in essence and spirit, lawfulness, not only for the strategic purpose of winning British sympathy, but also to sustain the self-image contained in their collective myth and the moral justification for their action which derived therefrom.

'Loyalty' defined an external relationship to the British state, not a wholehearted sense of incorporation into the British nation. Hugh de Fellenberg Montgomery, a Liberal Unionist landlord from County Tyrone, delineated, perhaps unwittingly, the Loyalist attitude in a 1918 letter[93] refuting a Sinn Féin pamphlet which had asserted 'that a man belonging to one country cannot be loyal to another country'. 'A citizen of any country', Montgomery wrote, 'can be loyal to any other country to whom he is bound by honour or by interest to be loyal. At the present time every Englishman is bound to be loyal to France, Italy, America, Belgium, Servia &c, and every Frenchman is bound to be loyal to England, Italy, America &c, and so forth.' This is a remarkable formulation, for it places political obligation not only on a contractual footing, but on the footing of that most fragile of contracts, the wartime alliance. Allegiance is not a matter of national feeling, but a bargain whose only sanctions are honour and interest. Actually, Montgomery continues, Irishmen are asked to be loyal to the United Kingdom, not to England, but it 'would ... be perfectly reasonable to ask any Irishman to be loyal to England, England being his best and chief customer for everything he produces.' Interestingly, when he comes to make this application of his general principle to the particular case of Ireland, there is no mention of 'honour', only of 'interest'. What he is tacitly admitting is that for the people whose 'loyalty' is actually in question, the Catholics, the contract of government is manifestly not regarded as a matter of honour; the best that can be hoped for is that they will live up to it out of a recognition of their own interest. In Ireland the honest people—the people who honour their bargains, who are loyal in the fullest sense—are the Protestants.

At the time Montgomery wrote, the last previous act of state (disregarding the Home Rule Act which was in suspension for the duration of the War) which could plausibly be represented as a treaty defining the relationship between Great Britain and Ireland was the 1800 Act of Union. That instrument, as applied and administered in the succeeding century, had manifestly failed to create a 'nation' corresponding to the whole British Isles capable of cementing the allegiance of either Catholics or Protestants with the emotional adhesive of nationality. For the Catholic community, the matter was simple : they were Irish and would be loyal only to an Irish state. For the Ulster Protestant community, the matter was much more complex : they had quasi-national feelings of attachment to Ireland, to 'Ulster' and to a Britain which was less the real Great Britain than a vague concept of a Greater Britain which somehow the Empire might come to embody. But at bottom, as Montgomery's letter suggests, they thought not in terms of nationality, but in terms of a treaty or contract. In the context of 1918 Montgomery's argument is hopelessly naïve, for the treaty between Great Britain and Ireland was clearly being repudiated. Within four years, however, two new 'treaties' would be entered into, and Montgomery's argument is directly germane to an understanding of how one of them worked.

4

'Those Districts which they could Control'
1914-1972

'More than a Mere Act of Parliament'

Although the Ulster Protestant community had essentially won its claim to separate treatment before the outbreak of World War I, the pre-war events did not predetermine that there would be a Northern Ireland state such as existed from 1921 to 1972. The issue before the 1914 Buckingham Palace conference had been the simple retention by the predominantly Protestant part of Ulster of exactly the status it already enjoyed. John Redmond, at least, hoped that the war, by joining Catholic and Protestant in common sacrifice, would radically transform Ulster Protestant attitudes. In the event, the spectacle of southern Catholics honouring the memory of those who died trying to exploit England's difficulty at Easter 1916, while they themselves mourned the near-annihilation of the Ulster Division at the Somme two months later, confirmed Ulster Protestants in their determination to resist Home Rule. Moreover, the drift of Irish nationalism from constitutional to revolutionary methods and goals crucially affected the process by which the Northern Ireland state took form, and, more crucially, the way in which Ulster Protestants perceived that process.

In constitutional theory, the foundation of Northern Ireland was the result of a simple act of parliament, the Government of Ireland Act, 1920. We would go rather seriously astray, however, if we tried to understand Ulster Protestants' feelings towards the Northern Ireland state solely in terms of this orderly legal process. To do so would be rather like naïvely assuming that the legal fiction of a 'provisional Government'—that fig leaf of constitutionality devised to cover the nakedness of southern Ireland's violent secession from the United Kingdom—was responsible for the consent which the Irish Free State came to enjoy from its populace. In 1968, when William Craig resigned from the Northern Ireland Cabinet after challenging the right of Westminster to interfere in the province's affairs, he declared that Northern Ireland's constitution was 'more than a mere act of Parliament';[1] it represented 'an agreed settlement'—'the settlement made when our grandfathers and fathers made their historic stand'.[2] To follow this reasoning, we must understand not only the constitutional process by which the Northern Ireland regime was formally established, but also the revolutionary events which brought the Northern Ireland *state* into being.

After the 1916 Rebellion, the Ulster Unionists had agreed to an ambiguous plan for immediate Home Rule, with 'temporary' exclusion of the six counties of Antrim, Armagh, Down, Fermanagh, Londonderry and Tyrone, but when the ambiguities were clarified the plan fell through. In 1917 and 1918, their delegation in a constitutional convention had stood firm against any significant compromise with the Nationalists, who themselves were now trying to find middle ground between their previous position and the shadowy demands of Sinn Féin rather than the crystal-clear demands of the Ulster Unionists. In the 1918 general election, the Unionists, profiting from a long-overdue redistribution act, won 26 Irish seats, and the old Irish Party was reduced to a mere six, four of which they owed to a last-minute deal with Sinn Féin to avoid triangular contests with Unionists. As the 73 Sinn Féiners elected set themselves up as Dáil Éireann, the legislature of an independent Irish Republic, it was clear that the Unionists would be the only effective Irish voice in the Parliament which would settle the issue deferred since 1914. Despite the fact that the wartime coalition which Lloyd George had kept together for the postwar reconstruction period was dominated by 'unionists', however, British opinion on the continued viability of the legislative union had shifted decisively.[3] While the Ulster Protestants could expect especially tender treatment of their particular interests, they could no longer find any significant British support for the denial of some sort of self-government to the rest of Ireland. Without a fresh legislative initiative, the 1914 Act would automatically come into effect with the ratification of the last peace treaty, so it was with some urgency that in the autumn of 1919 a Cabinet committee set about drafting a new Home

Rule Bill. Despite its partisan authorship, the new Bill was a sincere attempt to square the circle. There would be two Irish parliaments to make laws for the 'peace, order and good government' of Ulster and of the rest of Ireland respectively. As a symbol of Irish unity there would be a 'Council of Ireland' composed of an equal number of delegates from each parliament. The Council would have only very limited powers, but provision was made for the two parliaments acting concurrently to devolve further powers upon it or even ultimately to replace it with an all-Ireland parliament.

The Unionist 'party line' on the bill was that they had no desire for a parliament of their own. A few Protestants—e.g. temperance advocates[4]—were hopeful that their special interests might receive a friendlier hearing in a Belfast parliament than at Westminster. Moreover, Unionist spokesmen quickly came to recognise that the party line was a highly convenient argument for generous financial treatment by Westminster.[5] Nevertheless, the party line did reflect a genuine consensus in the Protestant community, whose leaders, however, quickly realised that the existence of a separate regime in Belfast would be a useful safeguard to their exclusion from the Dublin parliament, provided they enjoyed a secure majority in their own legislature. To guarantee such a majority they persuaded the government to reduce the area of its jurisdiction from nine counties, in which Protestants were only 56 per cent of the population, to the six counties for which they had negotiated exclusion in 1916, in which nearly 66 per cent of the population were Protestants. The Ulster Unionist Council endorsed the six-county arrangement over the protest of Unionists from Cavan, Donegal and Monaghan, who understandably felt that the covenant was being betrayed. Six-county men invoked the 'present calamity' clause of the covenant and argued that by this time there was 'a new calamity' and a 'new conspiracy', thereby incurring the indignation of three-county men who argued, quite plausibly, that even within the nine counties the Unionist majority would be adequate to forestall unification with the South.[6] Their protests were overridden and the Ulster Unionist Party at Westminster acquiesced in the Bill which, as a matter of principle, they could not go on record as supporting.

While the 'mere act of Parliament' which would create the

Northern Ireland regime was being drafted and debated, a full-scale guerrilla war was developing in the South of Ireland. Ulster Protestant response to that situation would consummate the state-building process begun in 1911. Although in early 1920 IRA attacks were still rare in the northern six counties, the fact that the crown forces had to be concentrated in disturbed areas made northern Protestants feel especially vulnerable. In country districts they responded by organising vigilante patrols or 'Protectionist Committees'.[7] In Belfast and several smaller towns, working-class Protestants responded in their traditional way, by rioting, which in their eyes was a form of defence. Though they defined the enemy as 'Sinn Féin' rather than Catholics *per se*, it would not be an overstatement to say that the burden of proof that he was not a Sinn Féiner rested with each individual Catholic. In troubled areas of Belfast, Protestants were enrolled as special constables on an *ad hoc* basis.[8] Steps were taken to reactivate the UVF. Late in the summer the Unionist leadership took an initiative designed to regularise these arrangements.

On 2 September, Sir James Craig, who, as Parliamentary and Financial Secretary to the Admiralty, was a member of the government (though not of the Cabinet), presented their proposals[9] to a conference of cabinet ministers. He proposed that, without waiting for the Government of Ireland Bill to come into effect, the government ought immediately to set up a quasi-autonomous administration for the six counties, particularly in matters of law and order. The day-to-day administration of the Irish government in Dublin Castle was, at this point, carried on by two Under Secretaries—a Catholic and a Protestant. The Ulster Unionists wanted a third Under Secretary[10] to take charge of law and order in the six counties and, incidentally, to make arrangements for the transfer of power to the projected Northern Ireland government. They wanted the command structure of the police and military to be immediately revised to make the crown forces in the six counties independent of Dublin Castle. They proposed that a force of some 2,000 armed and apparently full-time Special Constables be raised 'to ensure that adequate Police posts are re-established throughout the six Counties, and that any new measures ordered by the Government are properly enacted'. Craig also called for the enrolment of a 'reserve force of

Special Constables' and a 'Special Constabulary Reserve'. Although it is not entirely clear whether he conceived these as distinct forces, Craig did make plain that what he had in mind was to reactivate the UVF with official sanction.

Obviously one Unionist motive for taking this initiative was to meet a real need for security. Another motive was to get their supporters under responsible control and thereby sustain their image as the law-abiding section in Ireland, which was being seriously compromised, for example, by sectarian rioting.[11] At least as early as April, the Ulster Unionist MPs had become gravely apprehensive that IRA activities in the province might provoke retaliation by 'our people . . . and if they once [got] out of hand a [disastrous] position would arise which would probably bring our own friends into collision with the authorities'.[12] It was Craig's intention that the 'Special Constabulary Reserve' should be organised by a proposed RIC Commissioner for the six counties 'but should be commanded by their own local Leaders'. For the 'reserve force of Special Constables' he suggested, 'Possibly it would be well to swear in a very much larger number of persons than would be required for duty at one time. This would enable reliefs to be formed, and would also ensure that a large proportion of the population is brought under discipline.'[13] Though the government was apparently unwilling to break up the formal command structure of the regular security forces to meet the Ulster Unionists' wishes, they did implement the proposals to the extent of promptly appointing an official representative, Sir Ernest Clark, to be resident in Belfast, to take charge of forming a Special Constabulary and to handle the 'political' business of the Chief Secretary's Office in the six counties (though not, except for 'special problems', the ordinary supervisory functions of the Office with respect to specific Irish government departments).[14] To the annoyance of local Unionist leaders, Clark was styled only Assistant Under Secretary rather than, as they thought had been promised, Under Secretary.[15] They managed, however, to wheedle out of the Chief Secretary an assurance that in practice Clark would report only to the Protestant Under Secretary rather than to his Catholic colleague, whom they suspected of leaking information to Sinn Féin.[16] Whatever Clark's official title, a 'sane, stolid representative Unionist' from Co. Tyrone probably expressed the general understanding of the former's role when he referred to him as 'our new Ulster secretary'.[17]

Clark set about his task by collecting information on the existing vigilance forces throughout the province.[18] Within a few weeks a scheme was developed and published for enrolling three classes of special constables. Class A were to be paid, full-time constables serving with the RIC and different from ordinary police mainly in that they could not be transferred to other parts of Ireland. Class B were to be unpaid (except for small allowances) and ordinarily to serve on one night patrol per week. Class C, also unpaid, were to be enrolled for emergency duty only. As Class A was in effect, a device for filling up the ranks of the RIC which had been depleted by the troubles, and Class C was never extensively deployed, popular and historical interest has rightly focused on the 'B' Specials. Recruiting for Class B seems to have gone fairly briskly in country districts,[19] where it was in part simply a matter of swearing in existing vigilance forces and reactivated UVF units. In Belfast, where high postwar unemployment created far more interest in paid Class A service, recruitment for the B Specials proceeded more slowly.[20] Nevertheless, within a year some 16,000 B Specials had been enrolled in the six counties.

Thus in the nine months prior to the opening of the Northern Ireland parliament in June 1921, the sources of civil authority had assumed a most curious configuration in the North. Formally, government departments operating in the area, including the demoralised RIC, were administered through Dublin Castle under a Chief Secretary responsible to parliament at Westminster. Throughout the South of Ireland that administration had manifestly lost the most elemental prerequisite of a state—a credible monopoly of physical force. But in an important sense it had also surrendered that monopoly in the North as well. An informed observer of Belfast in early 1921 would have recognised that such civil authority as the six counties enjoyed reposed as much in the former town hall, where R. Dawson Bates presided over the Unionist organisation, as in the Scottish Provident Building, where Clark had taken offices. It was from old town hall, for example, that a Catholic expelled from the shipyards might get assistance in recovering his job.[21] Indeed, the fact that Clark seems already to have envisaged a career for himself in the service of the Northern Ireland government[22]—a course which, in the event, he adopted—probably did not encourage him to wield such shadowy power as he enjoyed in opposition to the will of those who were heirs-designate to genuine civil authority in the province.

The Government of Ireland Act received the royal assent in December 1920, and elections for the two parliaments were held the following May. Although the unopposed return of Sinn Féin for nearly all seats in the South rendered the Act a dead letter there, the Northern parliament, with a handsome Unionist majority, was opened by the king on 22 June 1921. The new regime had been established. But if the Northern government had at this point enjoyed only the authority conferred by legislation, we would not be entitled to call Northern Ireland a 'state', for in law its 'government' wielded no instruments of physical force. The 1920 Act withheld police from the Northern (and Southern) government for a period of up to three years, at the discretion of the Westminster government. For five months Northern Ireland, if we consult only the statute book and the orders in council, did not constitute a state at all, but only a territory enjoying somewhat more extensive local government than an English county. These were five crucial months, for in early July the Westminster government entered into a truce with the rebels and opened negotiations with their leaders. The new Northern regime was one of the stakes in this game, and northern opinion feared that Westminster would be tempted to sacrifice their independence from the South. Had the Northern government been *de facto* the mere administrative arrangement which it still was *de jure*, that temptation and the hopes of the southern negotiators of capitalising on it might have been substantial. In fact, however, it was the government of a state. The community whose support it enjoyed had seceded from Dublin Castle rule almost as thoroughly as their southern Catholic counterpart. They had endowed their provincial government in advance with the physical force necessary for the existence of a state. Everyone knew that—irrespective of the technical legal position—if forced to choose, the Special Constabulary and the less formal organs of community defence, would serve Belfast, not Westminster. When the transfer of security powers occurred, on 22 November, it was a mere formality. At that point, in the words of their official historian,

'The Special Constabulary which had in fact been controlled from Belfast since its inception, ceased even in theory to owe allegiance to General Tudor in Dublin.'[23]

Two weeks later an 'Anglo-Irish treaty' was signed. It provided dominion status for Ireland, but gave Northern Ireland the right to opt out of the new Irish Free State and remain within the United Kingdom. In the event that the Northern parliament exercised this option, the treaty provided for a tripartite boundary commission to make adjustments in the border. Exactly one year elapsed between the signing of the treaty and the final approval of the Free State's constitution by the Westminster parliament. On the following day the Northern parliament, as expected, exercised its option and thus automatically set in motion the boundary commission mechanism, with which, however, its own government refused to co-operate. That year in Irish history embraced a good deal more than an orderly process of constitution-making. The Dáil and the IRA both split into pro-treaty and anti-treaty factions, not over the status of the North, but over the issue of abandoning the symbols, though not the substance, of an absolutely independent republic. Indeed, both pro- and anti-treaty factions within the IRA kept up guerrilla activity in the North, especially along the border. Michael Collins, the pro-treaty leader who headed the Free State's 'Provisional Government', had several meetings with Sir James Craig, now the Northern Prime Minister, in early 1921 in which they made statesmanlike efforts to barter concessions to the northern Catholics for an end to IRA activities in the North. Neither of the leaders had sufficient control over his followers to effect either the letter or the spirit of their agreement, and Northern Ireland continued in a real state of siege until the summer when open hostilities broke out between the two IRA factions, diverting their attention away from the North and into an internecine civil war in the South.

'Peace, Order and Good Government'

The Northern Ireland regime—usually called Stormont, after the site of its parliamentary building, which was opened in 1932 —lasted for fifty years and nine months, at the end of which not only the regime, but, I shall argue, the state corresponding to it, collapsed. To understand first the persistence and then the collapse of the state it is useful to think generally about how states acquire support. One way to conceptualise this issue is to divide support into two categories: specific and diffuse.[24] Specific support is the support a state receives in return for specific benefits it provides to its citizens. For the purpose of an historical analysis, it is convenient to subdivide these specific benefits into two further categories, classic and modern. The classic functions of the state include the provision of such benefits as public order and personal liberty which classic political theorists tended to regard as the whole duty of government and which modern economists, for example, call 'indivisible' benefits. In the modern world, states are also increasingly expected to provide material benefits. To be sure, pre-modern governments could be in jeopardy if there was widespread economic distress, but modern assumptions of human efficacy and the solubility of problems place on governments a much heavier burden of expectations that they can and should create conditions for constantly increasing affluence.

For a state to persist in time, however, it is also important that it generate 'diffuse' support—an attachment which is uncondi-tional or at least dependent only upon conditions unlikely to change in the short run. It is diffuse support which enables states and regimes, if not governments, to weather crises in which specific demands for benefits cannot be met. It has been the argument of this essay that feelings of common nationality and a nationalist myth-structure are normally the most important sources of diffuse support for political institutions in a modernising society. We have seen that in the course of modernisation the Ulster Protestant community developed feelings of nationality which were, at best, confused, ambivalent and fragile. How then did their state develop enough diffuse support to last for as long as it did? Why did they work the settlement, which they had said they did not want, with scarcely-disguised alacrity, never troubling Westminster with pleas to restore them to the *status quo ante* 1921? For Ulster Protestants did not treat Stormont as the glorified county council which was contemplated in the 1920 Act but rather made it, more authentically than Westminster, the centre of their political life and a potential focus for allegiance. As early as 1936 a careful student of the new political system could observe that 'in Northern Ireland public interest is centred almost exclusively upon the local parliamentary institutions'.

Candidates for the Westminster House of Commons defined their policy 'in relation to local issues', not 'to the wider issues of the day'.[25] Northern public opinion, he wrote,

> has enjoyed the power, indefinable, but none the less real, of interpreting the Constituent Act [of 1920]; and that public opinion (especially Unionist opinion) had decreed that interest shall be directed towards the local parliamentary institutions and the activities of their members. As a consequence, the subordinate legislature has filled a more important role than that foreseen by British statesmen in 1920.[26]

Some observers have, in effect, regarded all the support enjoyed by the Northern Ireland state as what I have called 'specific'. For example, it is sometimes suggested that working-class Protestants supported the state primarily because its regime protected their privileged access to employment and otherwise discriminated in their favour. No doubt allegedly discriminatory policies practiced or encouraged by the regime did help muster Protestant support for the Northern Ireland state, though Protestants tended to think of such policies in terms of the classic, rather than the modern, functions of government: full employment for Catholics, for example, might threaten the kind of order and liberty which mattered most—self-determination separate from the South—if it eroded the overall Protestant electoral majority. Indeed, the notion that support for the state ought to be the citizen's side of a bargain over the 'specific' classic benefits of government is fully consistent with contractarian thinking. One should not be misled by the rational precedents of the contractarian culture, however, into overlooking the mythic function it might perform under certain circumstances—e.g. those which obtained after 1921.

The Northern Ireland state—in contrast to the Westminster regime, which retained a sovereignty in law which was not matched by unconditional attachment on the part of Ulster Protestants—did enjoy some diffuse support. The mere existence of the state was perhaps sufficient, as Professor Beckett argued in 1971, to produce 'a sort of "Ulster patriotism" '—'a kind of embryonic nationalism; or, at least, a state of mind out of which a sense of national, rather than merely regional, distinctiveness might, in certain circumstances, emerge'.[27] The generally disappointing response which promoters of an Ulster nationalism have managed to evoke in the quite extraordinary 'circumstances' which have arisen since Beckett wrote is a reminder of the wisdom of his cautious qualification of terms like 'nationalism' and 'patriotism' when applied to Ulster Protestants.

Indeed, nationalism was not dominant in the political culture of the Northern Ireland state : the source of such diffuse support as it enjoyed was not a perception on the part of its citizens that it was composed of persons they defined as 'like' themselves. Given the contractarian tradition, what was important to Ulster Protestants was that their state had come into existence by a process which seemed to conform to contractarian assumptions as to what was normal and right. A band had been entered into, its adherents had stood on their guard against the enemy, and in the end the sovereign authority seemed to have contracted with the banded community to exercise its sovereignty in the territory in question : to hold the pass against the king's enemies and their own. The 1920 Act, to quote one contemporary Unionist, simply 'gave Ulster what she had prepared to fight for, if necessary, before the war. It was the fulfilment of the Craig-avon resolution [of 23 September 1911]—to take over the government "of those districts which they would control". The parliament of Northern Ireland established by the Act was in fact the legalisation of the Ulster Provisional Government of 1913.'[28] Much as the Scots had compelled their sovereign, Charles II, to sign the covenant in 1651, so the Ulster Protestants compelled the sovereign parliament to sign the covenant in 1920.

In the minds of Ulster Protestants this contractarian myth-structure received two kinds of continuing verification, each of which concealed a fundamental weakness in the Northern Ireland state. In the first place, Westminster, by its actions and inactions, seemed to have accepted a central contractarian premise : that the public band, now embodied in the Northern government and its special constabulary, being the only reliable source of public order in Ireland, had been given a free hand to exercise in 'those districts which they could control' the sovereignty which reposed nominally at Westminster. The Westminster House of Commons evolved procedures—in no way mandated by the 1920 Act—to bar discussion of devolved matters.[29] Westminster's power to refuse the royal assent to acts of the Northern parliament was

never exercised. Westminster politicians probably did not intend
by this behaviour to endorse the contractarian culture. In dealing with Irish affairs, they did not feel embattled, merely
annoyed.

The southern government's decision to remain neutral in
World War II, however, did for a time shift British perspectives
more into line with those of Ulster Protestants. This is not to say
that Ulster Protestants saw the war effort in quite the same light
as the English. Englishmen went to war for king *and country*,
and an appeal to fight simply for the king might have struck
many of them as more quaint than stirring. Churchill's famous
speech after Dunkirk ('We shall fight on the beaches, we shall
fight on the landing grounds, . . .')[30] is a pure nationalist appeal to
defend the fatherland. It is instructive to compare these words
with the peroration of the broadcast by Sir James Craig (now
Lord Craigavon) promising Northern Ireland's support for the
war effort. 'We are King's men', he declared, using words reminiscent of the feudal contract. 'We will be with you to the end.'[31]
More significant, however, than Ulster Protestants' conception at
the time of why they were fighting was their sense after the war
that the British recognised that they had kept their side of the
contract of government through the sacrifices of the war years.
Certainly in the years following the war Northern Ireland enjoyed
more sympathy in Britain than at any time before or since.
When southern Ireland broke the last formal link with the Commonwealth in 1949 and became a republic, the Unionists
appealed to that sympathy for a reinsurance of their position.
Unionist headquarters gave wide circulation to a pamphlet, *Ulster
Is British*,[32] whose central message, buttressed by pages of electoral
statistics and analysis, was more 'Ulster chooses to remain in the
British Commonwealth' than, as one might expect from the title,
'Ulstermen are like Britons'. The campaign bore fruit in a clause
of the 1949 Ireland Act which guaranteed that Northern Ireland
would not cease to be part of the United Kingdom without the
consent of the province's parliament—an action which was doubly
significant since the Labour Party, which had always been
suspicious of the Ulster Unionists, was in office at the time. In
law, this pledge meant very little, for, as was pointed out in
debates on it,[33] no parliament can bind its successors. It certainly
did not alter the provision of the 1920 Act reserving to West-

minster ultimate sovereignty over all 'persons, matters and things' in Northern Ireland. 'The pledge', however, did give the appearance of a *quid pro quo* offered by a grateful Britain in return for the province's loyalty in time of real need. As such it seemed to many Ulster Protestants to represent explicit acceptance of the contractual relationship which, for them, was implicit in the 1920–22 settlement.

In general, however, the belief that Britain had accepted the contractarian assumptions was mistaken. The same world-shaking events which occasioned the warm glow which produced 'the pledge' also signalled the demise of Britain's overseas empire, and with it a popular rejection in Britain of imperial glory as an attainable or even a worthwhile objective. Sandy Row residents who, as late as the early 1970s, could speak of their neighbourhood as the 'heart of the empire'[34] were out of touch not only with the realities of world politics, but, more importantly, with the psychological adaptation which the mainland British had made to those realities. In the context of an end to imperial ambition, 'the pledge' meant exactly what it said, and not a word more. Britain was merely affirming the local majority's right to self-determination, not any active desire on her own part to retain the territory in question and certainly not any conception that the Catholic Irish were an enemy against which Ulster loyalists were an essential bulwark. Indeed, the same legislation which contained 'the pledge' also contained curious provisions to prevent southern Irishmen in Britain from being treated as aliens even though their country was now fully independent. Insofar as Ulster Protestants invested the pledge with greater meaning than it had—e.g., by inferring that the Northern Ireland parliament could now never be abolished—their illusion weakened the state.

The contractarian myth received a second sort of continuing verification: the myth called for the existence of an enemy, and for the first forty years of the state's existence the Catholic minority seemed perfectly willing to play that role. In marked contrast to the (proportionately much smaller) southern Protestant minority, which accepted the Irish Free State and willingly played an active, if modest role in its institutions, the northern minority refused to accept the legitimacy or permanence of the new institutions in the North. The divergence between the allegiance-patterns of the two minorities can be understood in terms of the two political cultures—nationalist and contractarian —which underlay the two states.

The nationalist myth fostered among Catholics, especially southern Catholics, the assumption that it was natural, inevitable and right for the nation to attract the allegiance of all her sons and daughters. To be sure, de Valera did at least once publicly describe Ireland as 'a Catholic nation'[35]—the myth was not entirely impervious to reality. Nevertheless, the Irish nation was commonly understood to be the whole body of inhabitants of the island. The division of Ireland was 'unnatural', and if the northern Protestants, for the time being, said that they felt no allegiance to Dublin, that was no guide to their 'true' feelings, which would come to light as soon as the 'artificial' divisions maintained by 'the English' were somehow—perhaps by force, perhaps by diplomacy—eliminated.

The nationalist myth had consequences for the minority problems in both states. In the South, where it had the character of a self-fulfilling prophecy, it was a salutary and socially constructive myth. The leaders of the Free State leaned over backwards to satisfy, even gratify, their Protestant minority. Over half of the government's nominations to the first Free State Senate went to Protestants,[36] for example, and expensive arrangements have been made to keep Protestant schools open even in areas where a Protestant school-age population has almost vanished.

At the same time, the nationalist myth had socially destructive effects in the North. Northern Catholics were realistic enough to know that their Protestant neighbours would never welcome southern Catholics as liberators, but they did generally accept the teleology implicit in the nationalist myth : eventually deliverance must come. For four years their hopes were sustained by an anticipation that the boundary commission would award such huge tracts of territory to the Free State that Northern Ireland would cease to be economically viable and choose to join the South. When the commission's work ended in fiasco—a finding that only minor border changes were in order, a leak of its conclusions to the press, and a hasty decision by the Free State government to drop the whole matter in return for certain financial concessions[37] —representatives of the northern minority from border districts were prompted to take their seats in the northern Parliament.[38]

However, by declining to act as official (i.e. 'loyal') opposition, they continued to deny the legitimacy of the state. They clung to the nationalist myth with a tenacity which increased with the return to respectable southern politics in 1927 of the purer bearers of that myth: Eamon de Valera and other anti-treaty leaders who had earlier refused to take their seats in the Dáil, but who would dominate southern politics for the next genera- tion.

The contractarian myth also conditioned the allegiance- patterns of both minorities.. Like the nationalist myth, it had a salutary effect in the South. Whereas the northern Catholics were in some sense the South's irredentist population, the southern Protestants were not in the same position *vis-à-vis* their northern co-religionists. One consequence of thinking in terms of the public band was the presumption that if one remained out- side the *laager*, nothing could be done for him. Between 1912 and 1920, when northern Unionists thought at all about the plight of the southern Protestants they contemplated either wrecking Home Rule altogether or providing a 'refuge'. Failing the first possibility, southern Protestants knew very well by 1920 that nothing would be done on their behalf unless they 'fled' to the North. Thus the North's contractarian myth increased the readiness of southern Protestant leaders to co-operate with the Free State, whose leaders were impelled by their own nationalist myth to reciprocate.

By contrast, the contractarian myth exacerbated the alienation of the northern minority. Whereas southern nationalists assumed that it was natural and inevitable for the nation-state to enjoy the willing adherence of all members of the nation—even those who for the time being rejected it—many northern Protestants assumed that it was natural and inevitable for their state to be rejected by their 'natural enemies'. The behaviour of the northern minority tended to be regarded as regrettable but unavoidable, and—another self-fulfilling prophecy—northern Protestants there- fore did practically nothing to woo Catholics into allegiance to their state. The Dublin government's eagerness to meet any reasonable need of its minority contrasts sharply with the fact that during fifty years the permanent Unionist majority accepted only one minor legislative proposal from the Nationalist benches, the Wild Bird Act of 1931.[39] In 1959, when two progressive

Unionist spokesmen advocated efforts to recruit Catholics into the Unionist Party, their suggestions received a chilly reception from the Unionist leadership.[40] When, in 1929, the northern parliament abolished the system of proportional representation for parliamentary elections, it did so not to weaken the Nationalist Party, but to eliminate third parties and render the unionist-nationalist dichotomy all the sharper.[41] Though there was no doubt an element of specifically party, rather than communal, self-interest in this action—Unionist leaders suffered from recurrent fears of a significant defection by Protestant workers to Labour—it reflects more basically a belief that clear polarisation into friends and enemies is the normal, and indeed desirable, state of affairs. Thus both the contractarian culture and the nationalist culture contributed to the successful integration of the South's minority into the Free State; both contributed to the continued alienation of the North's minority from the Northern Ireland state.

One subject on which a departure from previous policy might have been expected once the Protestants had a government of their own was the regulation of communal demonstrations, towards which Dublin Castle's response had vexed extreme Protestants since the time of William Johnston of Ballykilbeg. The characteristic form in which Stormont faced this problem was the issue of the display of the Union Jack and the Irish tricolour. Theoretically, Stormont might have adopted any of three policies. (1) It might have treated the display of either flag in any public place as a legitimate exercise of free expression and provided protection for anyone who wanted to express himself in that way. (2) It might have treated only the display of the Union Jack as legitimate and taken effective measures to prevent display of the tricolour and protect display of the Union Jack in any part of the state. (3) It might have confined each flag to the areas where it would not be 'provocative'.

The consistent and successful pursuit of either of the first two policies would have enhanced the authority of the Northern Ireland state. Either of these policies would have made plain that public order throughout the state's territory derived from the state and not from the 'self-defence' of either community. The first policy would have had the added advantage of demonstrating that not only order but civil liberties, even those of the minority, derive from the state. Such is the message conveyed by the rows of *gardai* who accompany the little Orange processions which are still held in the Republic. Many Protestants would have preferred the second policy and agreed with the Rev. Ian Paisley when he declared, 'I don't accept that any area in Ulster is Republican and I don't want to see the Tricolour flying here. I intend to see that the Union Jack flies everywhere and that it keeps flying.'[42] Though the state occasionally yielded to demands such as this one for the second policy, in general it has tried to pursue the third.

Under the Flags and Emblems (Display) Act (NI), 1954, the police were indeed empowered to remove a tricolour, but only— the qualification is significant—*if* they believed its display would cause a breach of the peace.[43] The obvious intention of the legislation was to confine tricolours to Catholic territory. Prosecutions under the Act have been infrequent, and tricolours were and are regularly flown in Catholic areas, for example at Gaelic football grounds throughout the province.[44] To be sure, extreme Protestants have occasionally goaded the government into removing tricolours being displayed in Catholic areas—most dramatically in the case of a Republican Party headquarters in Divis Street in 1964, where the police action triggered several nights of rioting. The sequel to this episode, however, confirms that it represented a reluctant deviation by Stormont from its settled policy: a week later a Republican parade, 5,000 strong and headed by a tricolour, marched more than a mile through West Belfast, including Divis Street, along a route lined with police, who made no attempt to interfere.[45]

The Flags and Emblems Act did not, of course, put the Union Jack upon the same footing as the tricolour; indeed, display of the former on private property was specifically protected. In practice, however, the only way to display a Union Jack in a Catholic area was to mount a formidable procession to carry it there. Under the Public Order Act (NI), 1951, advance notice of such a procession had to be given to the police, who were empowered to reroute it if they feared serious public disorder. Again, the government sometimes yielded to pressure to permit such processions—notably on the Longstone Road, Annalong, in the mid-1950s[46]—but in general the government tried to keep loyalist processions out of Catholic areas.

Government policy toward demonstrations tended to legitimate the existence of areas within the state's territory over which it did not fully exercise sovereignty. No doubt policymakers, like their Dublin Castle predecessors, were partly motivated by a pragmatic desire to avoid trouble. They were also, however, emphasising rather than ameliorating the division of Northern Ireland society into two enemy camps, a fact which was central to the contractarian myth-structure from which the state derived such diffuse support as it enjoyed. It is noteworthy that the 1951 Public Order Act differed from the 1936 British Public Order Act, with which it is sometimes compared, in one significant particular; it did not prohibit the wearing of military or quasi-military uniforms.[47] The state did not attempt to play down the polarisation of its society but adopted policies which maintained a heightened awareness of communal fracture lines throughout its territory.

Although the Northern Ireland state's performance of its 'classic' functions changed little before the 1960s, from the end of World War II changes were occurring in its economic environment which would decisively alter its performance of the 'modern' functions of government. First the establishment of the welfare state in Britain naturally induced expectations that the Nothern Ireland state would provide new sorts of economic benefits. Secondly, a sharp decline in demand for linen, together with increasingly efficient competition in agriculture and, following the reconstruction of Japan and West Germany, in ship-building, placed the three mainstays of the province's economy in deep trouble.[48] Thirdly, the Republic's government was moving away from the autarkic policies begun in the 1930s and toward frank acceptance of interdependence with the United Kingdom —a policy consummated in the Anglo-Irish free trade agreement of 1965.

Stormont responded to postwar welfare legislation by getting Westminster to agree that as Britain introduced new social benefits Northern Ireland might also enact similar measures 'step-by-step' and—a principle which Ulster Unionists had been trying to establish since 1922—the difference between revenue and expenditure would be made up by the British exchequer. Beginning in the 1950s, Stormont took steps to attract new industries which would replace the jobs being lost in Ulster's traditional industries. Both these responses by the state to economic change were to have momentous consequences. Whatever truth there may have been to allegations that Stormont had hitherto carried out its 'modern' functions in a discriminatory way, these postwar developments meant that in vast new areas of state activity Catholics would inevitably benefit along with Protestants. Westminster was obviously not going to underwrite social benefits on an overtly Protestant-only basis (though, of course, there might be unfairness in the local administration of such benefits as housing), and outside investors in new industries were indifferent, if not actively opposed, to the restrictive employment patterns condoned in some of the older industries (though it was believed that Stormont managed to direct such investment disproportionately towards Protestant population centres).

The fact that industrial development was becoming such a crucial function of Stormont generated some cabinet-level leadership sensitive to the need to create at least the impression that the province was discarding old sectarian animosities. Prominently associated with the industrial development efforts was Captain Terence O'Neill, who served as Minister of Finance in the last years of Lord Brookeborough's two decades as Prime Minister, and who succeeded the latter in 1963. The third postwar change in the economic environment—the South's growing interest in co-operation—evoked little response from Brookeborough, but O'Neill took the dramatic step of initiating an exchange of visits in 1965 with his counterpart in the Republic, Seán Lemass. Moreover, he indicated a desire for reconciliation with the northern minority through various gestures, such as canvassing for votes in Catholic neighbourhoods and making highly publicised courtesy visits to convents.

These postwar developments had important and lasting political consequences. As the level of social benefits in the North rose significantly above that available in the Republic, continued United Kingdom membership began to offer some advantages to Catholics, who began to have second thoughts about their traditional 'enemy' role. Although there seemed initially to be significant support in the Catholic community for the IRA campaign in 1956–62, such support evaporated rather quickly. Late in 1964, the Nationalist Party adopted a policy of working for reform within the constitution, and shortly after the O'Neill-

Lemass talks they finally accepted the role of official opposition at Stormont.

A second consequence of the postwar developments was the crystallisation of a significant Protestant group who no longer accepted the basic assumptions of the public band. This group was largely middle-class—the northern business community, which stood to gain from freer access to southern markets, had applauded the O'Neill-Lemass talks—and amounted to perhaps ten per cent of the Protestant population.

A third consequence was a Protestant backlash against O'Neill's policies led by the Rev. Dr Ian Paisley. Paisley, the founder of the Free Presbyterian Church, attracted public attention through his colourful anti-ecumenical protests, notably on the occasion of the Archbishop of Canterbury's visit to the Pope and at the 1966 Irish Presbyterian General Assembly, in which he had managed to discern a 'Romeward trend'. A corollary of his religious message was that the Catholics could not be trusted in the political arena, and for those Protestants who were responsive to his appeal, any gestures by Catholics suggesting the contrary were merely further evidence of the latter's treachery and duplicity. Paisley spoke for a segment—perhaps fifteen per cent—of the Protestant community whose distrust of the Catholics was *a priori* and did not require the empirical corroboration which events were to provide for other Protestants after 1968.

The province's history since 1969 is crowded with personalities and shifting configurations of political movements. To make sense of this complex pattern of events it is useful to remember that the three developments just noted—Catholic reassessment of the 'enemy' role, middle-class Protestant disillusion with the contractarian political culture, and *a priori* Protestant backlash —all predate the crisis. The first two of these, precisely because they were consequences of fundamental economic change, represent permanent departures from the political patterns of half a century. Each was to take institutional form in a new political party. A new Catholic communal party, the Social Democratic and Labour Party (SDLP) founded in 1970 upon the principle that Irish unification could only come about through majority consent in the North (rather than by majority demand from the island as a whole) has established a secure claim to about two-thirds of the Catholic vote. In the same year, middle-class Protestants disillusioned with the contractarian myth, together with many middle-class Catholics, formed the Alliance Party, which manages to attract about ten per cent of the vote in each community. Alongside these permanent new features of the political landscape, the Paisleyite backlash represents a permanent old feature, whose relative importance would for a time be obfuscated by the rush of events, but can now be assessed and placed in perspective.

'Persons, Matters and Things'

Until the 1960s, Catholic adherence to the nationalist myth, ironically, meant that their community made relatively low 'specific' demands upon Stormont. The regime was not really expected to redress their grievances, each of which was merely put forward as one more piece of evidence that nothing would go well until the state was abolished in favour of a united Ireland. The regime had learned to rely on the diffuse and specific support it received from the Protestant community and to write off Catholic support. Captain O'Neill's attempt to obtain at least 'specific' support for the regime from Catholics, by creating an 'Opportunity State'[49] in which they would benefit fully from the 'modern' functions of government, created two difficulties. In the first place it eroded the diffuse support the regime enjoyed among those Protestants who distrusted the Catholics *a priori*, and thereby made it urgent that the Catholic support he sought be forthcoming quickly. Secondly, it generated rising expectations in Catholics that they should benefit from the 'classic' functions of government as well as the 'modern' functions.

In 1968 these expectations found expression in a vigorous civil rights movement, whose marches and other protests focused attention on some of the laws and practices which worked to the disadvantages of Catholics, such as plural voting, gerrymandering of local government electoral boundaries, and discrimination in the allocation of public housing for the purpose of maintaining local Protestant electoral majorities. Several of the reforms being demanded were granted, and O'Neill called an election early in 1969 in hopes of obtaining a mandate for proceeding with others. The results were ambiguous, but it was clear that O'Neill's candidates did not carry a Catholic vote impressive enough to offset the support which his opponents within the Unionist party gained from exploiting the Protestant backlash. Two months later, unable to command the confidence of the Unionist parliamentary party, he resigned. The last straw had been a series of acts of sabotage against public utility installations, for which several Protestant extremists were subsequently tried, though only one was convicted.[50]

Though a great deal of the original civil rights programme was actually put into effect during O'Neill's last few months in office and during the two-year administration of his cousin and successor, Major James Chichester-Clark, the cashiering of O'Neill by his party and the appearance of enacting reform only at the insistence of Westminster insured that Stormont would get no credit from the Catholics for redressing their grievances.

In any event, the regime's capacity to guarantee the rights of its citizens was most severely challenged not by the demands of the civil rights movement, but by their tactics. Because they enjoyed some support from liberal Protestants and because they rested their case on Northern Ireland's deviation from 'British' standards of equal citizenship, the civil rights leaders quite honestly regarded their movement as distinct from traditional Catholic nationalism. Their protests, and especially those of their more radical student allies, the People's Democracy (PD), took a form which raised the vital issue of the citizen's right to free expression in public places throughout the territory of his state. The protesters refused to consider themselves a 'side' in the sectarian conflict[51] and tended to demand the right to march through areas, such as town centres, hitherto understood to be Protestant territory. Predictably, Orange and Paisleyite elements regarded the civil rights movement as, in the words of Harry West, merely a 'cloak' for their 'old, traditional enemies'.[52] Demonstrations were attacked, counter-demonstrations were mounted, and the authorities fell back upon the hoary precedent of deeming 'provocation' the thing to be stopped. Rather than trying to guarantee free expression in all public places, they tried to confine demonstrations and counter-demonstrations to recognised sectarian territory—civil rights demonstrations being defined as 'Catholic'. While Stormont was also willing to reroute *ad hoc* (e.g., Paisleyite) Protestant demonstrations, however, it was reluctant to interfere with the routing of 'traditional' (i.e., mainly Orange) parades.

It is impossible here to give a full account of the events which triggered the regime's collapse, but many of the basic causes of that collapse can be discerned in events in Dungiven, County Londonderry, in the summer of 1969.[53] Dungiven is a village with a 90 per cent Catholic majority, where Orange parades can only take place either on the sufferance of the local Catholics or by virtue of an overwhelming show of force by the authorities. The latter had occasionally happened in the past, but in general local Orangemen had learned to keep a low profile. In 1968, however, the local lodge's banner had been stolen, and custom called for an elaborate ceremony to unfurl a new banner in time for the 1969 marching season. Civil rights and PD spokesmen descended on the village, and local Catholics were persuaded, contrary to their initial inclinations, to permit the planned procession to take place. PD members festooned the village with posters and banners bearing such slogans as 'You can march. Can others[?]' and 'We believe in civil rights. Do you[?]' Significantly, the Master of the local Orange lodge perceived the message 'You can march' as 'We allow you to walk', and the RUC District Inspector remembered it as 'We allow you to march because of civil rights.'[54] Despite the fact that Orangemen insisted on tearing down these signs before proceeding through the village, the day passed off, remarkably, without violence.

Two weeks later, however, sit-down demonstrators tried to stop the local Orange lodge from holding a much more modest procession through the village *en route* to the 12th of July celebrations at Limavady, on the ground that in Dungiven such a procession was not 'traditional'. The demonstrators were arrested, and the Orangemen marched to their bus and moved on to Limavady, where most of the 110 policemen present in Dungiven that morning were now redeployed. During the day the Dungiven Orange Hall suffered minor vandalism, and Orange leaders, with difficulty, prevented a massive influx of Orangemen into the little Catholic village to 'protect' the hall. On the next day, the Stormont Minister of Home Affairs tried to mollify local Orange leaders by ordering police protection for the hall and, apparently, by agreeing to use the 'B' Specials (whose District Commandant was also the Dungiven Orange Master) armed with truncheons only.

Some 50 policemen—nearly the whole locally-available force, now that major disturbances in Derry had drained police away from the vicinity—were concentrated in the hall, an action which immediately drew a hostile Catholic crowd to the scene. In a baton charge to clear the street, an elderly man was fatally injured. When the police retreated into the hall, the crowd set fire to their tenders and managed to do a good deal of damage to the hall with petrol bombs and burning tyres. Nearly half the policemen were injured. Meanwhile, the 'B' Specials failed to follow orders to assemble at either of two locations where they could be held in reserve to deal with trouble outside the Orange Hall. Instead, they proceeded to a point opposite a ballroom where a dance attended by some 1,400 Catholics was in progress. Predictably, as people left the dance, the 'B' Specials found themselves facing a hostile crowd. Thereupon, they obtained arms, contrary to their instructions, and dispersed the crowd with warning shots. Two hours later, when the RUC District Inspector interrogated the party of 'B' Specials, they declined to give information about the firing.

Two lessons of general significance for the situation in 1969 emerge from the Dungiven episodes. First, the civil rights leaders' notion that everyone should be guaranteed free expression in any public place was, at best, imperfectly grasped by both Catholics and Protestants. The Orange Master construed the very toleration of the first procession by the Dungiven Catholics as an inverse assertion of dominance on their part. Moreover, when his lodge tried to take advantage of the precedent set by the first procession, Catholics, free from the intense promptings of civil rights leaders, tried to reassert their local dominance directly. Although the results of that assertion may have seemed equivocal in July, the ambiguities were clarified a month later. During the widespread disturbances of 12–15 August, Dungiven Catholics mounted a direct assault upon the police station and successfully completed the work of burning the Orange Hall, as well as the courthouse. By this time the fragmentation of Northern Ireland's territory along the fracture lines delimiting Catholic areas was being consummated in Belfast, Derry and elsewhere by the erection of barricades. Dungiven's geographical situation rendered barricades unnecessary, and on 15 August the local Ancient Order of Hibernians went ahead with a planned procession in defiance of a government ban on all parades. Two policemen who tried to enforce the ban were 'escorted to safety' by the local priest, a civil rights leader and some Hibernian leaders.[55] Stormont had lost all pretence to a monopoly of physical force in Dungiven.

That loss represented more than the heightened territorial assertiveness of the Catholics which, ironically, was one consequence of the civil rights movement's attempt to override the territorial conventions. A second lesson reflected in the Dungiven experience was that even if Stormont had been disposed to undertake the responsibility, so often eschewed by Dublin Castle, of protecting the right of free expression, it simply lacked the force to do so. An ordinary government, faced with great risks of disorder, would have called in troops to supplement its ordinary police, but Stormont's only 'troops' were the 'B' Specials. The Dungiven episode illustrated how unamenable the Specials were to discipline, and though by good fortune their introduction into this situation did not lead directly to disaster, their use in other places during this period did demonstrate that their mere presence was certain to intensify Catholic anger and exacerbate disorder. These considerations were well-understood at Stormont, where the government was already sponsoring legislation which, had it not been overtaken by events, would have deprived the Specials of all police functions. The primary value of the Specials to the regime was to help muster diffuse support for it among Protestants by acting out an important role in the contractarian myth; in the absence of an IRA campaign they could contribute little to the actual maintenance of public order.

The only alternative to extensive deployment of the Specials was to ask Westminster for troops—an option which, as Stormont was well aware, would entail at least some increment of Westminster intervention in the province's affairs. Stormont procrastinated before making any such request, but also deployed the Specials only fitfully, until the annual Apprentice Boys celebrations of 12 August, which became the occasion in Derry of the worst rioting since the demonstrations had commenced a year earlier. During the lesser troubles of the preceding few months barricades had been erected by Catholics in the Bogside, and at least some precedent had been established for the withdrawal of police from the area.[56] Now when police, accompanied by a

Protestant mob, tried to pursue Catholic rioters into the Bogside, the action resembled an invasion of a territory with the rudiments of sovereignty. As violence spread to other parts of the province, and barricades went up in West Belfast, a mood of revolutionary expectancy was enhanced when Jack Lynch the Taoiseach (prime minister of the Republic), broadcast a statement which was widely understood in both northern communities to presage an actual invasion or 'liberation' by southern troops, though southerners probably recognised his words as simply another example of the ambiguous posturing they had come to expect from their politicians. Lynch was speaking the sober truth, however, when he asserted that Stormont had lost control of the situation. The RUC was stretched to its limit, the 'B' Specials were mobilised, and on the afternoon of 14 August Stormont requested troops from Westminster.

The events of the preceding year demonstrated that Stormont was fundamentally incapable of performing the 'classic' function of guaranteeing civil rights to its Catholic citizens, even when the latter were willing to suspend their insistence that Irish unity was the *sine qua non* of such rights. The regime simply lacked sufficient agencies of coercive force capable of establishing that public order which is prerequisite to meaningful civil rights, without treating the Catholics as enemies rather than citizens. In this context, the Catholic community had effectively excluded the regime from those ethnic territorial entities which public policy, both before and after 1920, had done so much to maintain intact. The regime's admission of failure, by calling for troops from Westminster, raised a new question: Had the Catholic enclaves—'Free Derry', 'Free Belfast' and many rural areas where barricades were irrelevant—seceded from the United Kingdom state as well as from the Northern Ireland state?

During the early days of the army presence it seemed just possible that Westminster might be able to regain the recognised and credible monopoly of physical force throughout Northern Ireland's territory which Stormont had forfeited. Catholics welcomed the troops as deliverers from what they perceived as the attacks of police, Specials and Protestant extremists; in some places they served cups of tea to the soldiers. Nevertheless, this 'honeymoon' period was too brief, the basis for trust too slender, and troops too ill-suited to the role of ordinary policemen for them

F

to succeed in the vital task of protecting Catholics from ordinary malefactors within their own community and/or from extreme Protestants. They were thus unable to perform that classic function of government, the provision of public order, which was essential if the United Kingdom state was to become an object of allegiance on the part of ghetto Catholics. More important, Westminster hesitated, for two and a half crucial years, to take the step which, if taken immediately, might have allowed the United Kingdom to become an object of direct allegiance, without the intervening presence of the hated Stormont regime. Despite the territorial fragmentation of the state which it nominally governed, that regime was left intact, and while Protestants perceived its powers being whittled away, Catholics had a different perception. In July, 1970, when soldiers carried out widespread house searches in the Falls Road area only two weeks after the return of a Conservative government at a United Kingdom general election, many Catholics were convinced that their Unionist enemies, with the connivance of the latter's traditional British allies, had taken control of the army.

From August of 1969, the mere absence of ordinary policing had inevitably called forth vigilante-style forces in barricaded Catholic areas, and while in a few areas 'defence' might be organised by an *ad hoc* 'community defence association',[57] it was on the whole equally inevitable that the IRA would reappear to perform this function. To the extent that the 'official' leadership of the IRA—which had become increasingly committed to socialist objectives in recent years at the expense of the pure nationalist gospel—was slow to provide defence, they were superseded by a new 'provisional' leadership, who saw the issue in familiar terms of British oppression, now visibly manifested in a military presence. By 1971 the 'Provisionals'—or in some areas the 'Officials', kept up to the mark now by competing Provisional militancy—were firmly established in Catholic ghetto areas, where they carried out police and defence functions and executed what passed for justice, and from which their 'volunteers' sallied forth to engage in urban guerrilla warfare, chiefly shoot-outs with soldiers and bomb attacks on commercial enterprises. Catholics in such 'no-go' areas, where the police seldom ventured, accepted the IRA as their legitimate defenders, perhaps not so much because they saw the British soldiers as the embodiment of

'British' dominance, but because increasingly they saw them as tools of Stormont.

Indeed, even though Westminster had forced Stormont in 1969 to disband the 'B' Specials and disarm the police (the latter reform lasting in practice only a few months), Stormont did retain the leading voice in security policy. The most important security decision of this period—the imposition of internment without trial in August, 1971—was taken on the initiative of Chichester-Clark's successor, Brian Faulkner. Internment is, by its very nature, haphazard : unavoidably a number of young Catholic men guilty only by association were swept into the net. Its use seemed to confirm that Stormont was capable of dealing with the Catholics only as enemies, not as citizens. Moreover, the security policy which Stormont had persuaded Westminster to sanction was a patent failure. Internment not only solidified IRA support in Catholic areas, but led to a dramatic rise in terrorist violence throughout the province : in the last five months of 1971 there were twice as many killings as in the preceding two and a half years. The fact that security forces were manifestly losing to terrorists their monopoly of physical force even outside Catholic neighbourhoods reflected a fundamental failure of the regime. Whereas in 1969 Stormont had lost this monopoly in Catholic territory largely because it lacked agencies of physical force capable of treating Catholics as citizens rather than as enemies, the events of 1969–72 demonstrated that even when ethnically neutral forces were placed at its disposal the regime was incapable of devising policies which would transform mere force into effective authority. Belatedly recognising this reality, in March, 1972, Westminster decided to take responsibility for security out of Stormont's hands, thus divesting it of a defining characteristic of the government of a state. Faced with the prospect of continuing as a mere glorified local authority, rather than a regime, Faulkner and his colleagues resigned. Westminster suspended the Northern Ireland parliament and introduced 'direct rule' under a Secretary of State, William Whitelaw, responsible to the United Kingdom Parliament. The Stormont regime had been extinguished.

Epilogue

State of Nature Revisited

What was abolished on 24 March 1972 was the regime created by the Government of Ireland Act 1920. It turned out, however, that not only that *regime*, but also the *state* into which the Ulster Protestant community had erected itself between 1911 and 1921, was collapsing. In concrete terms, that community has not tried to constitute a new state by taking the step, so often mooted for several years, of a unilateral declaration of independence (UDI). Moreover, when the Westminster regime supplanted Stormont, it did not regain the monopoly of physical force which Stormont had lost nor inherit such diffuse support as Stormont had enjoyed. The United Kingdom became in the province merely the *nominal* state: often its regime seemed to enjoy a recognised monopoly of physical force only in middle-class neighbourhoods, in some Protestant rural areas remote from ethnic frontiers, and in the 80-acre security zone in central Belfast. In many urban working-class neighbourhoods—Protestant as well as Catholic—and in large rural areas, superiority of physical force was, in effect, conceded to the paramilitaries of the dominant ethnic group. Even such functions as the allocation of publicly-financed housing were often tacitly devolved upon the paramilitaries.

The absence of a state became the essence of the Northern Ireland problem, subsuming all other candidates for the distinction of being *the* problem. For example, to the extent that there was still a civil rights problem in Northern Ireland, that problem resulted from the lack of a state to give effect to legislation passed by Stormont and Westminster since 1968 and from the fact that the nominal state was reduced to using the instruments of warfare, rather than those of civil administration. It does not necessarily follow from the protracted character of the crisis that in Northern Ireland there are more intense sources of social conflict than in other societies. There may indeed be, but the fact that the crisis has gone on for so long results primarily from the fact that the modern world's most effective instrument for resolving conflict—the state—has broken down in those parts.

Thus a 'solution' would consist in the successful erection of one or more states which, taken together, would embrace all the territory of Northern Ireland. Westminster could probably have produced such an outcome at any time by the simple expedient of withdrawing its troops. Such a withdrawal would no doubt have been followed by an outburst of much more severe inter-communal violence than has hitherto been witnessed, the flight of much of the Catholic population to the South, intervention by the Republic's armed forces, and a military standoff along a line running from perhaps Limavady to Dundrum. It is important to recognise that this 'doomsday' scenario would very probably produce a 'solution'—namely, the emergence of a new, smaller, all-Protestant state in the North and the incorporation of the rest of Northern Ireland into the Republic. Each state would quickly come to enjoy enough support from its ethnically-homogenous population to legitimate its monopoly of force within its new *de facto* boundaries. The killing would stop.

The likely cost of this 'solution', however, would be a blood-bath and, for tens of thousands of persons, the lot of refugees. British statesmen have generally been unwilling to incur this frightful cost, for it is one of the salutary ironies of the Anglo-Irish nexus that despite their disdain for both Irish communities Englishmen cannot bring themselves to regard the Irish as foreigners in quite the same sense as Cypriots or Pakistanis. West-minster has implicitly used the modest power deriving from its military presence to impose upon the problem the constraint that its solution must not entail a 'bloodbath' or massive forced popula-tion transfers. Given this constraint, there were four potential solutions which competed for the attention of public men, together with one alternative which was not a potential solution, during and in the wake of Stormont's collapse. Each solution proposed the erection of a new state, and each was founded, in effect, on certain 'nationality' assumptions. By exploring the career of each 'solution', we can understand how and why the Northern Ireland state had collapsed along with its regime.

The first solution, incorporation of Northern Ireland into a new, 32-county, republic, was being put forward by the IRA. This solution rested on the traditional nationalist assumption that Ireland is one nation, though its proponents were willing to indulge some small diversity within the nation by proposing a federal structure within the projected new republic and to recognise the dangers of precipitate British withdrawal by accepting, in the short term, a 'declaration of intent' to withdraw the troops.[1] Of course the assumption was rejected by Ulster Protestants, but in addition many Catholics in the South were having second thoughts as to the practicability of a united Ireland. In part these doubts simply arose out of better information than had hitherto been available to the southern populace. Television made it possible for the first time for many southerners actually to see and hear Ulster Protestants affirming their absolute, total and unqualified rejection of a united Ireland. More fundamentally, nationalist rhetoric had encouraged the apocalyptic hope that if only Stormont would disappear, and the British abandon their imperialist designs, all difficulties would quickly resolve themselves. In fact Stormont was now gone, and all British parties were treating Northern Ireland as an unwanted burden. Nevertheless, difficulties seemed only to multiply and threatened to 'spill over' into the Republic itself. In February, 1973, voters in the Republic turned out the Fianna Fáil government, which was tainted by revelations that certain cabinet ministers had been covertly supplying arms to the Provisional IRA, in favour of a Fine Gael/Labour coalition whose leaders took seriously the rights as well as the fears of the Ulster Protestant community.

Few Irish Catholics were willing to forsake the nationalist myth altogether—only eleven per cent of a sample of the southern electorate in October, 1974, said that they would vote to delete the articles of the Republic's 1937 Constitution which claimed jurisdiction over the North[2]—but more and more of them were willing to relegate unification to the millenium. Ironically, this important shift in Catholic expectations roughly coincided with an increased willingness in British governing circles to contemplate a united Ireland as the solution to the problem. In 1971 Harold Wilson, as opposition leader, had put forward a plan for a 15-year transition to a united Ireland (within the Commonwealth), and in private conversation Conservative leaders were also speak-

ing of a united Ireland as the only long-term solution.[3] From an
English point of view, it was easy to reason from 'After all, they're
all Irish', to the notion that an all-Ireland state might be a
viable proposition. Once they had to grapple with the problems
of direct rule English statesmen came fairly quickly to their
senses, but the damage to Westminster's ability to command
support among Protestants for a more realistic solution had
already been done.

A second possible solution, 'an independent British Ulster', was
being contemplated by the Vanguard movement launched by
former Home Affairs Minister William Craig as 'an umbrella
for traditional Loyalist groups'[4] at a series of rallies throughout the
province during the six weeks prior to the suspension of Stormont.
Vanguard drew its apparent support from the formidable Protestant backlash which had materialised in reaction to the
upsurge of IRA violence in 1971. The Paisleyite backlash of the
1960s had been based on the assumption that any Catholic
political assertiveness was merely disguised IRA activity—a piece
of *a priori* reasoning unaffected by the fact that between 1962
and 1969 the IRA was notable mainly by its absence. In contrast, it was the solid empirical fact of an IRA campaign being
mounted from Catholic areas which, *a posteriori*, convinced the
anonymous authors of a leaflet distributed in working-class Protestant areas of Belfast during the violent internment week of
August, 1971, 'that the enemies of our Faith and Freedom are
determined to destroy the State of Northern Ireland and thereby
enslave the people of God'.[5] Their appeal for 'all members of
our loyalist Institutions, and other responsible citizens', to organise
themselves into platoons led to the formation of the Ulster
Defence Association (UDA),[6] a much more broadly-based movement than the little paramilitary units which had earlier sprung
up on the fringes of Paisleyite politics.

Within a few days after the imposition of direct rule, the UDA
issued a handbill declaring, 'We were once a proud and happy
nation', which had now been 'betrayed'.[7] This theme was
elaborated shortly thereafter in a Vanguard pamphlet entitled
Ulster—A Nation, which argues that the Ulster loyalists are 'an
old and historic community', for whom union with Britain had
never been 'an end in itself', but 'was always a means of
preserving Ulster's British tradition and the identity of her loyalist

people'.[8] British politicians, by 'dismantling Ulster's capacity for resistance to friend [*sic*] or foe' had 'unwittingly forged a nation that cannot entrust to them its security or national destiny'.[9] This must, I suppose, count as an expression of Ulster nationalism *à la Basque* for which we searched in vain in the literature of Unionism between 1912 and 1923.

The 'nation' in question is clearly the Ulster Protestant community, but the pamphlet, significantly, never uses the term 'nation' to describe that community as it existed before the 'betrayals' of 1969–72. Its central message is not that it is natural and right for the Ulster Protestant community to constitute a state, but that, regrettably, that community is now despised by the British nation and has been betrayed by the British state: '.... if Westminster by her own act divests the relationship with Ulster of all ties of sentiment, the product of a long history, and reduces it to a balance of material interests, then Ulster will, willy-nilly, be forced to do likewise.'[10] So this is a reluctant, matter-of-fact nationalism, perhaps a nationalism of despair, a nationalism arising out of immediate events and circumstances, not out of long-term social processes.

In the modern world, nationalism has been a prime secular alternative to traditional religion in the role of reaffirming the group, of sanctioning actual or projected authority relationships. It is certainly significant that at least a small group of Ulster Protestants finally felt a need to articulate such a secular myth-structure, but the authors of this pamphlet find it really difficult to give their nationalism a mythic dimension. When they come to define 'the heart of the matter', they use not the language of the enthusiast, but that of the social scientist: 'Two different communities in Great Britain and Ulster at different stages of development by virtue of different historical experience possess different scales of reference by which to measure, weigh and judge.'[11] Only in their concluding sentence do the authors slip into the kind of poetic language we associate with nationalist rhetoric: 'Let Ulster, the land of Ireland's foremost heroes, speak to the whole of Ireland again with the authority of a Cuchulainn, *fortissimus heros Scottorum*, and like Finn MacCool of old build a new Causeway to join all the people of these islands in a new community of spirit and endeavour.'[12] Indeed, this brief flash of eloquence itself illustrates the difficulties Ulster Protestants have in embracing a thoroughgoing nationalism, for it expresses the authors' ultimate hope that beyond independence for Ulster there may lie a new era of co-operation between Great Britain, 'Eire', and Ulster, and perhaps even a federal constitution for the British Isles.

Indeed, the dominant rhetoric of the pamphlet is not national-ist, but contractarian. Loyalty is described as 'not a unilateral relationship': it is no disloyalty to the Queen to refuse loyalty to 'ministers or governments that fail in their duty to give loyal subjects the blessing of the Queen's Peace'. 'Guarantees' of Northern Ireland's position are 'not worth a button', whether they rest on 'solemn promises by British statesmen' or on acts of parliament. Even the Conservatives have become 'dishonest, un-trustworthy and treacherous', and, indeed, British politicians themselves have no high opinion 'of each other's standards of promise-keeping and truth-telling'. Moreover, no parliament can bind its successors; in Churchill's words, 'Every parliament is entirely free to behave honestly or like a crook.' Thus the 1949 pledge and any subsequent guarantees which may be offered rest ultimately on the 'changing mood' of the British people; 'national honour' is subservient to 'national self-interest, as interpreted by the politicians in power'.[13] (A few months later, Craig worked out a more elaborate legal argument that the suspension of Stor-mont was, in itself a violation of the pledge.)[14] British politicians have 'inspired no confidence in their honesty of purpose or their resolve to do other than to betray the trust they undertook to discharge'. They 'have robbed Ulster of her own means of protection and then ... have failed in the moral duty to supply it themselves in honour of their explicit undertaking'.[15]

So the nationalism of *Ulster—A Nation*, interesting though it is, is only a thin veneer over the old contractarian modes of thought. More significantly, the Ulster nationalism theme seems to have struck only a momentary responsive chord in the Prot-estant community. After the initial shock of the Westminster take-over subsided, Vanguard tended to play down the nationalist arguments for its case. A leaflet, *Government without Right*,[16] published a few months later by the Newtownards branch of Vanguard, tends to avoid Ulster nationalist rhetoric, but is redolent of contractarian eloquence. Whitelaw's administration is described as 'the government of usurpation set up in flagrant breach of a constitutional compact made with our ancestors in 1920 and accepted by them for their posterity after a generation and more of political struggle'. Its acts are an exercise of that arbitrary power from which Englishmen and Ulstermen won freedom at the Glorious Revolution. The Bill of Rights underlies the 1920 Act, and the suspension of Stormont overthrew 'the pre-eminent rights of a community to a measure of self-govern-ment, conferred by agreement and solemnly written in law'. Resistance to Whitelaw's rule is therefore defended in language reminiscent of the seventeenth century. By having a conversa-tion with IRA leaders during a two-week truce in the summer of 1972, Whitelaw became guilty of 'treasonable conspiracy with the Queen's open enemies' : 'with the foreknowledge of the Prime Minister and other high officers of State he [Whitelaw] has been in secret negotiation with rebels, whose hands were still reeking with the blood of Her Majesty's liege subjects.' By failing to ensure the rule of law, Westminster has defaulted on its obliga-tions and forfeited the power 'entrusted to it by the Ulster people'. In classic Whig phrases, the authors declare that power to be 'a revocable trust', which Westminster has deserted 'by abdica-tion, if not by downright treachery'. Thus, unless Westminster promptly restores Stormont and holds an election, 'the Ulster people must set up, under the crown, their own parliament and government and negotiate the terms of a future relationship with Great Britain.'

This kind of rhetoric did undoubtedly reflect widespread feel-ings in the Ulster Protestant community, but we must evaluate its significance from the perspective of what actually happened and, more to the point, what did not happen at this time. Many of the elements for a replay of the 1911–14 phenomenon were ready to hand. A paramilitary force—indeed, several such forces —had been organised within the Protestant community. A 'covenant' reminiscent of the 1912 document was being handed about in 1971 under Orange auspices, and its sponsors claimed that it attracted about 500,000 signatures (including those of 'many' Catholics).[17] Moreover, at one of Vanguard's organising rallies early in 1972, Craig had read out another covenant-like document and called for verbal assent from the assemblage.[18] Nevertheless, the Protestant community mounted no ceremony remotely approaching the disciplined solemnity and convincing near-unanimity of the 1912 exercise. No 'Provisional Government' took counsel in the precincts of the Ulster Club. The Presbyterian Church commissioned scholarly studies of such topics as discrimination, republicanism and loyalism, and, as an institution, generally stayed out of 'politics'. Despite Vanguard's 'umbrella' pretensions, it was a symptom not of the unity, but of the division in the Protestant community, and especially in its elite. The defection of a sizable portion of the Protestant middle class from contractarian assumptions in the 1960s was proving to be permanent. Though such people were far from a majority, even within their own community, they were relatively influential and articulate and they lent their support to moderate Unionism or the Alliance Party. No credible replay of the 1912 scenario was possible without them. Moreover, even among those who still thought in contractarian terms, contractarian logic seemed to lead not to the conclusion that UDI should be undertaken, but to the need to keep Britain up to the mark in honouring her imputed obligations. The Ulster Protestant community, in other words, was not prepared to reconstitute the state they had created between 1912 and 1920. It is in this crucial sense that we can say that that state had collapsed.

A third solution being actively discussed around the time of the Westminster takeover was 'total integration'—the permanent absorption of the province's government departments into their United Kingdom counterparts, together with an increase in the province's Westminster representation, which had been reduced by the 1920 Act to somewhat less than what it deserved on the basis of population. Proponents of total integration were, in effect, arguing that, if Northern Ireland were placed on a footing 'just like Yorkshire', the United Kingdom might become really, rather than just nominally, the state in the province. The implicit nationality assumption of this solution was that Ulster is British —a proposition which required no new myth-making activity on the part of Ulster Protestants, who had long understood it to mean 'Ulster chooses to remain British' rather than 'Ulstermen are like Britons'.

Shortly before the Westminster takeover, the Rev. Ian Paisley indicated a preference for total integration over 'Mr Craig's UDI' in the event of any tampering with Stormont,[19] and he adhered to this line for the first several months of direct rule. Paisley and

Craig spoke for constituencies which could agree upon the goal of continued Protestant dominance. Elements of Craig's following, however, felt the need, at least briefly, for an up-to-date secular myth—i.e., a nationalism—to sanction that set of authority relationships. Paisley spoke most authentically for that segment of the Protestant community for whom this function was still performed well enough by a non-secular myth : men become truly free only through salvation according to the scriptural plan, so in the political realm the preservation of freedom entails, above all, guaranteeing that the minions of Rome never get the power to suppress scriptural truth.[20] Paisley's flirtation with total integration, therefore, represents not only the tactical manoeuvre of adopting a policy distinct from that of his principal rival for the affections of extreme Protestants, but also the fact that he and his most enthusiastic followers had no need for the secular myth which a few of Craig's followers were constructing to validate continued Protestant dominance in the province.

Total integration failed to attract much support from other Northern Ireland politicians, many of whom stood to lose the only arena in which they could hope to cut a figure. The overriding reason why this solution remained a purely academic proposition, however, was that British opinion was generally hostile to any suggestion for drawing the troublesome province even closer into the body politic. A subordinate reason was that the Irish Republic opposed any change which would not leave some mechanism by which eventually the province might express a determination to join the Republic. In nationality terms, Westminster and Dublin were agreed that Ulster was not British.

The fourth possible solution, some sort of shared government in the province, was the one which Westminster settled upon. The nationality assumption underlying such proposals was that Ulster Catholics and Protestants had, or might develop, a sense of common identity. While recognising that no such common identity yet existed, except perhaps in the Alliance Party, White-law formulated his policy in the faith that it might be created by 'working together'. Leaders of the Catholic community, the SDLP, were eager to 'work together' with Protestants and found it easy to adapt the projected common Ulster identity to their existing nationalist myth by reasoning that if Protestants came to have such an identity with them Protestant resistance to Irish unity might wane. On the Protestant side a largely middle-class segment of the Unionist Party led by Brian Faulkner stoically accepted that 'working together' would be imposed upon them.

As the British government moved toward the 'working together' solution, the forces of Paisley and Craig drifted away from their respective 'total integration' and 'independent British Ulster' solutions and into an alliance, together with anti-Faulkner elements of the Official Unionist Party, upon an alternative which was not a 'solution' as we are using that term. That alternative, the restoration of Stormont, would have meant the establishment of a regime without a state, and in diverting the attention of perhaps half the population of the province away from the crucial task of state-building for some two years, Craig and Paisley were acting with high irresponsibility. However, as Westminster pursued the 'working together' solution, it too shrank from facing up to that task.

Whitelaw's plan, put forward in a White Paper[21] in March, 1973, and given statutory form thereafter, was ingenious. A new Assembly would be elected, but given no powers until a Protestant-Catholic coalition prepared to share executive power, presented itself. By this procedure Whitelaw hoped to use the hunger of Protestant politicians for the power they had lost a year earlier to induce them to cooperate with the SDLP. Nevertheless, powers which had proved 'divisive' in the past would, for the time being, be left in Westminster hands. These powers included jurisdiction over police, courts and other law-and-order matters, i.e., the defining characteristics of a state. Whitelaw's strategy was to attempt to create consensus for shared, but less-than-state institutions and only if and when that consensus had been achieved to transform those institutions from a glorified local government into the government of a state.

Whitelaw came up with a subtle and apparently promising solution to the problem of how to gratify Catholic nationalist longings while simultaneously reassuring Protestants that they would not be thrust out of the United Kingdom. He resurrected the Council of Ireland proposal originally put forward in the 1920 Act, but never implemented. In so doing, he demonstrated that he had learned an important lesson about Irish nationalism: that most of its adherents are much more concerned with symbols than with substance. The Council, which would consist of equal representation from northern and southern legislatures, and which would exercise only very limited powers in areas of common interest (e.g. tourism), represented almost exactly what most Catholics, North and South, really wanted. It would legitimate an 'aspiration' to a united Ireland without actually threatening the higher standard of living enjoyed by northern Catholics by virtue of United Kingdom membership and without saddling southern Catholics with the unwanted burden of actually governing the troubled province over which their hearts and their constitution claimed jurisdiction. In consequence, it seemed that by reviving the Council proposal Whitelaw might be able to gain from the Dublin government explicit guarantees that Northern Ireland would remain in the United Kingdom as long as the majority so desired, a meaningful reinforcement of Britain's own reassurances on the point.

In June of 1973 the new Assembly was elected. After several months of haggling, a coalition consisting of the 19 SDLP members, 8 Alliance members and about 20 Official Unionists was put together. The coalition was opposed by 17 Loyalists, divided almost equally between Vanguard and Paisley's Democratic Unionist Party, and about a dozen Unionists who rejected Faulkner's leadership.[22] In December, a conference of leaders of the coalition parties and of representatives of the Westminster and Dublin governments was held at Sunningdale, near London. Plans were formalised for the Council of Ireland and for cross-border co-operation on security, and the Republic gave the anticipated guarantees of Northern Ireland's position in the United Kingdom. On 31 December, six Protestants and five Catholics were sworn in as the Northern Ireland Executive, using an oath which omitted all reference to the crown.

Two months later, a United Kingdom general election was held, and in Northern Ireland it was treated as a referendum on the Executive and the Sunningdale Agreement. The Ulster Unionist Council had repudiated Faulkner's leadership of the Official Unionist Party, and the anti-Faulkner Official Unionists joined with Vanguard and the DUP in a United Ulster Unionist Council (UUUC) to put up an agreed panel of anti-Sunningdale candidates. The UUUC garnered 50.8 per cent of the votes cast and won eleven of the twelve Northern Ireland seats. The Executive's difficulties were increased by constitutional problems in the South. The Dublin government's power to give the Sunningdale guarantees was challenged in the Republic's courts, and although the challenge was dismissed, the wording of the Supreme Court ruling raised doubts as to the status of the guarantees.[23] Meanwhile, the Republic's representatives on an Anglo-Irish Commission, established to find legal means of bringing fugitive terrorist offenders to trial, took the position that the obvious solution, extradition, would violate the Republic's constitution, and persuaded the British representatives to go along with their alternative: a system of extra-territorial courts. More important than legitimate doubts as to the workability of this proposal was the fact that the Commission's deliberations dragged on for nearly four months. Since the Northern Ireland Executive was not represented on the Commission, it was seen to be powerless to affect this matter which was at least believed by many Protestants to be the heart of the problem.

Loyalist assembly members, still in a minority within the Assembly, could do little but engage in disruptive behaviour in the chamber, and on 14 May the anti-Sunningdale initiative was seized from them by loyalist workers, who organised a general strike throughout the province. The strikers demanded dissolution of the Executive, new elections, abandonment of the Council of Ireland proposal 'even as a topic for discussion', and, following the new elections, an end to the Secretary of State's 'power of veto'.[24] Since the Executive had no security powers, decisions as to how to deal with the strike remained in Westminster's hands. In reality, the Executive shared not power but impotence. The new Labour government was indecisive; its most dramatic move in the crisis was a televised speech by the Prime Minister, Harold Wilson, whose reference to loyalists 'spending their lives sponging on Westminster and British democracy'[25] only served to solidify support for the strikers in the Protestant community. On 28 May, the Executive collapsed.

The Loyalist strike seemed to repudiate not only Whitelaw's solution, but the nationality assumptions underlying three of the four basic solutions which had been under discussion during the preceding two years. In the first place, it was most explicitly a condemnation of 'Ireland a nation' even in the attenuated form that concept assumed in the proposed Council of Ireland.

Secondly, insofar as it was an attack upon 'power-sharing', the strike was a refusal to entertain the possibility of a common identity among northern Catholics and Protestants. Actually, although the success of the strike represented unequivocal rejection of the Council of Ireland by most Ulster Protestants, the extent to which it also represented rejection of power-sharing is problematical. As late as mid-April, a poll showed that 74 per cent of the people in Northern Ireland favoured power-sharing, although only 41 per cent favoured the Council of Ireland.[26] No doubt some Protestants 'in favour of' power-sharing were simply expressing a stoical willingness to give it a chance so long as it seemed inevitable : once the power-sharing Executive had been toppled, support for power-sharing dropped to 46 per cent (33 per cent of Protestants and 74 per cent of Catholics).[27] A crucial element in the success of the strike had been the rallying of many middle-class Protestants behind it at the end of its first week.[28] This accession of strength to the strikers represented not, perhaps, irreconciliable hostility to power-sharing in any form, but the inability, for reasons which will be discussed below, of this particular experiment to evoke any real sense of 'common identity' with Catholics on the part of most Protestants.

In the third place, as a massive repudiation of parliament's will, the strike seemed to demonstrate that Ulster was not British—i.e., that a substantial share of the Protestants were unwilling to accept the democratically-formulated will of the British nation. Significantly, the contemptuous usage 'the Brits' was often on Protestant lips in the aftermath of the strike. The contractarian myth was, by its very nature, incapable of providing Westminster with the diffuse support which a genuine sense of British nationality might have induced. Westminster's actions were not being evaluated on the nationalist presumption that a people *like* oneself can be trusted. Indeed, a 1968 survey had revealed that, interestingly, Protestants were more inclined to regard the English than the southern Irish as 'different' from Northern Ireland folk.[29] Similarity and difference, however, were simply not the issue : the issue was demonstrated trustworthiness, unhallowed and unobscured by sentimental ties. To the true believers in the contractarian myth, the disbandment of the Specials and the suspension of Stormont had constituted default upon the 1920 bargain. For loyalists, the issue posed by Sunningdale was, above all else, whether the 1949 'pledge' was to be honoured. As Westminster had already forfeited whatever presumption of honesty it earlier enjoyed, its reiteration of 'the pledge' at Sunningdale was treated as duplicitous and the Council of Ireland as an earnest of its true and treacherous intent.

Significantly, however, the sequel to the strike seemed to demonstrate that the fourth nationality assumption under discussion over the preceding two years—an Ulster (i.e., Protestant) nationalism—was insubstantial. In the weeks after the strike there was a good deal of talk about Ulster nationalism, particularly from members of the British government, who gave the impression that they would welcome UDI as a way out of their difficulties. Nevertheless, UDI did not happen. A large segment of the Protestant middle-class, while prepared to second the work of the strikers, was unwilling to take the lead in the kind of counter-revolutionary movement which their grandfathers had mounted in 1912–14.

The shared emotions of Protestants in the strike and its aftermath were not so much a sense of Ulster nationalism—a term used mainly by the strike's detractors—as a sense of having evened up the score in the zero-sum game. The Catholics had been 'winning' consistently since 1968, and a sense of humiliation had been keenly felt on the Protestant side. Glen Barr, a young, working-class, Vanguard politician from Derry who was to emerge as a key figure in the strike, had warned the SDLP in the Assembly several weeks earlier against continuing to 'rub the noses of Loyalists in the dirt'.[30] In a post-mortem on the Executive, Faulkner noted, perceptively, that 'People were showing that we have had five years of being kicked around. . . .'[31] Such feelings, and their tendency to be held more strongly by working-class than middle-class Protestants, were appropriate to 'industrial action', but not to a revolution.

The fundamental flaw in the Whitelaw solution was not that it was based on the 'wrong' nationality assumption, but that it gave priority to nation-building over state-formation. By reserving security powers to itself, Westminster was insisting that something like a 'nation' be created (by 'working together') *before* a state was erected (by devolution of security powers). There might have been a very different outcome if an SDLP leader such as Paddy Devlin or John Hume had appeared regularly on television as, say, Attorney General or Home Secretary, to announce how many terrorists had been arrested and how many rounds of ammunition captured during the preceding week—a strange prospect, but no stranger than the roles in which the new leaders of the Irish Free State were cast in 1922–23. Power-sharing did not fail; power-sharing was never tried.

British policy-makers failed to understand that what counts, in legitimating a state in Ulster, is not nationality, but the public band. The central question posed by events was *not* 'Can Protestants and Catholics come to feel "like" one another?' but 'Can Catholics be admitted to the public band?' The question was posed as it was partly because Westminster in 1972–74 was unwilling to give meaningful assurances of a determination to make the United Kingdom the state in Northern Ireland. The regime did use the modest power deriving from its military presence to block certain outcomes—an IRA victory, open communal warfare with population transfers, the return of Protestant-dominated governmental institutions (though in this last case, Westminster's resolution might well have faltered had the Protestant community been determined to seize power after the pattern of 1912). Westminster, however, was hardly a credible candidate for the allegiance of either community so long as her principal spokesmen appeared eager for a settlement by divestiture.

As late as August of 1975, the question whether Catholics might be admitted to the public band was still paramount. It was being posed in a constitutional convention in the form, whether or not Loyalists might join with the SDLP for the duration of the present 'emergency' in a law-and-order administration enjoying security powers. In what looked like a deliberate double-cross of Craig, Paisley killed the scheme. Opponents of the scheme were able to appeal to that lodestar of the contractarian culture, honesty, by representing the UUUC election manifesto as a 'pledge to the electorate'. A later poll suggested, however, that a substantial majority of the Protestant community would have gone along with the scheme.[32] Whether the SDLP could have retained the support of their community while sharing the responsibility for arrests, house searches and all the other unpleasant imperatives of reimposing order is imponderable, though they were eager to try.

This scheme having miscarried, the question seeems to be subtly shifting toward whether the United Kingdom can become the state in the province. Westminster politicians have been disabused of the notion that they can somehow be rid of Northern Ireland without risking a holocaust. Meanwhile, and not coincidentally, the frequency of political violence appears to be declining and the Westminster regime thus to be gaining a credible monopoly of physical force in the province. If it succeeds, the Protestants' lack of a clear sense of nationality may indeed contribute to a solution rather than being the destabilising factor it constituted in 1972–75. Once Westminster really is performing the classic functions of government for both communities, it is altogether possible that it will become the object of allegiance and thereby gain legitimacy. It is well to remember that the protracted crisis through which Northern Ireland has been passing had its origins in a partial *rapprochement*, not a growing alienation, between at least some elements in the two communities. (In that respect, it resembles no previous crisis in Irish history, except perhaps that of the 1790s.) The institutions which existed in 1969 were incapable of accommodating *rapprochement*.

Those institutions are gone: the regime collapsed only to reveal that the state on which it had been erected was in ruins. Those who believe that a state ought not to be founded on assumptions which exclude one-third of its inhabitants from full citizenship can hardly mourn the passing of the Northern Ireland state, in itself. However, the fact that it was not immediately succeeded by some other state has meant that the province has been through a period in the state of nature, where life does indeed turn out to be nasty, brutish and short. This circumstance results from the Westminster regime's implicit determination not to admit a 'solution' whose cost might be a colossal bloodletting and massive forced population transfers, i.e., her refusal to withdraw her troops and let the two sides sort themselves out into two well-defined, ethnically-homogeneous states.

British statesmen have thus cast themselves, along with many Ulster folk, in the unlikely role of tragic figures—choosing good over the evil of holocaust—at great cost in the blood and treasure of all the peoples of the kingdom. They have not chosen to deem the Irish and their quarrel unworthy of sacrifice on the part of a people who unwittingly allowed that quarrel to fester. Whether all the undoubted private tragedies of these seven years will add up to one grand classic tragedy wherein great men struggle with forces which are beyond their control, we shall not know until we attain upon these years the perspective of 'history'. Yet the perspective *from* history upon the present is accessible now. The duty of the historian is to provide from that perspective the understanding which may enable the actors in this drama—if tragedy it be—to play the heroic rather than the ignoble part. Life is not art, and in life, tragedy understood can be tragedy overcome.

Notes

INTRODUCTION
(pp. 1–6)

1. Richard Rose, *Governing without Consensus: An Irish Perspective*, Boston 1971, 378.
2. *News Letter* (Belfast), 7 July 1975. (This newspaper, which was entitled *Belfast Newsletter* from 1737 until 1962, will be cited *BNL* hereafter.)
3. *Ibid.; Irish Times* (Dublin), 7 July 1975.
4. *BNL*, 9 July 1975.
5. *Irish Times*, 8 July 1975.
6. *Ibid.*, 7 July 1975.
7. *BNL*, 7 July 1975 (italics added).
8. Analogies are often drawn between Ulster Protestants and American white southerners. Up to the 1860s, white southerners did seriously maintain that a violation of the contract as they understood it would absolve them of their allegiance to the Union. In the 1960s, however, despite a good deal of posturing and claims that the contract was being violated (i.e., that Supreme Court rulings against segregation were 'unconstitutional') they did ultimately submit to 'the law of the land', i.e., to a *national* consensus, expressed through national institutions, radically reinterpreting the fundamental law. Ulster Loyalists would maintain that the analogy is false —that they face a British national consensus which would, or might, thrust them out of the U.K. Rose's data, however, demonstrates the strength of 'ultra' attitudes in 1968, when public discussion revolved around internal political and legal reforms, not around Northern Ireland's membership in the UK.
9. *BNL*, 8 July 1975.
10. For a discussion of the distinction, see J. W. Gough, *The Social Contract: A Critical Study of its Development*, 2nd ed., Oxford 1957, 2–3. Strictly speaking, the social contract is a

transaction among individuals in the 'state of nature' arranging for the establishment of a government where none had previously existed; the contract of government presupposes a state to be already in existence and purports to define the relation of the ruler to the ruled. In the history of contractarian thought and practice, the two are very much intertwined.

11. *Protestant Telegraph*, 19 Mar.–1 Apr. 1977.

Chapter One
'THE COMMENDABLE PRACTICE OF
THESE KINGDOMS' (1607–1784)
(pp. 7–42)

1. Somewhat confusingly, the district known as 'the Laggan' or 'the Lagan' in the seventeenth century is not the valley of the River Lagan which flows into Belfast Lough, but lies between the Rivers Foyle and Swilly, near Derry. I follow the practice of using the ancient place-name, Derry, for the town which has grown up on that site, but the seventeenth-century name, Londonderry, for the county which was constituted at the time of the Plantation.

2. Lord Ernest Hamilton, *The Irish Rebellion of 1641, with a History of the Events which Led up to and Succeeded It*, London 1920, 269.

3. John T. Gilbert, ed., *History of the Irish confederation and the War in Ireland, 1641–1643*, Dublin 1882, I, 163.

4. Together with those of a lesser chieftain who imprudently chose the following year to attempt a rebellion.

5. M. Perceval-Maxwell estimates the 'total adult population' of Ulster before the Plantation as 'probably between 25,000 and 40,000'. *The Scottish Migration to Ulster in the Reign of James I*, London 1973, 17.

6. H. S. Maine, *Ancient Law*, London 1917 (repr. 1927), 100.

7. T. W. Moody, 'The Treatment of the Native Population under the Scheme for the Plantation of Ulster'. *Irish Historical Studies*, I (No. 1, Mar. 1938), 59–63.

8. See Perceval-Maxwell, *Scottish Migration*.

9. T. W. Moody, *The Londonderry Plantation, 1609–41*, Belfast 1939.

10. Patrick Adair, *A True Narrative of the Rise and Progress of the Presbyterian Church in Ireland*, with introd. and notes by W. D. Killen, Belfast 1866, 102.

11. Gough, *Social Contract*, pp. 62–6; J. D. Douglas, *Light in the*

North: The Story of the Scottish Covenanters, The Paternoster
Church History VI, Exeter 1964, 1–60.

12. S. R. Gardiner, *History of England (1603–42)*, VIII, 329–30,
quoted in Gough, *Social Contract*, 95. S. A. Burrell, 'The
Covenant Idea as Revolutionary Symbol: Scotland, 1596–
1637', *Church History*, XXVII (No. 4, Dec. 1958), 338–50.
13. John Hill Burton, *The History of Scotland from Agricola's
Invasion to the Revolution of 1688*, V, Edinburgh 1870, 476.
14. Douglas, *Light*, 197–9.
15. S. A. Burrell, 'The Apocalyptic Vision of the Early Covenanters', *Scottish Historical Review*, XLIII (No. 135, April 1964),
12.
16. *Ibid.*, 13.
17. Gordon Donaldson, ed., *The Edinburgh History of Scotland*
III, Edinburgh 1965, 308–316. See I. B. Cowan, 'The Covenanters, A Revision Article', *Scottish Historical Review*, XLVII
(No. 143, April 1968), 39, for a discussion of the problems
of assessing support for the covenanting cause.
18. Douglas, *Light*, 203.
19. See J. C. Beckett, 'The Confederation of Kilkenny Reviewed',
Historical Studies II, London 1959, 32.
20. Adair, *Narrative*, 103.
21. M. Perceval-Maxwell, 'Strafford, the Ulster-Scots and the
Covenanters', *Irish Historical Studies*, XVIII (No. 72, Sept.
1973), 524–51.
22. Adair, *Narrative*, 91; Andrew Stewart, 'History of the Church
of Ireland, after the Scots were Naturalized,' *ibid.*, 313.
23. Adair, *Narrative*, 91.
24. *Ibid.*, 114.
25. *Ibid.*, 115.
26. Douglas, *Light*, 206–8.
27. *Ibid.*, 206 (italics added).
28. The presbytery's action called forth a rejoinder from John
Milton, and consequently their pronouncement is printed in
John Milton, *The Works of John Milton*, ed. F. A. Patterson,
et al., New York 1932, VI, 236–41.
29. *A Sample of Jet-Black Pr—tic Calumny*, Glasgow, 1713, 8.
McBride was a non-juror and therefore atypical among his
Presbyterian contemporaries. His argument states the characteristic Presbyterian position of a generation earlier, the full
implications of which most Presbyterians in his own day were
content to forget.
30. *Ibid.*, 9; cf. 218 for errata.

31. Clement Pike, 'The Origin of the Regium Donum', *Transactions of the Royal Historical Society*, 3rd Ser., III (1909), 205–69. In an apparent reference to Sir Arthur Forbes, who acted as an intermediary between the government and the Ulster Presbyterians, the Bishop of Derry complained in 1672 that 'the Presbyterian party have boasted their great interest at Court and that they shall be heard by the King himself— one of them saying they have a friend at the King's elbow who will see they shall be heard.' *Calendar of State Papers, Domestic*, May 18–Sept. 30, 1672, 607.

32. Public Record Office of Northern Ireland [hereafter, PRONI], transcript of minutes of the Meeting of Antrim, D1759/1A/2, 32, 306, 9 Apr. 1672, 7 June 1687.

33. In Rose's terms they were neither 'rebels' (low support, low compliance) nor 'fully allegiant' citizens (high support, high compliance). They took positions which ranged between his 'ultra' (high support, low compliance) and 'repressed' (low support, high compliance) categories.

34. Bodleian Library, Oxford, Carte MSS 45/274, 'A Letter from Ballymoney near Colerane to a freind [sic] at Dublin June 25 1679' [intended for publication] enclosed in *ibid.*, 45/273, Tho. Nisbett to Mrs. Crooke, 25 June 1679.

35. *Ibid.*, 221/220, Copy of Robert Rule to Sir William Stewart, Bart., [exact date illegible] 1679. Cf. *ibid.*, 45/348, Stewart to Ormond, 8 July 1679.

36. Killen buries the correct title in a footnote on p. 1 of his edition of Adair, puts his own ersatz version on the title page, and contents himself with 'A True Narrative, &c.' at the head of p. 1.

37. R. Dudley Edwards, *The History of the Laws against the Nonconforming Churches in Ireland in the Seventeenth and Eighteenth Centuries* (unpublished M.A. thesis, National University of Ireland), 206A.

38. James Seaton Reid, *History of the Presbyterian Church in Ireland*, 2nd ed., London 1853, II, 501. Though Trail denied having, to his knowledge or recollection, tried to dissuade people from taking the oath of supremacy, he had scruples over taking it himself without adding certain words from the thirty-nine articles (or the analogous Church of Ireland articles) to clarify its meaning. Clearly, the matter was a subject of dispute among Presbyterians themselves. In 1679 the Meeting (i.e., Presbytery) of Tyrone complained of the Laggan Meeting that 'They hear that some brethren of the M[eeting]

of Down, has said to the people, that they may take the Oath of Supremacy in some sense : & that others offend about it.' PRONI, transcript of minutes of the Laggan Meeting, D1752/1E/2, 17, 6 August 1679.

39. Reid, *History*, II, 501–2.
40. *Ibid.*, 503, 505.
41. *Ibid.*, 490.
42. In a summary of the ordination rules transmitted from the Antrim Meeting to the Laggan Meeting in 1673, specific reference to the Covenant is omitted : PRONI, transcript of minutes of Antrim Meeting, D1759/1A/2, 98, 8 July 1673. Trail, who had been ordained at St Johnstown in 1673, specifically denied before the Privy Council that he had ever taken the Solemn League and Covenant : Reid, *History*, II, 498.
43. Trinity College Dublin Library, Molyneux MSS. 883/1, 189.
44. Actually, these stipends may have been paid in only one year (1676) before Charles' death. Reid, *History*, II, 317n.
45. Classon Porter, *Ulster Biographical Sketches*, Belfast 1884, 23–30. Up to the very eve of William's expedition to England, the Meetings found themselves faced with 'the hazard of many in this country deserting ordinances upon false suspicions of a defection in the Min[isters] &c.' and were planning measures 'to avert or prevent the hurt of a growing schism breaking out in this country by some wild persons &c.' PRONI, transcript of minutes of Antrim Meeting, D1759/1A/2, 389f, 395f, 398f, 405f; 7 August, 4 Sept., 1 Oct., 6 Nov. 1688.
46. One minister of a parish near Derry reported later that his own prayers had been answered by a voice from heaven telling him 'Within a year and a half Ireland shall be a desolation!' whereupon he tried unsuccessfully to persuade his parishioners to cease work on a manse they were building for him. In less than a year the manse was destroyed during the siege of Derry : Robert Wodrow, *Analecta: or, Materials for a History of Remarkable Providences* . . . I, [Glasgow] 1842, 41–2. It is not necessary to credit the voice from heaven to recognise that what the minister believed he heard corresponded closely to the psychological needs of himself and his colleagues at this time.
47. In the minutes of the last sitting of the Antrim Meeting before the hostilities interrupted their business there is a tantalisingly ambiguous passage which can be read as implying that the

ministers hoped that William would 'declare' a Synod—a level of jurisdiction which they had prudently foregone for a generation—in the same sense that he, with the Scottish parliament, did in fact summon a General Assembly to meet by his authority in Scotland the following year. PRONI, transcript of minutes of Antrim Meeting, D1759/1A/2, 420–21, 5 Mar. 1688/89. Twenty years later a bishop claimed that he had seen a petition presented by commissioners from the Ulster Meetings to the King, containing 'a Project to Abolish Episcopacy in the North of *Ireland,* according to the Model of *Scotland'.* James Kirkpatrick, minister of Belfast's Second Presbyterian congregation, tried to refute this allegation, but the evidence he offers really does not disprove that some such trial balloon was floated. [James Kirkpatrick], *Presbyterian Loyalty . . .* Belfast 1713, 404–06.

48. *MacKenzie's Memorials of the Siege of Derry,* with intro. and notes by W. D. Killen, Belfast 1861, 78. Porter, *Ulster Biographical Sketches,* 27–28.

49. William M'Carmick, *A Farther Impartial Account of the Actions of the Inniskilling-Men,* ed. W. T. Latimer, Belfast 1896, 15.

50. *MacKenzie's Memorials,* 17.

51. M'Carmick, *Account,* 10.

52. *Ibid.,* 14.

53. *Mackenzie's Memorials,* 61.

54. Gordon Donaldson, *Scotland: Church and Nation through Sixteen Centuries,* New York 1973, 108, estimates the total number of Roman Catholics in eighteenth-century Scotland as between 20,000 and 30,000.

55. D. H. Smyth, *The Volunteer Movement in Ulster: Background and Development, 1745–85* (unpublished Ph.D. thesis, Queen's University Belfast, 1974), 26, 34–5. For an example of a spontaneous band in 1745 see J. W. Kernohan, *The Parishes of Kilrea and Tamlaght O'Crilly: A Sketch of their history with an account of Boveedy Congregation,* Coleraine 1912, 28: 'And we do hereby promise and engage to arm ourselves (to the utmost of our power) and to assemble together from time to time, as often as may be necessary to concert measures for effecting the purpose of this our Association, the defences of ourselves, our religion and liberties against Popery, France, and Arbitrary Power.'

56. Francis Godwin James, *Ireland in the Empire, 1688–1770,* Cambridge, Mass., 1973, 26–7.

57. These percentages are from J. G. Simms, *The Williamite Confiscation in Ireland, 1690–1703*, London 1956, 196.
58. J. G. Simms, 'Remembering 1690', *Studies*, LXIII (Autumn 1974), 231–42.
59. S. B. Chrimes, *English Constitutional History*, London 1948, 162.
60. Gough, *Social Contract*, 132–5.
61. Students of Locke will of course recognise that what follows is not an adequate account of Locke's contribution to political philosophy, but an attempt to capture the way his ideas were appropriated by active participants in politics. Cf. *Ibid.*, 135ff.
62. J. A. Froude, *The English in Ireland in the Eighteenth Century* II, London 1874, 21, quoting Arthur Young, *Tour in Ireland*.
63. Actually, there were considerably fewer than 150,000 Protestants in Ulster at this time, but nobody knew for certain how many there were. Contemporary rumour in England held that the Scottish covenanters expected the aid of 40,000 Ulster-Scots 'able to bear arms' (Reid, *History*, I, 214). Strafford, who knew perfectly well that it was an exaggeration (see Essex to Arlington, 12 October 1673, *Essex Papers*, ed. Osmund Airy, London 1890, I, 124) agreed with this estimate when it was put to him by Laud, and even inflated it to 60,000 in further private communication. As to the total Ulster-Scot population, Strafford at one time claimed there were 150,000 'of that nation, of like affection (as is to be feared)', though he later reduced this estimate to 100,000, a figure which he quoted in his public impeachment trial in 1641 and which accords well with the rumoured 40,000 'able to bear arms'. (Perceval-Maxwell, *IHS*, XVIII, 549; Perceval-Maxwell, *Migration*, 314; John Rushworth, *Historical Collections* VIII, London 1680, 499.) In addition, it was well known that there were some indeterminate number of English Protestants in Ulster. English opinion decided, upon the first news of the rebellion, that its object was to kill 'all' the Protestants of Ireland (Karl Bottigheimer, *English Money and Irish Land: The 'Adventurers' in the Cromwellian Settlement of Ireland*, Oxford 1971, 31). It did soon become evident that such massacres as occurred were largely confined to Ulster, and when the captors of a clergyman boasted that they had already killed 154,000 they hit upon a number in just the range which English opinion was prepared to believe. See also Keith J. Lindley, 'The Impact of the 1641 Rebellion upon England

and Wales, 1641–5', *IHS*, XVIII (No. 70, Sept., 1972), 143–76.

64. William Molyneux, *The Case of Ireland's Being Bound by Acts of Parliament in England, Stated*, Dublin : Pat. Dugan, 1725 (1st pub. 1698), 13.

65. [William Atwood], *The History and Reasons of the Dependency of Ireland upon the Imperial Crown of the Kingdom of England*, London 1698, 197–8. Cf. *An Answer to Mr. Molyneux . . .*, London 1698, 'Epistle Dedicatory' (pages unnumbered).

66. James, *Ireland*, 258, *et passim*.

67. *Historical Manuscripts Commission*, [hereafter *HMC*], *Charlemont*, I, 7.

68. *Ibid.*, 226.

69. *BNL*, 3 Sept. 1756.

70. *Ibid.*, 7 Sept. 1756.

71. W. E. H. Lecky, *History of Ireland in the Eighteenth Century*, II, new ed., London 1892, 220–21.

72. *HMC Charlemont*, I, 354.

73. Lecky, *Hist. Ire.*, II, 234–5.

74. *BNL*, 3–7 July 1778.

75. *Ibid.*, 30 Oct.–3 Nov. 1778; *Hibernian Journal* (Dublin), 4–6 Nov., 9–11 Nov. 1778.

76. *BNL*, 8–11 Dec. 1778.

77. John Rogers, *A Sermon Preached at Lisnavein, otherwise Ballybay New Erection, on Saturday, June 10, 1780 . . .*, Edinburgh 1780, 9.

78. *Hibernian Journal*, 22–24 March 1779.

79. James, *Ireland*, 27.

80. *Hibernian Journal*, 5–7 Apr. 1779.

81. *Ibid.*, 3–5 Nov. 1779.

82. Lecky, *Hist. Ire.*, II, 240.

83. *Hibernian Journal*, 24–26 Nov. 1779.

84. Lecky, *Hist. Ire.*, II, 303.

85. *Parliamentary Register*, I (16 Apr. 1782), 335.

86. Speech of Grattan, 27 May 1782, *ibid.*, 355.

87. Speech of John Hely Hutchinson, 16 Apr. 1782, *ibid.*, 333.

88. Speeches of Mr. Hartley and Sir H. Langrishe, 27 May 1782, *ibid.*, 363, 368; Temple to Townshend, 30 Nov. 1782, quoted in Lecky, *Hist. Ire*, II, 331–2.

89. Maureen Wall, *The Penal Laws, 1691–1760*, 2nd ed., Dundalk 1967, 17–20, 64.

90. Lecky, *Hist. Ire.*, II, 196.

91. *Hibernian Journal*, 9–10 Nov. 1778.
92. *Ibid.*, 11–14 June 1779.
93. Patrick Rogers, *The Irish Volunteers and Catholic Emancipation (1778–1793): A Neglected Phase of Ireland's History*, London 1934, 63, 75, 79.
94. [Arthur Brooke], *An Inquiry into the Policy of the Laws Affecting the Popish Inhabitants of Ireland*, Dublin 1775, 95.
95. See Elgy Gillespie, 'Kilodagh Barn Church', *Irish Times*, 2 Dec. 1975; Thomas P. Kennedy, 'Church Building', in Patrick J. Corish, ed., *A History of Irish Catholicism* vol. V, fasc. 8, Dublin 1970, 2. In the nineteenth century, Ulster Presbyterians, perhaps in emulation of Anglicanism, began to favour the longitudinal plan of church building, which can be seen in most Belfast Presbyterian churches today. The meeting house of the First Presbyterian Church of Dunmurry (now non-subscribing), erected in 1779, preserves the characteristic eighteenth-century ground plan.
96. Emmet Larkin, 'The Devotional Revolution in Ireland, 1850–75', *American Historical Review*, LXXVII (No. 3, June 1972), 625–52.
97. Rogers, *Irish Volunteers*, 147–8.
98. When it was suggested in the House of Commons in 1782 that a badly-drafted clause in a pending relief bill might inadvertently repeal the seventeenth-century acts upon which the land settlement rested, the house was thrown into what the attorney general called 'a *panic*'. *Parliamentary Register*, I (15 Feb. 1782), 243.
99. John Lawless, *Belfast Politics Enlarged*, Belfast 1818, 230.
100. Dennis Taaffe, *An Impartial History of Ireland*, IV, Dublin 1811, 206.

Chapter Two
FREEDOM, RELIGION AND LAWS
(1760–1886)
(pp. 43–86)

1. David M. Potter, 'The Historian's Use of Nationalism and Vice Versa', in *The South and the Sectional Conflict*, Baton Rouge 1968, 44.
2. Rupert Emerson, *From Empire to Nation: The Rise to Self-Assertion of Asian and African Peoples*, Cambridge, Mass., 1960, 96.
3. *One Island, Two Nations*, Workers' Association, n.p., 1973, 3, 34.

4. *Ibid.*, 20.
5. Peter Gibbon, *The Origins of Ulster Unionism*, Manchester 1975, 20. I am mystified, however, by Gibbon's apparent classification of (Catholic) Irish nationalism in this passage as a 'quasi-nationalist' movement as well.
6. For a convenient summary of such theories, see Anthony D. Smith, *Theories of Nationalism*, London 1971.
7. Alex Inkeles, 'The Modernization of Man', in Myron Weiner, ed., *Modernization: The Dynamics of Growth*, New York 1966, 138–50.
8. Ernest Gellner, *Thought and Change*, London 1964, 147–78.
9. *Ibid.*, 155.
10. *Ibid.*, 167.
11. *Ibid.*, 173.
12. See index of rents per acre for 1710–39 on the manor of Brownlow's-Derry, Co. Armagh, in W. H. Crawford, 'Landlord-Tenant Relations in Ulster, 1609–1820', *Irish Economic and Social History*, II (1975), 13.
13. Charles Coote, *Statistical Survey of County Armagh*, Dublin 1804, 261.
14. W. H. Crawford, 'Economy and Society in South Ulster in the Eighteenth Century', *Clogher Record*, 1975, 253–4. I have also profited from private conversation with Mr. Crawford on several points raised in this discussion.
15. W. H. Crawford, *Domestic Industry in Ireland*, Dublin 1972, 36.
16. T. W. Freeman, *Pre-Famine Ireland*, Manchester 1957, 273.
17. Conrad Gill, *The Rise of the Irish Linen Industry*, Oxford 1925, 110–12, 139–42.
18. W. H. Crawford and B. Trainor, eds., *Aspects of Irish Social History, 1750–1800*, Belfast 1969, 74.
19. J. Byrne, *An Impartial Account of the Late Disturbances in the County of Armagh*, Dublin 1792, 27.
20. George Cornewall Lewis, *On Local Disturbances in Ireland . . .*, London 1836, 34, quoting Hardy, *Charlemont*.
21. Crawford and Trainor, *Aspects*, 36.
22. PRONI, T 808/14898, copy of 'Intelligence from the North', 1 March 1772.
23. Froude, *English in Ireland*, II, 212.
24. F. J. Bigger, *The Ulster Land War of 1770*, Dublin 1910, 102.
25. Arthur Young, *A Tour in Ireland*, London 1780, II, 30.
26. Froude, *English in Ireland*, II, 121.
27. *Gentleman's Magazine*, 1773, 467–8.

28. W. A. Maguire, *The Downshire Estates in Ireland, 1801–1845*, Oxford 1972, 39.
29. See, e.g., *Hibernian Journal* (Dublin), 5–8 Nov. 1779 : 'Yesterday Evening a Party of the Lurgan Volunteers escorted one Killin, a notorious Rioter, to this town [Belfast], and sent him on board the Tender.'
30. *Belfast Mercury*, 14 May 1784.
31. Rev. Edward Hudson to Charlemont, 19 May 1798, *HMC Charlemont*, II, 322, but cf. 333, 341, 354–5.
32. *Report from the Select Committee Appointed to Inquire into the Nature, Character, Extent and tendency of the Orange Lodges . . .*, hereafter *Sel. Comm. Orange*, I, 88. The 1834 religious census found there to be 1,518,100 Protestants in Ireland, and from data in the 1831 census it seems reasonable to estimate that 24.1 per cent or 366,000 were males 20 years of age or over.
33. I develop this point in my forthcoming 'Presbyterianism and "Modernization" in Ulster' in *Past and Present*.
34. For an incident in 1827 near Dungannon which suggests that some Seceding laymen positively expected that their clergy would support the Orange cause see *Sel. Comm. Orange.* (1835), II, 48–69.
35. *Ibid.*, I, 114.
36. *Ibid.*, I, 127.
37. Ian Budge and Cornelius O'Leary, *Belfast: Approach to Crisis, A Study of Belfast Politics, 1613–1970*, London 1973, 32.
38. John Joseph Monaghan, *A Social and Economic History of Belfast, 1801–1825* (unpublished Ph.D.thesis, Queen's University Belfast, 1940), 585–90.
39. Budge and O'Leary, *Belfast*, 40.
40. As noted above, a spokesman for the Order claimed a membership of about 200,000 at the 1835 enquiry. In 1848, 'up to 100,000' Orangemen paraded on the 12th. (Hereward Senior, 'The Early Orange Order 1795–1870', in T. Desmond Williams, ed., *Secret Societies in Ireland*, Dublin 1973, 44.) Religious censuses were conducted in 1834 and 1861, and although they do not give the exact data we want, it is possible to guess from them that there were about 365,000 male Protestants over 20 years of age in 1834 and about 350,000 at the time of the 1851 census.
41. Budge and O'Leary, *Belfast*, 24.
42. *Ibid.*, 14–100.
43. Gibbon, *Origins*, 96–7.

44. Brian M. Walker, *Parliamentary Politics in Ulster, 1868–86* (unpublished Ph.D. thesis, Trinity College Dublin, 1976), 85–6.
45. Gibbon, *Origins*, 94–5.
46. This is the version formalised in the 1799 rules of the Order. *Sel. Comm. Orange.*, I, appendix, p. [3]. Other versions in circulation around 1796 used the terms 'Protestant cause' and 'Protestant Religion'. State Paper Office of Ireland, Rebellion Papers, hereafter SPOI, Reb. P. 620/24/82, R. Waddell to E. Cooke, 5 Aug. 1796, enclosure; 620/24/11, Holt Waring to Cooke, 4 July 1796, enclosure.
47. See evidence of William Swan in *Sel. Comm. Orange.*, I, 94–100, esp. qq. 1400–04, 1422–24, 1484.
48. Hereward Senior, *Orangeism in Ireland and Britain, 1795–1836*, London 1966, 206–7.
49. *Minutes of Evidence taken before the Select Committee of the House of Lords, appointed to inquire into the State of Ireland, 24 March–22 June, 1825*, H.C. 1825, ix (521), 337.
50. *Ibid.*, 356: Declaration of representatives of 340 Orange Lodges at Armagh, 11 Mar. 1823.
51. *Sel. Comm. Orange.*, I, 111.
52. Frank Wright, 'Protestant Ideology and Politics in Ulster', *European Journal of Sociology*, XIV (1973), 234.
53. Resolution of Ulster Protestant Defence Association, *BNL*, 1 Apr. 1869.
54. Walker, *Parliamentary Politics*, 219–20, quoting PRONI, Hertford Papers, CR 114A/538/6, Lt. Gen. F. H. Seymour to Sir G. F. Seymour, 14 Aug. 1869.
55. Gordon Donaldson, *Scotland: The Shaping of a Nation*, Newton Abbot 1974, 113.
56. Karl Deutsch, *Nationalism and Social Communication: An Inquiry into the Foundations of Nationality*, 2nd ed., Cambridge, Mass., 1966, 111. (Italics added to the word 'trust'.)
57. Emerson, *Empire to Nation*, 95–6.
58. Galen Broeker, *Rural Disorder and Police Reform in Ireland, 1812–1836*, London 1970, 58.
59. Oliver MacDonagh, *Ireland*, Englewood Cliffs, N.J., 1968, 22–42.
60. Conor Cruise O'Brien, 'Holy War', *New York Review of Books*, XIII (No. 8, 6 Nov., 1969), 11.
61. M. W. Dewar, John Brown, S. E. Long, *Orangeism: A New Historical Appreciation*, Belfast [1967], 118.

62. Sir Horace Plunkett, *Ireland in the New Century*, popular ed., London 1905, 191.
63. Wright, *Eur. Jn. Sociol.*, XIV, 250.
64. See Andrew Boyd, *Holy War in Belfast*, 2nd ed., Tralee 1970.
65. Quoted in *BNL*, 26 Aug. 1872.
66. *Hansard* 3, ccxi (7 May 1872), 363–8.
67. Quoted in *BNL*, 11 Sept. 1857. The article attracted attention in Belfast because it assumed that Protestants were in a minority 'even in Belfast', a claim which was mistaken unless the author was using the term 'Protestant' in the, by then archaic, sense of 'Church of Ireland'.
68. See, e.g., SPOI, Reb.P., 620/24/37, John Ogle [Sheriff of Armagh] to E. Cooke, 15 July 1796. *HMC Charlemont*, II, 69, William Campbell, D.D., to Charlemont, 9 Feb. 1788.
69. Gibbon, *Origins*, 67–86.
70. *Ibid.*, 74.
71. For a slightly different argument that the generations after 1848 marked the crucial phase of modernisation in southern Ireland, see Joseph Lee, *The Modernisation of Irish Society, 1848–1918*, Dublin 1973.
72. See Patrick J. Corish, 'The Origins of Catholic Nationalism,' in Patrick J. Corish, ed., *A History of Irish Catholicism*, vol. III, *fasc.* 8, Dublin 1968.
73. See Thomas N. Brown, 'Nationalism and the Irish Peasant, 1800–1848', *The Review of Politics*, XV (No. 4, Oct., 1953), 403–11.
74. *Ibid.*, 430–40.
75. For a treatment of the land campaign as a 'revolution of rising expectations', see James Donnelly, *The Land and the People of Nineteenth Century Cork*, London 1975. Cf. K. Theodore Hoppen, 'Landlords, Society and Electoral Politics in Mid-Nineteenth Century Ireland', *Past and Present*, No. 75 (May 1977), 62–95.
76. Sam Clark, 'The Social Composition of the Land League', *Irish Historical Studies*, XVII (No. 68, Sept. 1971), 447–69.
77. James M'Knight, *The Ulster Tenants' Claim of Right; or, Landownership a State Trust; The Ulster Tenant-right an Original Grant from the British Crown, and the Necessity of Extending its General Principle to the Other Provinces of Ireland, Demonstrated; in a Letter to the Right Honourable the Lord John Russell*, Dublin 1848. Cf. H.M. Commissioners of Inquiry into the State of the Law and Practice in respect to the Occupation of Land in Ireland, *Evidence*, Part I, (H.C.
G

1845, xix), 744, evidence of James Sinclair, q. 17. See also speech of Rev. John Downes at Lisburn, *BNL*, 5 April 1850 : '[he] then referred to the period of the Ulster plantation at the beginning of the seventeenth century. The crown of England expressly gave lands in Ulster to landlords on the condition that the tenantry under them should share in the benefit of the gift.'

78. See speech of Rev. John Kinnear at Letterkenny, *Londonderry Sentinel*, 8 Feb. 1870 : '. . . when King James settled Ulster he bound up the undertakers by these conditions—That they would "allow their tenants to hold by settled lease and easy rents".'

79. Speech of Rev. Mr Rutherford at Banbridge, *BNL*, 29 Jan. 1850.

80. Crawford, *Ir. Econ & Soc. Hist.*, II, 20.

81. See report of tenant right meeting in Saintfield, *BNL*, 18 Jan. 1850 : 'Three cheers for Sharman Crawford, tenant right, and no surrender'. Cf. Alexander R. Dinnen, *Ulster Tenant Right, Mr. James Sharman Crawford's Amendment Bill, and 'No Surrender'*, Belfast 1876.

82. *Londonderry Sentinel*, 22 Apr. 1886, quoting *Belfast Morning News*, 29 Dec. 1884 and 5 Jan. 1885. The complete articles can be found in *Freeman's Journal* (Dublin), 31 December 1884, 6 January 1885.

83. Emmet Larkin, *The Roman Catholic Church and the Creation of the Modern Irish State, 1878–1886*, Dublin 1975, 396.

84. Gellner, *Thought and Change*, 147–9.

85. See Smith, *Theories of Nationalism*, 41–64.

86. David W. Miller, 'Irish Catholicism and the Great Famine', *Journal of Social History*, IX (No. 1, Autumn 1975), 81–98. For a critique of my argument, see Eugene Hynes' forthcoming article, 'Irish Catholicism and the Great Hunger', in *Societas*. I am grateful to Mr Hynes for showing me the typescript of this article. In my judgement, his main line of explanation is consistent with my own (too brief) remarks on p. 93 concerning the Church's sanctioning of peasant desires for secure attachment to the soil.

87. The argument of the following paragraphs is developed in greater detail in my forthcoming 'Presbyterianism and "Modernization" in Ulster', in *Past and Present*.

88. Gibbon, *Origins*, 56. I disagree with Gibbon's argument that this emphasis was dominant in Ulster Presbyterianism up to the 1859 revival.

89. J. L. Porter, *Life and Times of Henry Cooke*, London : Belfast 1877, 236.
90. *Records of the General Synod of Ulster* III, Belfast 1898, 536. Robert J. Rodgers, *Presbyterian Missionary Activity among Irish Roman Catholics in the Nineteenth Century* (unpublished M.A. thesis, Queen's University Belfast, 1970), 96–7.
91. Rodgers, *Presbyterian Missionary Activity, passim.*
92. Wright, *Eur. Jn. Sociol.*, XIV, 213–80.
93. *Report of the Commissioners of Inquiry into the Origin and Character of the Riots in Belfast in July and September 1857; with Minutes of Evidence and Appendix*, H.C. 1857–58, xxvi (2039), 157 (q. 7904).

Chapter Three
'HERE WE STAND, A LOYAL BAND'
(1883–1920)
(pp. 87–121)

1. Richard Hawkins, 'The "Invasion of Ulster" ', *Irish Times*, 27 Jan., 28 Jan. 1969. Thomas MacKnight, *Ulster As It Is*, II, London 1896, 36.
2. *The Repealer Repulsed! A Correct Narrative of the Rise and Progress of the Repeal Invasion of Ulster: Dr Cooke's Challenge and Mr O'Connell's Declinature, Tactics, and Flight . . .*, Belfast, 1841.
3. PRONI, D627/252, H. de F. Montgomery Papers, W. Patterson to [Montgomery], 7 Dec. 1866.
4. See e.g., editorial in *Londonderry Sentinel*, 24 Dec. 1885. Cf. speech by Major Saunderson, *ibid.*, 9 Jan. 1886.
5. *Ibid.*, 22 Dec. 1885, 12 Jan., 16 Jan. (speech of Viscount Cole at Florencecourt), 26 Jan., 28 Jan. 1886. *BNL*, 5 April 1886.
6. MacKnight, *Ulster*, II, 380. F. Frankfort Moore, *The Truth about Ulster*, London 1914, 56. But cf. the deadly serious Fred H. Crawford, *Guns for Ulster*, Belfast 1947, 13f.
7. *Londonderry Sentinel*, 14 June 1886.
8. Belfast Riots Commission, 1886, *Minutes of Evidence*, H.C. 1887, xviii (c.4925–I), 384.
9. Alvin Gouldner, *The Hellenic World: A Sociological Analysis*, New York 1969, 49–51.
10. Foreword to W. S. Armour, *Armour of Ballymoney*, London 1934, xii.
11. See, for example, the case of Southern Protestant acceptance of the new situation described by Emmet Larkin, *Roman Catholic Church*, 343.

12. F. Frankfort Moore, *The Truth about Ulster*, London 1914, 54.
13. *Ibid.*, 58–9.
14. See *Pall Mall Gazette* interview of William Johnston reprinted in *BNL*, 6 April 1886 : 'It [Home Rule] is looked upon as so perfectly chimerical that no one has thought of taking active steps to resist it.'
15. MacKnight, *Ulster*, II, 379.
16. Walker, *Parliamentary Politics*, 85–86. Aiken McClelland, 'The Later Orange Order', in Williams, ed., *Secret Societies*, 131.
17. Speech of Robert Greer, *Northern Whig*, 18 June 1892.
18. *Ibid.*
19. Patrick Buckland, *Irish Unionism: Two: Ulster Unionism and the Origins of Northern Ireland, 1886–1922*, Dublin 1973, 17.
20. F. S. L. Lyons, 'The Irish Unionist Party and the Devolution Crisis of 1904–5', *Irish Historical Studies*, VI (No. 21, Mar., 1948), 1–22.
21. Ronald McNeill, *Ulster's Stand for Union*, London 1922, 48.
22. *Ibid.*, 53.
23. A. T. Q. Stewart, *The Ulster Crisis*, London 1967, 69.
24. McNeill, *Ulster's Stand*, 58.
25. *Ibid.*, 85.
26. *Ibid.*, 49.
27. *Ibid.*, 86, 101.
28. *Ibid.*, 103.
29. *Ibid.*, 104–5.
30. Kernohan, *Kilrea and Tamlaght O'Crilly*, 28.
31. Stewart, *Ulster Crisis*, 66. Another 19,162 men and 5,055 women outside Ulster also signed.
32. Ian Colvin, *The Life of Lord Carson*, II, London 1934, 143.
33. McNeill, *Ulster's Stand*, 107.
34. *Dictionary of National Biography, sub* James Craig.
35. David W. Miller, *Church, State and Nation in Ireland, 1898–1921*, Dublin : Pittsburgh, 1973, 289.
36. Northern Ireland Public Record Office, *Irish Unionism, 1885–1923: A Documentary History*, ed. Patrick Buckland, Belfast 1973, 78. (Hereafter cited NIPRO, *Irish Unionism*).
37. See the resolution to be moved at an 1893 Orange demonstration in Co. Tyrone, 'never to submit to laws enacted by an Irish Parliament of which the members would be the nominees & puppets of the Roman Priesthood—', *ibid.*, 180.

38. Such attitudes on the part of both Catholics and Protestants are revealed by documents on the politics of the almost evenly-divided Fermanagh County Council published in NIPRO, *Irish Unionism*, 185–94.
39. McNeill, *Ulster's Stand*, 21–6.
40. *Ibid.*, 91.
41. See, e.g., sermon to local Ulster Volunteers by Rev. R. Moore, Ringsend, June 1914, quoted in H. S. Morrison, *Modern Ulster: Its Character, Customs, Politics and Industries*, London n.d. [1920], 94–99 : '. . . Let us hope on, pray on, and prepare on, so that when the hour of crisis arrives we may be ready, under the guidance of our leaders, to strike such a blow as shall for ever damn conspiracy and trickery in the government of these realms, and shall resound for liberty and truth throughout the civilised world.'
42. Cf. the proposed resolution of a Co. Tyrone Orange demonstration accusing Gladstone of trying to 'smuggle' the Second Home Rule Bill through the Commons, NIPRO, *Irish Unionism*, 179.
43. U.U.C. resolution attached to the covenant, McNeill, *Ulster's Stand*, 107. Italics added.
44. Roy Jenkins, *Asquith: Portrait of a Man and an Era*, New York 1966, 294.
45. Antrim, Down, Londonderry and Armagh. The border towns of Derry and Newry, which had Catholic majorities were to be treated as separate entities, a provision which was vital in securing Nationalist support for the scheme.
46. Though the British Conservatives went along with their Ulster allies for reasons that were probably mainly tactical, Bonar Law's rationale for their action suggests that Ulster's heightened awareness that parliament can make no binding promises was seeping into English politics as well. Even if the first general election produced a Unionist majority which would enact permanent exclusion, he argued, the second might return the Liberals again and allow the Unionist decision to be reversed (*Hansard* 5, lix (9 March 1914), cols. 922–3). The fact that the operations of the Parliament Act would almost certainly prevent such a reversal before the expiry of six years does not seem to have occurred to him.
47. Stewart, *Ulster Crisis*, 176–212.
48. Denis Gwynn, *The Life of John Redmond*, London 1932, 338.
49. McNeill, *Ulster's Stand*, 53.
50. Buckland, *Irish Unionism, Two*, 125.

51. Gibbon, *Origins*, 136.
52. London 1914.
53. An Irishman, *Is Ulster Right? A Statement of the Question at Issue between Ulster and the Nationalist Party, and of the Reasons—Historical, Political, and Financial—Why Ulster is Justified in Opposing Home Rule*, London 1913.
54. T. M. Johnstone, *Ulstermen: Their Fight for Fortune, Faith and Freedom*, Belfast 1914, 37–43.
55. James Logan, *Ulster in the X-Rays*, London n.d. [1923], 16–17.
56. See photograph in Gibbon, *Origins*, 134.
57. Johnstone, *Ulstermen*, 44.
58. See, e.g., NIPRO, *Irish Unionism*, 78, 81.
59. Edward Saunderson, *Two Irelands: or, Loyalty versus Treason*, London 1884, 3.
60. McNeill, *Ulster's Stand*, 15.
61. *Is Ulster Right?*, 232.
62. *Ibid.*, vii.
63. *Hansard* 5, cxxvii (31 Mar. 1920), col. 1298.
64. McNeill, *Ulster's Stand*, 169.
65. *BNL*, 5 Apr. 1920.
66. Herbert Moore Pim, *Sinn Fein*, Belfast 1920, 28–29.
67. Belfast 1919, 31–86.
68. 2nd ed., London 1917, 117–8.
69. *Ibid.*, 26–8, 68–71.
70. *Ibid.*, 112.
71. *Ibid.*, 40.
72. *Ibid.*, 194.
73. *Ibid.*, 172.
74. *Ibid.*, 176.
75. *Ibid.*, 174.
76. Sarah Nelson, 'Protestant "Ideology" Considered : The Case of "Discrimination" ', *British Political Sociology Yearbook*, vol. 2, *The Politics of race*, ed. Ivor Crewe, London 1975, 166–7.
77. Hamilton, *Soul*, 200.
78. Logan, *Ulster in X-Rays*, 55.
79. *Ibid.*, 39.
80. NIPRO, *Irish Unionism*, 6, 60.
81. Editorial in *Londonderry Sentinel*, 24 Dec. 1885.
82. NIPRO, *Irish Unionism*, 196.
83. See letter from Rev. Abraham Jagoe under heading 'Can We Trust Roman Catholics?—Are Roman Catholic Promises Trustworthy?' in *Londonderry Sentinel*, 9 Mar. 1886.

84. See, e.g., speech of Samuel Walker, *ibid.*, 31 Oct. 1885.
85. J. S. Drennan, 'We Meet!' printed in NIPRO, *Irish Unionism*, 14.
86. Logan, *Ulster in X-Rays*, 41. Italics added.
87. In the past several years, however, there has been some conscious imitation of the nationalist ballad tradition in loyalist pubs, which may foreshadow fundamental changes in this culture.
88. Johnstone, *Ulstermen*, 88.
89. Quoted from *Dublin Mail*, 2 Nov. 1888, in Irish Unionist Alliance Leaflet no. 26, 6th ser., I.U.A. Publications I, 141.
90. Johnstone, *Ulstermen*, 39–40, derives Ulster's claim to be 'the Imperial and Sovereign Province of Ireland' from the assertion that the high kingship of Ireland was confined to Ulster candidates for 600 years.
91. Indeed, in the early nineteenth century, the term 'Imperial Parliament' was used to connote that the U.K. itself constituted an empire.
92. William Arthur, *Shall the Loyal Be Deserted and the Disloyal Set over Them? An Appeal to Liberals and Nonconformists*, London n.d. (c. 1886).
93. NIPRO, *Irish Unionism*, 51–53.

Chapter Four
'THOSE DISTRICTS WHICH THEY COULD
CONTROL' (1914–1972)
(pp. 122–149)

1. *BNL*, 12 Dec. 1968.
2. *Ibid.*, text of Craig's letter to O'Neill.
3. D. G. Boyce, *Englishmen and Irish Troubles*, London 1972, 25–42.
4. See speech of T. W. Brown, MP, to Newtownards branch of the Ulster Temperance Council, *BNL*, 3 Apr. 1920. Cf. speech of H. T. Barrie, MP, to North Derry Women's Unionist Association at Coleraine, *ibid.*, 9 Apr. 1920.
5. Speech of H. L. Garrett at annual meeting of Belfast Chamber of Commerce, *ibid.*, 13 Apr. 1920. Speech of Sir James Johnston at monthly meeting of Belfast Corporation, *ibid.*, 2 Apr. 1920. Cf. Patrick Buckland, 'The Unity of Ulster Unionism, 1886–1939', in *History*, LX (No. 199, June 1975), 218–19.
6. NIPRO, *Irish Unionism*, 412–16.

7. Rev. John Redmond, *Church, State, Industry, 1827–1929, in East Belfast: Vivid Records of Social and Political Upheavals in the Nineteen-Twenties*, Belfast n.d. [1960], 23–4. Sir Arthur Hezlet, *The 'B' Specials: A History of the Ulster Special Constabulary*, London 1972, 10.

8. Rev. J. Redmond, *Church, State, Industry*, 17–23.

9. In extracts from the memorandum he presented which are printed in Thomas Jones, *Whitehall Diary*, III, ed. Keith Middlemas, London 1971, 38, Craig represents himself as speaking for the 'Ulster Loyalists'.

10. Craig's presentation referred discreetly to 'a Government Authority, e.g. an Undersecretary', but stipulated that he 'should have direct access to the Chief Secretary', which would make him an Under Secretary in fact, if not in title. P.R.O. Cab. 23/22 fol. 238, 2 Sept. 1920.

11. Boyce, *Englishmen*, 107–8.

12. PRONI, Carson Papers, D1507/1/1920/16, unsigned copy of letter to Bonar Law, Apr. 1920. Quotation taken from calendar entry; actual document unavailable at the time of this research.

13. P.R.O. Cab. 23/22, fol. 239. Cf. Jones, *Diary*, III, 38.

14. PRONI, Clark Papers, D 1022/9, extracts from Sir John Anderson to [Sir Ernest Clark], 12 Oct. 1920.

15. *Ibid.*, 'Notes Taken At Unionist Council Deputation Meeting 28/9/20', remarks of Mr Garrett.

16. *Ibid.*, D1022, Box 9, 'Conference between the Chief Secretary . . . and Standing Committee of Ulster Unionist Council . . . 13th October 1920', 12–14.

17. *Ibid.*, D1022/9, 'Extract of a letter by a sane, stolid representative Unionist in a disturbed part of the country', 26 September 1920.

18. *Ibid.*, notes on flap of folder labelled *'Special Constabulary Based on Special Constables Act of 1832'*.

19. Hezlet, *'B' Specials*, 27–28.

20. PRONI, Clark Papers, D1022/9, Copy of Clark to Anderson, 19 Nov. 1920.

21. See the correspondence regarding a certain Catholic ex-serviceman in PRONI, unlisted Craig Registered Papers, Cab. 6, Box 1, items 958, 1005, and 1033.

22. PRONI, Clark Papers, D1022/9, copy of Clark to Anderson, 19 Nov. 1920 : 'I am very intensely interested in the future problem here should the Government of Ireland Bill become law.'

23. Hezlet, *'B' Specials*, 48.
24. Easton, *Systems Analysis*, 267–88.
25. Nicholas Mansergh, *The Government of Northern Ireland: A Study in Devolution*, London 1936, 145.
26. *Ibid.*, 146.
27. J. C. Beckett, 'Northern Ireland', *Journal of Contemporary History*, VI (No. 1, 1971), 130–31.
28. McNeill, *Ulster's Stand*, 280.
29. Rose, *Governing without Consensus*, 117.
30. *Hansard 5*, ccclxi (4 June 1940), col. 796.
31. *BNL*, 6 Feb. 1940.
32. *Ulster Is British: A Reaffirmation of Ulster's Political Outlook, with a Report on Northern Ireland's General Election of 19th February 1949*, Belfast 1949.
33. *Hansard 5*, cccclxv (16 May 1949), cols. 43–44.
34. William Van Voris, *Violence in Ulster: An Oral Documentary*, Amherst 1975, 40.
35. J. H. Whyte, *Church and State in Modern Ireland*, Dublin 1971, 48.
36. Jack White, *Minority Report: The Protestant Community in the Irish Republic*, Dublin 1975, 92–3.
37. See Introduction by Geoffrey Hand to *Report of the Irish Boundary Commission*, Shannon 1969, vii–xxii. See also the same author's 'MacNeill and the Boundary Commission', in *The Scholar Revolutionary: Eoin MacNeill, 1867–1945, and the Making of the New Ireland*, ed. F. X. Martin and F. J. Byrne, Shannon 1973, 199–275.
38. Michael Farrell, *Northern Ireland: The Orange State*, London 1976, 108. Two Nationalists from West Belfast and County Antrim, areas which could not conceivably be affected by any decision of the boundary commission, had taken their seats several months earlier.
39. John Harbinson, *The Ulster Unionist Party, 1882–1973: Its Development and Organisation*, Belfast 1973, 119.
40. *Ibid.*, 43–5.
41. See statement by Craig, quoted in Farrell, *Northern Ireland*, 111 : 'What I want to get in this House and what I believe we will get very much better in this House under the old-fashioned plain and simple system, are men who are for the Union on the one hand, or who are against it and want to go into a Dublin parliament on the other.'
42. Patrick Marrinan, *Paisley: Man of Wrath*, Tralee 1973, 82.
43. For a useful summary of the legal issues discussed here see

Martin Wallace, *Northern Ireland: 50 Years of Self-Government*, New York 1971, 96–100.

44. Marrinan, *Paisley*, 81.
45. Boyd, *Holy War*, 182.
46. Farrell, *Northern Ireland*, 207–8, 213, 222.
47. Wallace, *Northern Ireland*, 96.
48. M. A. Busteed, *Northern Ireland*, London 1974, 7–18, in series 'Problem Regions of Europe'. For an interesting Marxist analysis of these developments see Anders Boserup, 'Contradictions and Struggles in Northern Ireland', *Socialist Register*, 1972, 157–92.
49. Richard Deutsch and Vivien Magowan, *Northern Ireland, 1968–73: A Chronology of Events*, Belfast 1973, I, 3b. (The title of the third volume of this invaluable work extends the terminal dates to 1974, but I shall cite all volumes hereafter as Deutsch and Magowan, *Chronology*.)
50. David Boulton, *The UVF, 1966–73: An Anatomy of Loyalist Rebellion*, Dublin 1973, 92–107.
51. See, e.g., remarks of Thomas Keane on 5 July 1969, Deutsch and Magowan, *Chronology*, I, 33a.
52. *Ibid.*, I, 18a.
53. This account is based mainly on *Violence and Civil Disturbances in Northern Ireland in 1969* [The Scarman Report] (Cmd. 566), I, 40–47. See also Paul Arthur, *The People's Democracy, 1968–1973*, Belfast 1974, 63.
54. *Violence and Civil Disturbances*, I, 42.
55. *Ibid.*, I, 112–4.
56. Deutsch and Magowan, *Chronology*, I, 24b, 25a.
57. *Sunday Times* Insight Team, *Ulster*, Harmondsworth 1972, 196.

EPILOGUE
(pp. 150–166)

1. See John Magee, *Northern Ireland: Crisis and Conflict*, London 1974, 153–5.
2. Deutsch and Magowan, *Chronology*, III, 156b.
3. *Ibid.*, I, 140b; Cecil King, *The Cecil King Diary 1970–1974*, London 1975, 151, 178; *Economist*, 15 Jan. 1972, p. 12.
4. Henry Kelly, *How Stormont Fell*, Dublin 1972, 122.
5. Linenhall Library, Belfast, collection of Northern Ireland political ephemera, E/2.23, mimeographed handbill with MS heading, 'Distributed 12/8/1971 on Newtownards Road'.
6. Boulton, *UVF*, 144–6. Simon Winchester, *Northern Ireland*

in Crisis: Reporting the Ulster Troubles, New York 1975, 216ff.
7. Linenhall Library ephemera collection, E/2.31, handbill headed 'The Attack! Bulletin 2 : No Law with WHITELAW.'
8. n.p., April 1972, 9, 13.
9. *Ibid.,* 7.
10. *Ibid.,* 14.
11. *Ibid.,* 10.
12. *Ibid.,* 15.
13. *Ibid.,* 4–7.
14. William Craig, *The Future of Northern Ireland,* n.p., n.d. [1972].
15. *Ulster—A Nation,* 7.
16. Linenhall Library, Belfast collection of Northern Ireland political ephemera, E/3.9, Ulster Vanguard, Newtownards Branch, *Government without Right* (n.p., n.d. [1972]). On internal evidence this item can be dated later than 10 July 1972.
17. Deutsch and Magowan, *Chronology,* I, 130b.
18. Henry Kelly, *How Stormont Fell,* Dublin 1972, 123–4.
19. Deutsch and Magowan, *Chronology,* II, 163b.
20. Wright, *Eur. Jn. Sociol.,* XIV, 213–80.
21. *Northern Ireland Constitutional Proposals* (Cmd. 5259), London, March 1973.
22. The one Northern Ireland Labour Party representative pursued an independent line, but generally gave encouragement to the coalition.
23. Deutsch and Magowan, *Chronology,* III, 6ab, 20ab, 23a, 28a.
24. *Ibid.,* 187.
25. *Ibid.,* 188–9.
26. *Ibid.,* 43b.
27. *Ibid.,* 93b.
28. Robert Fisk, *Point of No Return:The Strike That Broke the British in Ulster,* London 1975, 160–2.
29. Rose, *Governing without Consensus,* 486.
30. Deutsch and Magowan, *Chronology,* III, 33b.
31. *Ibid.,* 82a.
32. *Belfast Telegraph,* 19 March 1976.

Index